COLORADO'S
BEST

To Mary + Ron,
Happy Colorado Travels!
"Best" wishes—
Ing Whitehead

COLORADO'S

BEST

SECOND EDITION

THE ESSENTIAL GUIDE TO FAVORITE PLACES

COLORADO'S
BEST

BRUCE CAUGHEY & DOUG WHITEHEAD
With Accounts by Tamra Monahan

FULCRUM PUBLISHING
Golden, Colorado

SECOND EDITION THE ESSENTIAL GUIDE TO FAVORITE PLACES

COLORADO'S **BEST**

The information in *Colorado's Best, Second Edition,* is accurate as of July 2005. Prices, hours of operation, addresses, phone numbers, Web sites, and other items change rapidly. If something in the book is incorrect, please write to the authors in care of Fulcrum Publishing, 16100 Table Mountain Parkway, Suite 300, Golden, Colorado, 80403.

Library of Congress Cataloging-in-Publication Data

Caughey, Bruce, 1960-
  Colorado's best : the essential guide to favorite places / Bruce Caughey and Doug Whitehead ; with accounts by Tamra Monahan.-- 2nd ed.
    p. cm.
  ISBN 1-55591-575-2 (pbk.)
  1. Colorado--Guidebooks. I. Whitehead, Doug. II. Monahan, Tamra, 1958- III. Title.
  F774.3.C39 2005
  917.88'0434--dc22

                      2005014200

ISBN 1-55591-575-2

Printed in the United States of America
0 9 8 7 6 5 4 3 2 1

Editorial: Katie Raymond, Faith Marcovecchio
Design: Ann Douden
Cover image: Wendy Shattil/Bob Rozinski, from *Valley of the Dunes: Great Sand Dunes National Park & Preserve*
Back cover image: Jack Lenzo, of the Denver skyline as seen from the Denver Museum of Nature & Science (**BEST** place to photograph the skyline)
Map: Marge Mueller, Gray Mouse Graphics

FULCRUM PUBLISHING
16100 Table Mountain Parkway, Suite 300, Golden, Colorado 80403
(800) 992-2908 • (303) 277-1623 • www.fulcrum-books.com

To our daughters,
Julia and Shannon Caughey,
and Mara and Emma Whitehead,
for the joy and laughter they share each day.

Emma Whitehead, Julia Caughey, Mara
Whitehead, and Shannon Caughey.

View of Mount Antero from Chalk Creek
Canyon in the Upper Arkansas River
Valley. PHOTO BY DOUG WHITEHEAD

CONTENTS

THE FRONT RANGE **1**

Cultural & Historical

Outdoor Activities & Events

Where to Eat, Drink, & Stay

NORTHWEST

Cultural & Historical

Outdoor Activities & Events

Where to Eat, Drink, & Stay

Outdoor Activities & Events

Where to Eat, Drink, & Stay

SOUTH-CENTRAL

Cultural & Historical

Outdoor Activities & Events

Where to Eat, Drink, & Stay

SOUTHWEST **167**

Cultural & Historical

ACKNOWLEDGMENTS

We did it the second time around with a lot of help. We would like to start out with the locals in small towns and big cities across the state who remain the true "experts" and who helped write this book with their easygoing sharing of insights and directions to their favorite places.

The Colorado Historical Society has been an invaluable resource over the years, especially Eric Paddock and former staffers Stan Oliner and Peg Ekstrand. Thanks to Dianne Howie, formerly with Fulcrum Publishing, for her unbridled enthusiasm for this project from the beginning, and to Sam Scinta, for his continued support of the project. The expert editorial support of Katie Raymond greatly helped the second edition of this book. Thanks to the dedicated professionals, too numerous to mention by name, of the National Park Service, U.S. Forest Service, Bureau of Land Management, Colorado State Parks, and various museums, open-space districts, and other custodians of Colorado's heritage for happily sharing their knowledge. We would also like to recognize the many ski area and chamber of commerce folks who contributed their valuable assistance and advice.

Thanks for research assistance and good suggestions from Mark Stevens and Roy Burley. Loads of appreciation to Linda and Les Liman, Claudia Carbone, and Susan Spackman for excellent ideas on covering their hometowns. We also thank the many experts who sprinkle this edition of *Colorado's Best* with a new and very welcome element. A very important thank-you goes to Dean Winstanley, who continues to support this project with his understanding and good humor.

Especially from Bruce:

Special thanks to my wife, Tanya, who helps make sense of a sometimes-complicated world. She has helped out in so many ways and has encouraged my ongoing involvement with this book. You are the best!

To Shannon and Julia, who will forever light up my days with laughter and curiosity. I admire your willingness to learn and grow. I always look forward to your company when we head out on research trips around the state. And, yes, we will try to take a real vacation sometime, without a notebook to gather information.

And to my parents, Ken and Judith Caughey, who instilled a curiosity in Colorado from early on and helped me to believe in what I can accomplish with effort and perseverance.

This revision would not have been possible without the research and very welcome assistance of Tamra Monahan. She has captured many new inclusions for this edition, and I am so grateful.

Thanks also to my friends and colleagues in the Douglas County School District for encouraging my dual careers and for staying focused on what is truly important.

I love traveling the blue highways and back roads of Colorado, skiing, hiking, and biking in places so beautiful that they render words almost useless. We have tried our best to capture what is so wonderful about Colorado, and it is my hope that this book will provide the spark for you to get up out of your chair! Days, weeks, and months sometimes fly by in the workaday world, but we can always pause long enough, for a weekend or even a sunset, to appreciate all of our gifts.

Especially from Doug:

Much of my contribution to this book comes from my years producing, shooting, writing, and editing for CBS 4's *Colorado Getaways*. Thanks to all of the talented reporters, photographers, and editors who helped to expand my knowledge of the state, especially to retired reporter Leo McGuire for setting a high standard of travel writing for me to follow.

Special thanks to my wife, Barb, for being a wonderful travel and life companion. Because of her enthusiastic help in carving out time for me to write in the midst of our busy lives with two young daughters, this project became a far more pleasant undertaking than I might have imagined. Finally, thanks to my father, Orrick, for bringing me out to Colorado in 1971, driving me over Monarch Pass, and dropping me off in Gunnison into an unknown and exciting Colorado future. God rest his soul.

During my travels to gather information and experiences for this second edition of *Colorado's Best*, I was struck by how it felt like I was seeing the state for the first time. I have made a living writing about Colorado for fourteen years, on television and in print, and still I was amazed

by what I saw. One trip took me, over several days, on a grand traverse through the midsection of the state: from Cortez over Lizard Head Pass to Telluride, over to Ridgway and up to Montrose, along Blue Mesa Reservoir through Gunnison and over Monarch Pass, along the Arkansas River and through South Park, along U.S. Hwy. 285 and back to Denver. From canyon country to alpine vistas, through river valleys and over mountain passes, in wide-open spaces and on narrow, winding, two-lane roads, Colorado does not let up, its scenery unrelenting. I consider it a privilege to offer my take on how to best experience the Centennial State.

A refurbished steam engine still plies the winding route between Georgetown and Silver Plume despite some recent changes in ownership and equipment.

PHOTO BY BRUCE CAUGHEY

INTRODUCTION

My days and nights, as I travel here—
what an exhilaration—
not the air alone, and the sense of vastness,
but every local sight and feature.
Everywhere something characteristic ...

—WALT WHITMAN, *Aerial Affects*

This book of "bests" doesn't promise to be everything to everyone. However, we have managed to write this revised edition so that absolutely
anyone can find something valuable and interesting to do in Colorado.
While we may not cover your specialized hobby adequately, you'll be
able to enjoy some incredible Colorado places that we highlight within
these pages. Our mission has been to surprise and delight you with our
choices. To do so, we headed back out on the road during the past year
with a massive, brainstormed list of potential new inclusions. We have
winnowed, deleted, added, and changed our favorites, sometimes debat-
ing their merits long into the night.

To be sure, the following chapters are full of bias and opinions; our
research method could hardly be considered scientifically valid. With
some apologies, we have left out certain niches of activity and included
others based solely on our interests. But even if you can't find the state's
best snowmobile trails or duck-hunting blinds, you will learn that this
book comes from our hearts, and our passion and love for this state
should be easy to detect. It comes from a true desire to share hidden
gems and out-of-the-way places without skipping over some of the obvious, still-compelling choices. So whether you are heading up the I-70
corridor for some great skiing or pulling off the road for the best burrito
in the San Luis Valley, we've got something for you. We did intentionally
leave out a few hidden gems (for example, Bruce's favorite fishing hole),
but mostly, we give you the complete scoop.

Here we are: two guys who have spent the *past two-plus decades*
exploring, researching, writing, photographing, and sharing our firsthand
knowledge of the state in books and on television. We decided to reener-
gize and put our heads together to write this new edition. Although our
guide will never be comprehensive, it does highlight places and activities
that we're sure you will just love. We hope you'll enjoy this new book
and have some great experiences traveling in our wonderful home.

Practical Considerations

Colorado's Best covers a range of year-round activities and has been organized with the reader in mind. With the state broken into logical regions—The Front Range, Northwest, North-Central, The Eastern Plains, South-Central, Southwest—you'll be able to get a sense of where to look on the map to plan your itinerary. So flip through the book, check out the write-ups, and find where your interests lie.

In addition to regional breakouts, we have grouped the "bests" into three categories to match your interests within each region: (1) Cultural & Historical; (2) Outdoor Activities & Events; and (3) Where to Eat, Drink, & Stay. In the back, a cross-reference guide and an index can help you determine whether we have covered your favorite places or perhaps help you track down a place when you already know the name.

Gold Medal waters attract fly-fishing enthusiasts to free-flowing rivers on both sides of the Continental Divide.

PHOTO BY BURNHAM ARNDT, ASPEN CHAMBER RESORT ASSOCIATION

Because we love traveling with our kids, you'll find plenty of family-friendly outings within these pages. We have selected many kid-friendly activities and hope you will head out to enjoy the activities and places sure to create lasting memories with your children. In addition to places to go with the kids, when you want to get out of town for romance or other quiet adult times, we provide ideas.

We have also asked experts about some of their favorites and these "Expert Picks" are sprinkled throughout the book. We thought you might enjoy hearing from a brewmaster about his favorite beers, a mountain climber about the best routes, and even a renowned chef about the best restaurants in the state. Enjoy!

Colorado Highlights

In addition to the main body of entries, we want to reference some of the best of the best. Because of geographic disparity, many of our choices cross boundary lines. For example, few places on the planet boast more great peaks to climb: in Colorado, fifty-four of them top out at more than 14,000 feet (affectionately known as "Fourteeners"). We also have a fondness for climbing the more isolated ridges of 13,000-foot peaks and find great joy in early-season hiking in the lower elevations. Another "best" feature has to be the 471-mile Colorado Trail. Stretching from Denver to Durango, this amazing route encompasses a diversity of scenery, landscape, history, and culture; it can be taken in its entirety or in chunks over time.

Colorado has so much to offer. The task of picking "Colorado's best" challenges even those of us who have, perhaps, traveled and studied the state more than the average tourist. Colorado never ceases to amaze anglers, art lovers, climbers and runners, history buffs, wildlife watchers, festivalgoers, river rats, skiers, mountain bikers, hikers and motorists, buyers of fresh produce and diners of fine cuisine, hot-springs soakers, train riders, beer drinkers and wine connoisseurs, those who like to rough it and those who like to be pampered, fun seekers, truth seekers, sojourners, risk takers, and adventurers of all kinds. It's easy to run out of adjectives to describe the state's majestic and varied scenery and its history— including the days of the Gold Rush, the Santa Fe Trail, Mexican and Spanish Territory, Ute ancestral lands and the Anasazi, and woolly mammoth and dinosaurs. Colorado's sheer variety is astonishing in its breadth and impact.

Pick the "best"? For skiing, snowboarding, museums, galleries, nightlife, history, people, music festivals, culture, hut trips, stage rides, fishing, golf, and numerous other activities, you'll find our favorites. We hope you'll do everything in your power to head out in all seasons to enjoy this great state.

Early-morning sun casts a long shadow on the ruins of Lowry Pueblo. PHOTO BY DOUG WHITEHEAD

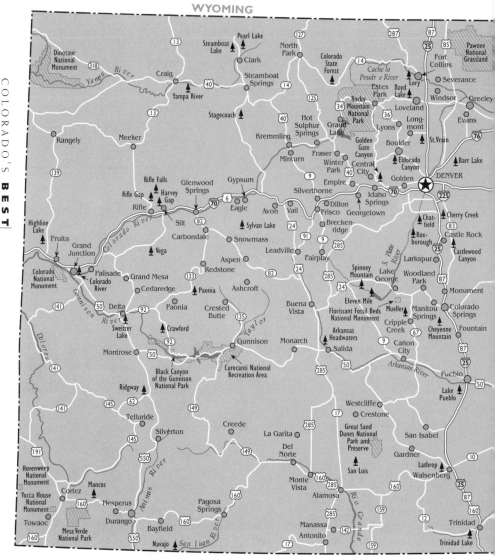

WYOMING

Dinosaur
National
Monument

318

Yampa River

Craig

13

Rangely

Meeker

139

Highline
Lake

Fruita

Grand
Junction

Colorado
National
Monument

141

Palisade
Colorado
River

Delta

Grand Mesa

Cedaredge

Paonia

Sweitzer
Lake

92

Montrose

50

Steamboat
Lake

Pearl Lake

Clark

Steamboat
Springs

14

Stagecoach

40

North
Park

127

Colorado
State
Forest

125

Kremmling

Minturn

Hot
Sulphur
Springs

Fraser
Winter
Park

40

Empire

287

Cache la
Poudr e River

34

Rocky
Mountain
National
Park

Grand
Lake

36

Golden
Gate
Canyon

Central
City

Lyons

Boulder

Eldorado
Canyon

287

25

Fort
Collins

85

Pawnee
National
Grassland

Lory

Boyd
Lake

Loveland

Estes
Park

Severance

Windsor

Greeley

Evans

76

St.Vrain

Barr Lake

DENVER

225

Rifle Falls

Rifle Gap

Rifle

Silt

Carbondale

Harvey
Gap

82

Glenwood
Springs

Gypsum

6

Eagle

Avon

Vail

Sylvan Lake

Snowmass

Vega

Aspen

Redstone

133

Paonia

Ashcroft

Crested
Butte

135

Crawford

92

Gunnison

Silverthorne

Dillon
Frisco
Breckenridge

24

91

Leadville

82

24

Fairplay

285

285

Idaho
Springs

Golden

Georgetown

9

9

Spinney
Mountain

Lake
George

Eleven
Mile

Buena
Vista

24

Florissant Fossil Beds
National Monument

Mueller

70

Chatfield

Roxborough

83

Cherry Creek

Castle Rock

25

Castlewood
Canyon

Larkspur

Woodland
Park

Manitou
Springs

Cripple
Creek

67

87

Monument

Colorado
Springs

Cheyenne
Mountain

Fountain

Monarch

Curecanti National
Recreation Area

285

Arkansas
Headwaters

Salida

9

50

Cañon
City

Arkansas River

Pueblo

87

25

141

Dolores
River

Black Canyon
of the Gunnison
National Park

Ridgway

62

145

149

Lake
Pueblo

50

Telluride

145

Creede

La Garita

285

17

Westcliffe

Crestone

San Isabel

10

191

Silverton

550

149

Del
Norte

Great Sand
Dunes National
Park and
Preserve

San Luis

Gardner

Lathrop

Walsenberg

25

87

Hovenweep
National
Monument

Cortez

Mancos

Yucca House
National
Monument

160

Hesperus

Towaoc

Durango

Bayfield

Mesa Verde
National Park

550

Pagosa
Springs

160

Navajo

San Juan River

160

Monte
Vista

285

Alamosa

Manassa

Antonito

142

285

159

Rio Grande

159

12

Trinidad

160

Trinidad Lake

NEW MEXICO

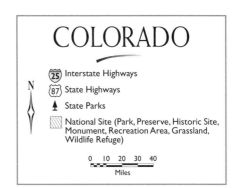

The western view from Cheeseman Park shows
downtown Denver with a backdrop of Front
Range peaks. PHOTO BY BRUCE CAUGHEY

THE FRONT RANGE

*From the very beginning, the confluence of Cherry Creek with the
South Platte River acted like a magnet in drawing the immigrants to
it. Despite the lack of trees and the somewhat barren aspects of the
infant town [Denver], it was a welcome sight to the traveler, weary
from the long and tiring stage ride across the plains. Miners
deserting the high hills during the winter months found it equally
attractive. Every year the place grew more civilized.*

—CARL UBBELOHDE, MAXINE BENSON,
AND DUANE A. SMITH, *A Colorado History*

Connecting from south to north, a string of cities—Pueblo, Colorado
Springs, Denver, Boulder, Fort Collins—began popping up along the
Front Range of the Rocky Mountains in the mid-1800s. These vibrant
places started as centers of commerce, shuttling and refining the ore
mined from the mountains as well as supporting the agricultural and
ranching economies of the eastern plains.

Today, with sustained growth and change driven by the economic
engine of Metro Denver and a more-than-desirable quality of life, the
urban edges seem to be getting less defined all the time. It used to seem
like a stretch of the imagination to think of a great Front Range city, but
now it's just a matter of time. After a century of boom-and-bust economic
swings, it seems like this linear concentration of civilization nestled
against the Rockies has finally come into its own, thanks in large measure
to the wellspring of talented individuals who have decided to live, learn,
work, and play here.

When organizing this book into regions, it became clear to us that
this logical grouping of urban, suburban, and rural areas known as the
Front Range may, in fact, be the most identifiable resource in the Rocky
Mountain West. With dramatic mountain views from many street corners, it's easy to see the appeal and the balance of life that keeps attracting newcomers.

Our mission to uncover the very best attributes of the Front Range
by nature causes us to turn away from the hassles that have come with
growth and change. It's not that we are unaware of them, but problems
and concerns get enough ink and airtime already. Our effort has been to
delve into what "best" attributes can be found along the Front Range. We
came across incredible places, including historical markers of the past,
romantic retreats, and great things to do with the kids.

We have skipped some of the obvious attractions, such as the
Museum of Nature and Science (and IMAX Theater) and the Colorado
History Museum. This doesn't mean you should consider skipping these
wonderful resources; it just means we wanted to uncover some less

obvious places and so have included the small towns to the north and south of Metro Denver. Instead of getting caught in a rut, perhaps you'll get a charge out of something new and unexpected. Whether you are coming to this area for a short vacation or have already put down roots, these fifty-plus "bests" from all along the Front Range should be on your short list of things to see and do.

Cultural & Historical

BEST Unsung Heroes of the West
Black American West Museum & Heritage Center (Denver)

In the classic conflict between cowboys and Indians, history is written by the winners. But even the losers have gotten far more ink than the Black cowboys. Consider this fact: nearly a third of all cowboys in the Old West were Black. Knowledge of their little-recognized contributions to conquering and settling the West was lost to generations of Americans.

When Paul Stewart came to Denver in the early 1960s, he began scouring the West for anything that told stories of those African American pioneers: old saddles, spurs, rare photographs, letters, oral histories. Characters such as rodeo king Bill Pickett and the feared gunslinger Mary Fields found their way into Western lore. Today, Stewart's collection forms the foundation of this small but indispensable museum in the heart of Denver's Five Points neighborhood.

The story does not stop there. The museum is housed in the renovated home of Dr. Justina Ford. Denied hospital privileges because of her race and gender, this Colorado medical pioneer delivered more than 7,000 babies in the homes of Denver's poor and disadvantaged during the first half of the twentieth century. The legacy of the Lady Doctor, and many other heroes, is preserved here. Loyal Buffalo Soldiers fought in the Indian Wars of the nineteenth century. The all-Black 10th Cavalry took San Juan Hill with Theodore Roosevelt in the Spanish-American War. The Tuskegee Airmen were some of the best pilots during World War II.

Guided tours, traveling exhibits, and a book- and gift shop add to your experience. Located across from the last light-rail station. 3091 California St.; 303-292-2566; www.blackamericanwest.org.

BEST Radio Show
etown

This eclectic, nationally syndicated, weekly radio show brings together music and a mission. The mission is to entertain, educate, and protect the cultural and environmental landscape through the live radio broadcast. The show features diverse musical acts—James Taylor, Big Head Todd and the Monsters, David Crosby, and Michelle Shocked. Other featured guests include everyone from poets and authors to policy makers. The show features the e-achievement awards to individuals who truly make a difference in their communities for the good of humankind. Usually the show emanates from the classic art-deco confines of the Boulder Theatre. Hosts Nick and Helen Forster lead the show with an earnest energy that does not come off as hokey. Stick around until the end and you will hear a synergistic live performance that serves as a fitting finale. Shawn Colvin, who has performed on the show, says, "I like where [etown] is coming from. I really appreciate the ecological overview … and the e-tones are one of the best bands I've ever played with." James Taylor said, "etown allows us to celebrate and honor the Earth and this remarkable community that sustains us." Their Web site features a schedule of musical guests and information on how to support the program or attend a broadcast. Contact the show at 303-443-8696 or e-mail them at info@etown.org. www.etown.org.

BEST Architectural Statement
Denver Art Museum Expansion

The fortresslike confines, narrow glass windows, and austere tiled shell of the 1971 vintage Denver Art Museum have been loved and hated over the years. But everyone seems fascinated by the jutting geometric angles of the new titanium-and-glass Frederic C. Hamilton building, which will be connected to the original building by a 100-foot bridge and will open in 2006. Designed by Daniel Libeskind, who is responsible for the design of the new, 1,776-foot-high World Trade Center Towers in New York City, the Denver Art Museum is moving into a world of international acclaim. Denver Art Museum Director Lewis Sharp says Libeskind is "one of the most innovative and passionate architects working today." Libeskind also designed the Jewish Museum in Berlin. The Denver project will be his first completed building in North America. The 146,000-square-foot addition will more than double the size of the current museum, making this the primary not-to-be-missed artists' showcase in the Rocky Mountain region. Traveling exhibitions will be drawn to the excitement of the heralded museum, and permanent displays will be expanded to include collections that have never had the chance to find a true home. Even during the construction period, you can gain an excellent sense of what kind of architectural marvel this museum will soon become. The excellent Palette's Restaurant is closed until 2006 for renovation. 100 W. 14th Ave. Pkwy.; 720-865-5000; www.denverart museum.org.

BEST Venue for Live Music on Planet Earth
Red Rocks Amphitheater (near Denver)

Red Rocks's incredible natural setting has been improved upon with the recent renovation of the crown jewel of live-music venues. Without question, this is the finest outdoor concert hall to enjoy big-name concerts along the Front Range, if not on the planet. Since 1941, this 8,000-seat theater has been attracting concertgoers to shows ranging from the Beatles to Bonnie Raitt to B. B. King. It remains the musicians' choice, thanks in part to acoustics perfected by Wolfgang Wagner, son of the great opera composer Richard Wagner. On summer evenings, as you listen to the music, the hard wooden bleachers hardly matter as the moon rises above the twinkling city lights. All the while you sit surrounded between immense slabs of red rock. Get concert information by calling Ticket-Master of Colorado at 303-596-4636.

Every Easter the sunrise service attracts thousands from across the Denver Metro area. On some summer nights, families and couples gather to watch movies projected on a large screen. Red Rocks Amphitheater is just part of an outdoor park that features hiking trails and great picnic spots. If you don't feel much like a picnic, you can stop in at the new Ship Rock Grille restaurant, which is located a short elevator ride down from the back of the amphitheater, with a deck and views to the west. The southwestern fare is worth checking out. Adjacent to the new Colorado-style restaurant, be sure to check out the Red Rocks Performers Hall of Fame, with massive concert pictures from live shows on the rocks—including the Beatles, Santana, U2, Sting, Willie Nelson, Stevie Ray Vaughn, and the Grateful Dead—and sound stations for visitors to listen down their own private memory lane.

To get here from Denver, take I-70 west to Morrison. Then drive south to the park entrance. For more information about the park, call the Trading Post at 303-697-8935. www.redrocks online.com.

Red Rocks Amphitheater.

BEST Stately College Campus
University of Colorado at Boulder

The stately, 600-acre University of Colorado at Boulder (CU Boulder) campus, with its attractive sandstone-and-red-tile-roofed buildings, massive trees, and long walkways, captures a welcome backdrop to higher learning. In the shadow of the dramatic uplift of the Flatirons, the campus emanates beauty and a strong architectural connection to its surroundings. To the uninitiated, students seem aimless as they wander to and from classes and hang out at the outdoor fountains at the University Memorial Center (UMC) courtyard. The UMC draws people inside for lunch at the Alfred Packer Grill, to buy a CU mug at the University Bookstore, or down the hall for video games and bowling.

At times, especially with several high-profile issues related to football-team recruiting, it feels like CU has not yet shed the party-school image—and it may never. For the most part, students still maintain an easygoing atmosphere that has existed in Boulder for decades. Despite obvious pressures to the contrary, Boulder manages to stay apart from and unhurried by nearby Denver. As one prominent resident puts it, "Boulder is fifteen square miles of land surrounded by reality."

To get a feel for the campus, wander past Old Main, the university's first stately building, which was already under construction when Colorado became a state in 1876. "It loomed before us gaunt and alone in the pitiless clear light—no tree nor shrub nor any human habitation was in sight," wrote Jane Sewall, daughter of CU's first president, in 1877. In the intervening years, the campus has come a long way, and Old Main still stands as a spruced-up reminder of the days of yore. The initial freshman class of twelve students has grown to more than 25,000 students today.

To learn about the storied history of the university, tour the inside of Old Main and visit the CU Heritage Center (Mon. through Fri. 10 A.M. to 4 P.M.; Sat. 10 A.M. to 2 P.M.). The CU Museum, Norlin Library, and Folsom Field (home of the CU Buffaloes Big 12 football team) are other good stops while on campus.

To get to the campus, drive north on I-25 from Denver to the Boulder Turnpike (U.S. Hwy. 36) and continue twenty-seven miles northwest. Follow the signs to the campus. 303-492-1411; www.colorado.edu.

BEST Collection of Tourist Traps
Colorado Springs

Colorado Springs has become the Colorado capital of cheesy, albeit sometimes very worthwhile, attractions. Its slightly tarnished distinction continues to be vigorously promoted by the city's elite, who have always welcomed tourists to pull off the highway to enjoy a numbing quantity of attractions.

The Colorado Springs Convention and Visitors Bureau can't stand the idea that we came up with this "best" category, but heck, it's true! And the Colorado Springs founding fathers should be proud of the fact that you truly can see it all in this modern city nestled at the base of 14,110-foot Pikes Peak, from Anasazi ruins moved 350 miles from their home (Manitou Cliff Dwellings) to the Pro Rodeo Hall of Fame (719-528-4761). On CO Hwy. 115, it's tough to miss the RV-size beetle that announces a massive collection of bugs at the May Natural History Museum.

With its paved underground walkways and a humongous, above-ground gift shop, Cave of the Winds still packs 'em in with impressive crowd management; they claim you can't miss their laser-light show on the nearby canyon walls. You really should head underground to see what secrets these caves hold, but do not expect to find one iota of solitude, even in the cool confines of the cave.

We're not here to cast aspersions. For example, it's understandable that Santa's North Pole is, without a doubt, a young child's favorite detour. The lights, music, elves, and kiddy rides all complement Santa Claus's (real beard) newfound home at the foot of Pikes Peak. And the World Figure Skating Museum and Hall of Fame is just the ticket for some visitors. So, too, the Flying W Ranch, which has served up chuck-wagon dinners and cowboy music since the 1950s.

The nerve of some local entrepreneurs can be stunning. For example, the "Grandest Mile of Scenery in Colorado" at Seven Falls is pretty nice but, to us, hardly worth the steep admission price. More than a quarter-million visitors pay up annually to see a so-called natural waterfall and canyon illuminated by a thousand multicolored lights and "enhanced" by piped-in music. You can skip the entrance fee and still get a good view of the falls by heading up North Cheyenne Canyon Rd. and hiking up the mellow, mile-long Mount Cutler Trail to the falls. Remember, free national forests comprise one-fifth of Colorado's land, not to even mention national parks, state parks, Bureau of Land Management land, and designated wilderness areas. Alas, it's so much sweeter to find your very own waterfalls and canyons!

BEST Weather Laboratory
National Center for Atmospheric Research (Boulder)

Few places rival the National Center for Atmospheric Research (NCAR) for its picture-perfect setting in the foothills above Boulder. In a striking facility designed by I. M. Pei to resemble cliff dwellings built by Colorado's ancient residents, visitors learn about weather research and then go out into the weather for a hike on open-space trails. NCAR's Mesa Lab welcomes visitors for free, self-guided tours or, with some advance notice, will arrange customized tours for groups of adults or children. Sponsored in part by the National Science Foundation, the lab serves as a place for visitors to appreciate scientific research that impacts our everyday lives.

Technical research includes efforts to determine the dynamics and impacts of everything from global warming to wind shear. Scientists delve into mathematical models of sea-surface temperature impacts on weather to atmospheric changes due to the use of chlorofluorocarbons. With the help of Cray supercomputers, a range of computer simulations analyze various climatic components that interact to create our weather. Although some of the multisyllable words you will encounter at NCAR may intimidate you at first, the interactive displays and helpful staff manage to make sense of the complex research.

And when you get tired of it all, head outside for some hiking or a picnic in the adjacent Boulder County Open Space. Many trail options, including a wheelchair-accessible trail, leave right from NCAR's backdoor. Keep your eyes peeled for deer along the pretty drive up to the lab and take some time to enjoy the top-of-the-world views back east over the plains. 1850 Table Mesa Dr.; 303-497-1000; www.ncar.ucar.edu.

BEST Dino Evidence
Dinosaur Ridge (west of Denver)

Dinosaur Ridge.
PHOTO BY JACK LENZO

To the untrained eye it's just another hill in a state full of mountains. But look a little closer and you'll see that the ridge known locally as the Hogback is really an ancient landscape tilted on its side. Look closer still and discover dinosaur tracks from huge beasts that roamed the area eons ago. The first stegosaurus bones ever discovered were found right here along Dinosaur Ridge.

Once a month from May through October, the road over the Hogback to Morrison is closed to car traffic. Volunteers from the Friends of Dinosaur Ridge, including retired geologists and paleontologists, station themselves at various points along the way, each filling in for visitors a different piece of the geologic puzzle revealed in the exposed layers. From mysterious orbs in the rock thought to be footprints of an apatosaur to small imprints made from the tiny shells of ancient crustaceans, a picture of life along the edge of a onetime sea emerges; this was a popular thoroughfare for theropods and their brethren.

If the theory holds true that today's birds are yesterday's dinosaurs, then maybe it makes sense that this landform has now become known as a highway for hawks. Any day throughout the year, you can make the fifteen-minute hike up to the top of the ridge to join researchers on the Hawk Watch Project counting thousands of hawks, eagles, falcons, and other raptors as they ride the air currents on their northward migration. The connection between dinosaurs and birds notwithstanding, this spine along the foothills continues to attract nature's travelers to this particular spot on Earth.

The Dinosaur Ridge Visitors Center is located on the east side of the Hogback, where Alameda Ave. crosses C-470. 303-697-DINO (3466); www.dinoridge.org.

BEST Place to Feel Like a Giant
Tiny Town (west of Denver)

To be perfectly honest, this "best" pick ended as a coin toss between the ever-popular Children's Museum of Denver and Tiny Town. We decided to give the nod to Tiny Town after a summer expedition with a few members of the under-four-foot-tall set. They loved every moment of peering inside the miniature fire station, homes, churches, stores, and, of course, taking the dwarf railway (with actual-size conductor) around the village. Sharing a picnic on a shaded grassy area at the twenty-acre facility topped off the day. The best part? Watching kids imagine themselves as giants, bending over to peer inside windows at the realistic-looking furnishings and miniature figures of people.

Open daily from Memorial Day to Labor Day. Small fee. Located south of Denver off U.S. Hwy. 285 and Turkey Creek Rd. 6249 S. Turkey Creek Rd.; 303-697-6829; www.tinytownrailroad.com.

BEST Bookstore of All Time
Tattered Cover (Denver)

With four levels packed with all manner of publications, the Tattered Cover in Cherry Creek remains Colorado's favorite book-buying destination. Add a funky café and a gourmet restaurant atop its more than 150,000 titles, as well as an extensive newsstand, and this store becomes a magnet for book lovers. People go out of their way to shop here—not only due to the breadth and depth of the books available but because of the well-versed sales staff. They excel at helping you find that hard-to-name volume you heard about from a friend but cannot quite remember.

Despite the name, this store does not sell used or tattered books.

Customers are, however, encouraged to plop down on a comfortable, overstuffed chair or couch and leaf through books while bathed in soft lamplight. Nobody's going to hurry you—and if you get hungry, you can retreat to the first-floor café or upstairs to the fancier confines of the Fourth Story Restaurant and Bar.

Book aficionados appreciate the large number of signings and readings the store offers. Everybody from local authors to megastars claim status as a result of a Tattered Cover appearance. When owner Joyce Meskis opened her first bookstore just two blocks away from the Cherry Creek location some twenty-five years ago, she found the neighborhood receptive, but her dreams soon outgrew her space. After several expansions, Meskis enlisted employees and even some of her loyal customers to haul boxes of books into her current Cherry Creek location, at 2955 E. First Ave. 303-322-7727; www.tatteredcover.com. Check out the lower-downtown sister store at 1628 16th St. 303-436-1070. Though it's a bit smaller, it offers a similar book-buying ambiance. A new, suburban branch in Highlands Ranch has a home in the Town Center.

BEST Throwback in Time
Renaissance Festival (Larkspur)

Blink twice, rub your eyes, and realize that you have traveled 400 years backward to the days of King Henry VIII and Queen Anne Boleyn. In a village setting in the woods near Larkspur a costumed cast of hundreds engages guests in a Renaissance fantasy complete with jousters, jugglers, and jigglers (the ladies' dress of the day features ample cleavage). More than 200 village artisans create original crafts and, though many art forms are not authentic to the times, nothing is mass produced. Of course, along with all the music and merrymaking comes a wealth of hearty food (roasted turkey legs and corn on the cob are perennial favorites), sweets, and drink.

Jousting matches take place in front of the King's Royal Court on summer weekends at the Renaissance Festival. PHOTO BY DOUG WHITEHEAD

This sometimes-bizarre, always-unpredictable festival has been running during summer weekends since the mid-1970s. You can participate in the scene just by walking around and not being shy. The leather goblets, flowered head wreaths, gargoyles, jewelry, and clothing seem perfectly appropriate at the festival, but you might want to consider how they'll look back home. Various scheduled shows include the pageantry of knights in a jousting match before the king and queen and the amazing antics of a hypnotist. Don't miss the coarse hilarity of Puke and Snot. "This is the version of *Robin Hood* your parents rent when you're off at camp!" they said while bounding around the stage in tights and making audience members blush between guffaws. The Endangered Cat Show, Tortuga Twins, and sword swallowing by Thom Sellectomy continue to delight crowds.

Kids will likely see and hear stuff outside their parents' normal bounds, but they absolutely love the magic of this place. In addition to the memorable highlight of combat jousting, they can enter the Children's Realm and ride a camel, pet a potbellied pig, or climb into the dragon swing; all this happens in the midst of a living museum.

Located in Larkspur, off I-25 between Denver and Colorado Springs, the festival takes place during eight summer weekends from mid-June through early August. Admission is charged; bring plenty of cash (or credit cards) for what's in store inside. Free for kids under five. 303-688-6010; www.coloradorenaissance.com.

BEST Cultural Festival
Greek Festival (Denver)

The rapid-fire strains of oddly tuned string instruments bring an upbeat tempo to Denver's annual Greek Festival in late June. Novices learn how to folk dance to the music, but when the experts show up in traditional costumes, most newcomers back away from the spotlight and join the circle. Male Greek dancers delight festivalgoers with leaping, high-energy moves, and the more subtle steps of female dancers bring a quiet beauty to the forefront. This festival appeals greatly to all the senses—the most memorable being the smells and tastes of traditional food, which can be purchased at the many stands. Not much compares with the scent of grilling souvlaki as you wander around the Greek marketplace. The squid, too, tastes wonderful when prepared by people who have eaten this delicacy for generations. And don't even think about skipping a slice of baklava, a honey-laden pastry, or a custard dish called *galaktobouriko*. Vendors sell authentic crafts, clothing, and jewelry as you get lost in the feel of a traditional Greek village.

The festival takes place adjacent to the unique gold dome of the Greek Orthodox Cathedral of the Assumption. If you have time, take a tour inside to see the impressive collection of Byzantine icons. The festival has been going strong since the mid-1960s, and we predict it will continue to be a draw for generations to come. Small admission fee. 4610 E. Alameda Ave.; 303-388-9314; www.assumptioncathedral.org.

BEST Culture in Suburbia
Arvada Center for the Performing Arts

The depth of culture in suburbia has always been shallower than in urban settings, college towns, and artisan communities. Thankfully, the movers and shakers in Old Town Arvada felt they could avoid cultural dearth by putting together this center. And the Arvada Town Council recently approved a multimillion-dollar show of thanks to allow for an expansion of this important cultural center. It sits on a large plot of land in northwest Metro Denver and features a 500-seat indoor theater, 1,200-seat outdoor amphitheater, art display areas, and dance areas. The complex, with its large, grassy slope, now features a terrific playground, replete with a colorful serpent that twists its way along a high-tech padded flooring. Little ones climb, hang, explore, and enjoy every part from the tip of its scaled tail to the dragon's massive head, with its toothy grin, flared nostrils, and large, arched eyeballs.

Check the listings to see what's happening here. You can enjoy everything from professionally produced plays and musical or dance events to a variety of classes and a very popular craft show in winter. Located at 6901 Wadsworth Ave., Arvada. Listen to a recording on classes, concerts, and plays at 720-898-7201; www.arvadacenter.org.

BEST College Sports Scene
University of Denver Ice Hockey

This category presented one of the most difficult choices in the entire book. In a not-too-scientific methodology, having rooted out our alumni bias and natural sports preferences, we came up with the most dynamic sports legacy in the entire state. University of Denver (DU) hockey has been a dominant force and has won national championships. Sure, we thought about college football, including the once-dominant CU Buffaloes, the CSU Rams, and even the always-feisty Air Force Academy Falcons with their lightning-bolt helmets and pristine foothills location north of Colorado Springs. But truly nothing compares to the energy and longtime traditions of the DU Pioneers, which, invariably, can be found among the country's top NCAA Division I hockey teams. Even its archrival, Colorado College, cannot quite compete with the energy, enthusiasm, and traditions that come with the Pioneers.

You can forget about the bench-clearing brawls that make pro hockey seem, at times, a parody of what the sport intended. Sit up close in the new 6,200-seat Magness Ice Arena, part of the copper-skinned Daniel L. Ritchie Center (just west of University Blvd. and I-25) and you'll benefit twice: (1) you won't run up the limit on your gold card; and (2) you'll get an up-close view of muscle, grit, and finesse on ice. The rowdy student section and band ensemble help energize the entire arena. With no red line, the pace of this game can reach frenzied pitches as the puck slides frantically back and forth across the ice. At utterly fair prices, the DU Pioneers provide a value guarantee on your entertainment dollar.

The season runs from October to mid-March. Call 303-871-2336 for tickets and information. www.denverpioneers.collegesports.com.

BEST Place to See Junk Transformed
Swetsville Zoo (near Fort Collins)

Bill Swets, a soft-spoken man in faded-blue overalls, rules over an imaginary kingdom of fanciful dinosaurs, bizarre creatures, and imaginary friends. Swets decided to do something with all the rubbish that collects outside of farmhouses and slowly rusts away. He transformed what must have been a mountain of accumulated throwaway gears, flywheels, scrap metal, and defunct machinery into more than seventy offbeat sculptures. Some playful, some sinister, these sculptures make every adult visitor wonder: "What could possibly motivate someone to do this?" The kids, however, couldn't care less. They will go nuts over this place, enjoying all of the strange sculptures that lie in wait along the winding, grassy pathway. Bring a lunch and hang out for a while.

Besides all of the sculptures, Swets operates a miniature steam railway that plies a .75-mile route beside the Poudre River. It's all free, but Swets says donations are accepted. Be sure to check out the welded metal turrets that dwarf the front entrance to Swets's small home, which lies adjacent to the sculpture garden. To get here from Denver, take I-25 north to the Harmony Rd. exit (265), which is just south of Fort Collins. Drive east of the interstate to the zoo at 4801 E. Harmony Rd.

BEST One-Stop Shopping Experience
McGuckin Hardware (Boulder)

One-stop shopping takes on new meaning when you enter this family-owned Boulder institution. Despite increased competition from chain megastores, for forty-five years McGuckins has reigned as king of the hardwares, thanks to its immense collection of eclectic stuff. The store's motto rings true: "If we don't have it, you don't need it." And customers do arrive with unusual requests. One man showed up at the store with his dad's ashes in a bag under his arm, trying to find an appropriate container. He couldn't pass up a good deal on a thermos, but it wasn't quite large enough to hold all the ashes. Before leaving, the son actually spread the remaining ashes outside of the store, saying Dad would have been pleased. Yeah, right.

You don't have to buy anything as you wander among this amassed collection of some 200,000 items, including everything from tools and camping equipment to wheelbarrows and toasters. But buying every variety of nails, screws, and bolts (up to an inch in diameter) has never been easier, especially when you enlist the help of one of the staff's easy-to-find green-vested employees. And, if you ever need a gift for a hard-to-buy-for relative, stop here and be guaranteed to find something to make them smile. McGuckin has one of the best collections of unusual Christmas ornaments we've ever encountered.

Located inside a hangar-size store off 2525 Arapahoe Ave. 303-443-1822; www.mcguckin.com.

BEST Place to Float Like a Butterfly
Butterfly Pavilion and Insect Center (Westminster)

Like a peaceful dreamscape filled with thousands of fluorescent, fluttering images, the domed environs of the Butterfly Pavilion create a memorable and unique experience. Pathways wind among a verdant botanical garden complete with ponds stocked with ornamental carp. The humid temperature hovers above 80° F, making this a perfect escape for a winter day. Benches stationed here and there encourage leisurely viewing. Take your time, look closely through the foliage and up along the ceiling nets, and you will see an array of patterns and colors created by nature.

In addition to legions of fluttering butterflies, you can actually feel a hairy tarantula in Westminster. PHOTO BY BRUCE CAUGHEY

There's nothing like a bright-blue butterfly landing on your shoulder to elicit smiles from all those around. Watch your step, however, and before you leave, be careful to check for any hitchhikers in the mirrored enclosure between the double sets of glass doors.

A glass case shows the butterflies emerging from their egg-shaped chrysalides, battling through the hard cases to spread their fragile, wet wings. Another room features an interesting collection of insects. If you ever wanted to feel a hairy tarantula march up your arm or stroke the slippery brown back of a pinecone-size Madagascar hissing cockroach, be sure to stop here. A relatively recent addition showcases hands-on tidal pools, a real draw for the younger kids, who can touch sea stars and other clingy creatures that exist on the fringe between ocean and land.

The gift shop draws visitors inside to buy a multitude of butterfly and insect paraphernalia, from science kits to tacky coffee mugs. Open year-round, seven days a week, except for Thanksgiving and Christmas. Located just off the Boulder Turnpike (U.S. Hwy. 36) in Westminster at 6252 W. 104th Ave. 303-469-5441; www.butterflies.org.

Outdoor Activities & Events

BEST Spectator Event
Colorado Mammoth (Denver)

It feels a bit like a college party when you attend games of Colorado's first professional indoor lacrosse league. Rock music reaches the rafters of the Pepsi Center during play, a hot tub sits just behind the glass for some lucky fans, and halftime antics ensue, including sumo-suit stunts, tricycle races, and beer chugging, along with the requisite fireworks and cheerleaders. Oh, and between all the action, a fast-paced, indoor lacrosse game takes place. You will undoubtedly spend more on concessions and parking than the game tickets, which you can pick up starting at about five bucks. It is a perfect place to scream loud for your team and enjoy all the distractions you can imagine. Even if you don't know the intricacies of the game, the announcers will explain what is happening; understanding hockey helps with some of the mechanics of the sport. And the huge, sometimes-sellout crowds always yell in unison when there is a penalty on the opposing team: "Get in the box!" Some people border on the fanaticism you might see at a World Wide Wrestling Federation event. Yes, they will be sitting all around you. Enjoy the not-totally-serious sporting experience and let yourself be entertained by the entirety of the scene. 303-405-1101; www.coloradomammoth.com.

BEST Place to Show off Your Snakeskin Boots
National Western Stock Show, Rodeo, and Horse Show (Denver)

The National Western Stock Show, Rodeo, and Horse Show has come to Denver every January since 1906 (when it was held in a tent!), but it is never cold enough to put a chill on the hundreds of cowboys who come to town. It is undoubtedly the biggest and best show in Denver, with many more than a half million paying visitors, so dig into that closet for a ten-gallon hat, snakeskin boots, and some tight Wrangler jeans. That is, if you want to fit in! Everyone is welcome to the friendly, slightly smelly confines of the National Western Complex in Denver. The rodeo brings out the best bull and bronc riders in the region, but some folks prefer the

children's mutton-bustin' competition.
Precision horseback-barrel riding and the
Clydesdales always bring out good
crowds. For a shift, try visiting the colorful Mexican rodeo, which serves as a
tribute to Hispanic culture. The exhibit
hall has all sorts of gadgets—from
always-sharp knife ware to never-stick
pans to ladders that twist into many con-
figurations. You will need some serious
willpower to walk through without buying any number of necessities. 4-H teams
from across the land come to display
their very finest stock, some of which
are sold at auction. You will see
incredibly groomed bulls, sheep, rabbits, birds, and, of course, llamas. The
whole family will enjoy this event.

A bull rider loses his grip at the National
Western Rodeo in Denver. COURTESY OF THE
NATIONAL WESTERN STOCK SHOW

For information about the National Western Stock Show, Rodeo,
and Horse Show, call 303-297-1166, extension 810, or visit www.national
western.com.

BEST Walking Mall
Pearl St. Mall (Boulder)

Maybe you've heard that Boulderites, even temporary residents attending
the University of Colorado, march to distinctly different drummers. It's
especially true while walking down the brick-lined Pearl St. Mall, where,
depending on the night, you might hear African drums, steel drums, or
bongo drums. If that isn't enough, street guitarists, violinists, and saxo-
phonists set up in doorways or between turn-of-the-century historic
buildings vying for your spare dollar.

On summer evenings you'll also catch magicians, mimes, comedi-
ans, and acrobats who sometimes draw astonishing numbers of people for
their short acts. All this hyperactivity happens amidst some terrific shops,
galleries, cafés, and restaurants. Despite all the racket, the mall really is a
place to converse on one of the many benches or while hanging out at a
restaurant courtyard sipping a beer and taking in the essence of what
Boulder is all about. One of our favorite places to catch a sunset over the
Flatirons is from the rooftop tables at the West End Tavern (926 Pearl
St.; 303-444-3535). The streets surrounding the Pearl St. Mall host more
of Boulder's nightlife and shopping district. So find a parking space and
wander around the entire area surrounding Pearl St. between 9th and
15th Sts. www.downtownboulder.com.

BEST Afternoon Stroll, Skate, or Ride
Washington Park (Denver)

The heart of a city lies in its public places, and Washington Park remains Denver's pulsing lifeline, especially in summer. Whether walking around Grasmere Lake, jogging the park's perimeter trail, or pedaling your bike in the park's interior, you'll encounter a rich mix of the city's inhabitants. Old couples gaze at the replica of George Washington's colorful garden at Mount Vernon while in-line skaters whir around the wide asphalt road. On warm days, volleyball nets and boundary ropes sprout by the tens along grassy areas of the park, vying for space with ultimate Frisbee, soccer, and touch-football games. Everyone shares the park's beauty and diversity.

Kids love the place, flocking to a couple of large playgrounds with their parents in tow—the one adjacent to the historic boathouse blends the best aspects of a medieval castle and a McDonald's Playland. The park's outdoor tennis courts, indoor pool, and gym all attract fitness buffs.

To see people totally immersed in their element, check out the older, mostly male crowd at the dozen or so well-used horseshoe pits on the park's west side and those impeccably dressed denizens at the manicured croquet greens to the east. There's even a small section of the park reserved for the venerable sport of lawn bowling! A phalanx of tennis courts can be found on the southern edge of the park.

Washington Park lies to the east of Downing St. between Virginia and Louisiana Aves.

BEST Amusement Park
Six Flags/Elitch Gardens (Denver)

As if they heard that faint tune coming from the ice-cream truck, the urge to let the inner child come out and play sweeps over drivers on I-25 as they approach the Platte Valley. They look out at an incredible juxtaposition of thrilling rides nestled right up against the jagged skyline of downtown Denver. This sight becomes Denver, but many of us still hanker for a time when Elitch's meant heading to historic North Denver to enjoy the rickety wooden Mr. Twister; mature, landscaped gardens; picnic tables; and the famous Trocadero Ballroom. The old place held a quaint charm for sixty-six years that will never quite be replicated.

But then who could be thinking about a charming setting when riding face-first down a 125-foot drop before careening through inverted loops on the Boomerang? If you find it frightening that your eyeballs practically pop out of their sockets, you might find some comfort in knowing you're not alone. Just when you think you've had enough, the cars launch into the twisting, turning loops backward! An expanded children's area and plenty of water rides make this state-of-the-art park an all-ages experience. The rides, shows, attractions, and food will keep you busy all day and into the night.

The park now flies the banner of Six Flags as it entered a massive building program and added Looney Tunes and DC Comics characters such as Batman, Bugs Bunny, Sylvester, Tweety, and Daffy Duck to the merchandising and marketing program.

In addition to the amusement park, hot summer days see visitors in swimsuits enjoying massive slides, the perpetual wave pool, and the lazy river.

Children three and under get in free, but everyone else pays a pretty hefty admission, although special deals abound. Open April through October. Located at 2000 Elitch Cir. From I-25, go south on Speer Blvd. (exit 212A), then turn onto Elitch Cir. 303-595-4386; www.sixflags.com/elitchgardens.

BEST "Primitive" State Park
Roxborough (Littleton)

Jutting vertical slabs of red sandstone rise spectacularly in the diverse transition zone between prairie and mountains just forty-five minutes south of downtown Denver. Created by 500 million years of geological turmoil combined with erosion, this state park comprises a "primitive" nature preserve close to home. Having barely escaped the developer's blade, Roxborough now plays an important role in safeguarding nature for its visitors. It's an absolutely great place to escape the city, and it is so close that you only need two to three hours to get a real sense of the area's beauty.

Late-day shadows enhance the beauty of the red-sandstone rocks that march along the Front Range just south of Denver.
PHOTO BY BRUCE CAUGHEY

Hikers enjoy miles of easy-to-moderate trails through nine ecotypes, including verdant meadows, thickets of Ponderosa pine, and desert terrain interspersed with yucca and colored with patches of thick gambel oak. Even if you just want to enjoy a picnic at one of the close-in overlooks, this destination provides a strong connection with nature. Spiked with ever-present reddish towers of stone, some as flat as upturned serving trays, the landscape plays on your imagination. Check in at the visitors center, nestled among the rocks, to see what recent wildlife sightings have been made. They will likely include deer, mountain lion, hawks, and eagles, among many other species. Talk with rangers for in-depth information about the flora, fauna, and geology of the entire area. Small admission fee to the park.

To reach Roxborough State Park, take U.S. Hwy. 85 (Santa Fe Dr.) south to Titan Rd. Turn right and proceed 3.5 miles. Follow the curve left (south) three miles to a signed entrance to the park. 4751 N. Roxborough Dr.; 303-973-3959; www.parks.state.co.us.

BEST Place to Spend a Lazy Afternoon
Chautauqua Park (Boulder)

From the sloping, grassy expanse of Boulder's Chautauqua Park next to the jutting rocks of the Flatirons, you can lose yourself in deep thoughts, superficial musings, or your favorite trashy novel. Spread out your blanket and share some gourmet treats with a special friend or dive into some PB and Js and potato chips with your kids. Toss the Frisbee, visit the playground, or take a hike. What you do in this glorious setting doesn't matter much—just being here and enjoying the moment counts volumes.

Head out on the miles of well-marked trails in the Boulder Open Space. A favorite afternoon hike leads up toward the Flatirons and Bluebell Shelter. Be sure to keep your eyes peeled for wildlife along the way, especially deer (and an occasional mountain lion) and, in season, a colorful spectrum of birds. You can often see technical climbers inching their way up the nearly vertical rocks with the help of ropes. Other walking trails lead to the top of nearby Flagstaff Mountain or south to the National Center for Atmospheric Research (NCAR). If you don't feel like hiking, bring along a kite; this park is often buffeted by a steady breeze. On many summer nights you can catch a concert in the historic barnlike setting of the Chatauqua Auditorium. All of this and we haven't yet mentioned the venerable Chautauqua Dining Hall, which offers great American fare.

To reach the park, drive west on Baseline Rd. Chautauqua Park is on the south side of the street before the road curves up Flagstaff Mountain.

BEST Urban Oasis
Jefferson County Open Space

Since 1972, millions of dollars set aside by the citizens of Jefferson County have purchased hundreds of thousands of acres of land along the foothills. In the face of unprecedented urban sprawl, Jeffco has done us all a huge favor. Large tracts of open spaces remain undeveloped, protecting an important aspect of Colorado's heritage. Eighteen Jefferson

County Open Space Parks provide miles of hiking, mountain biking, and horse trails, and nature and history programs. They also help to keep open important wildlife corridors and dramatic vistas of the Front Range.

One of the early acquisitions wasn't open space at all. The Hiwan Homestead Museum in Evergreen preserves a log home and many of its furnishings from the 1800s. Mount Falcon Park, above Parmalee Gulch, was the site of an ambitious, turn-of-the-century project by John Brisben Walker. Enlisting Colorado schoolkids and their penny-size donations in the effort, he hoped to build a summer White House for U.S. presidents. Getting only as far as the cornerstone and foundation, the ruins of his attempt still lie on trails that bring impressive views of downtown Denver far below. The remains of his own stone house, which burned down, also sit in the park. The trails of Pine Valley Ranch Park, about five miles off of U.S. Hwy. 285 from Pine Junction, connect with trailheads of the Pike National Forest. An observatory in the park provides a perfect venue for stargazing. At the Lookout Mountain Nature Center, north of I-70, scores of nature hikes and programs keep urban kids in touch with the outdoors. Lair O' The Bear offers secluded walks in the woods along Bear Creek.

New properties are being added to Jefferson County Open Space every year. Maps and other information are available at its Golden offices. 303-271-5925; www.co.jefferson.co.us.

BEST Backyard Camping
Golden Gate Canyon State Park (Golden)

Close to the city, Golden Gate Canyon State Park might as well be a hundred miles from civilization. Lush meadows, aspen forests, and abundant wildlife once attracted Utes, Cheyenne, and Arapaho to this rugged country. City folks today find solitude and sanctuary from smog and busy streets. Urbanites escape to this close-by park to replace a skyline of tall buildings with expansive views of Front Range mountain peaks.

Located in the foothills between Nederland, Central City, and Golden, the park offers camping that runs the gamut from developed campgrounds to primitive backcountry sites. At Reverend's Ridge, you'll find more than a hundred cushy campsites with hookups. A camper-services building offers hiking information along with showers and laundry machines. Summertime nature programs are held Friday and Saturday nights next to a roaring campfire in the amphitheater. Other areas in the park are reserved just for tents, and a few sites are for horseback riders only. If you really want to get away from the city, twenty-three first-come, first-served backcountry sites are spread throughout Golden Gate. Permits can be obtained at the visitors center. In addition, four primitive shelters styled like those along the Appalachian Trail are located in remote corners of the wilderness.

Miles of trails crisscross this country through which a toll road once carried supplies to the nearby booming mining towns of Central City and Blackhawk. Call the visitors center for more information: 303-582-3707. Reservations should be made well in advance of your visit. Call Colorado State Parks at 303-470-1144. www.parks.state.co.us.

BEST Moderate Mountain Biking
Horsetooth Mountain Park and Lory State Park (Fort Collins)

Mountain biking doesn't have to be only for adrenaline junkies. Many of us appreciate the way a bike provides access to nature. The rolling landscape of these two interconnected parks provides a perfect escape only fifteen minutes from the urban trails of Fort Collins. These parks lie in a transition zone between the plains and the mountains, with dramatic rock outcroppings above (including one that looks a bit like a horse's tooth and another famous one called Arthur's Rock) and the snaking shoreline of Horsetooth Reservoir along the eastern boundary of the parks.

With more than thirty miles of trails just behind the red-sandstone hogback, riders have a great opportunity to explore a lovely area that encompasses the short-grass prairie as well as thick ponderosa forest. As a recognized equestrian area, though, trails must be shared with horseback riders, and consideration is expected. (Horses can be rented on the premises at Double Diamond Stables.) Hikers also love this area.

One of our favorites is the 1.9-mile Overlook Trail. It connects with other, tougher trails and offers sweeping views as it winds along the red-sandstone hogback that marks the mountains' final descent to the plains. The six-mile-long Foothills Trail also offers a moderate introduction to the area and gorgeous views of the reservoir, as it parallels the shoreline much of the way.

For more information, contact Lory State Park at 970-493-1623. www.parks.state.co.us.

A lone mountain biker shares the trail with horses at Lory State Park. PHOTO BY BRUCE CAUGHEY

BEST Soaking after a Hike
Eldorado Artesian Springs (near Boulder)

Because the forbidding rock walls in Eldorado Canyon appear impenetrable, this area remains a slice of heaven close by. First things first. Take a hike on one of Eldorado Canyon State Park's many trails that lead steadily upward from the canyon floor. Or, sit back next to South Boulder Creek and watch technical climbers muscle their way upward while on belay. Whatever you choose, just be sure to make your way to Eldorado Artesian Springs during the heat of the day.

This slice of vintage America has been here since becoming a fashionable spa in the early 1900s. Today, it has definitely slipped from its former heights, when there was a choice of restaurants and a nice hotel, and it was, for a time, a favorite stopping-off place for Dwight D. Eisenhower. But the springs, nonetheless, remains a fantastic place to spend some time and soak away the trail dust. Heated by natural geothermal water more than a mile beneath the surface, the old concrete pool remains a comfortable swimming temperature. A long steel slide descends into the clear water from one corner. Sunbathers find spots on balcony overlooks or down along a narrow grassy area next to the creek. If you get thirsty or want to buy some bottles of Eldorado artesian water for the road, be sure to stop in at the snack bar.

Fee charged. Open from Memorial Day to Labor Day from 10 A.M. to 6 P.M. To get here, take CO Hwy. 93 (Broadway) south from Boulder for 5.5 miles. Turn right on Eldorado Springs Dr. and continue for three miles to the park entrance. The pool lies off to your right just before the park entrance. 303-499-1316; www.eldoradosprings.com.

BEST Trailhead
Colorado Trail/Waterton Canyon (Denver)

While you are pulling up to any trailhead, a sense of expectation and an openness to discovery accompany you. Whether you're out for a day hike or planning to trek along the 469-mile Colorado Trail from Denver to Durango, the Waterton Canyon trailhead awaits.

A dusty parking area, often filled with cars left behind by day hikers and mountain bikers, announces your arrival at the beginning of the trail. Due to its location at the head of a canyon, you find yourself secluded from the city only moments after setting off on the mellow-grade road. Keep your eyes peeled for the bighorn sheep that scramble along the upper reaches of the rocky canyon; beware of other wildlife sightings, including an occasional stealthy mountain lion. The initial route follows an old Denver South Park and Pacific Railway bed. The train used to take Denver residents six miles up the canyon beside the

South Platte River to Strontia Springs Resort. The resort no longer exists, replaced by a dam of the same name; nonetheless, this historic area remains a compelling draw to hikers, bikers, and an occasional, hopeful sportsperson fishing in the trout-laden waters.

The dirt road ends at the base of Strontia Springs Dam, becoming a single-track trail that, after about ten miles, arrives at the confluence of two forks of the South Platte River. From here, a road continues up into Cheesman Canyon and, eventually, to the small town of Deckers and some of the best trout fishing near the Front Range. To reach Waterton Canyon, head west on C-470 to Wadsworth Blvd. (CO Hwy. 121) and then south for several miles to the parking area.

BEST Country Walk in the City
Highline Canal (Denver)

The Highline Canal was formed by the siphoning off of rushing waters of the South Platte River southwest of Denver in Waterton Canyon. This steep-walled canyon represents a mecca for day-trippers from along the Front Range, as it follows the route of the defunct Denver South Park and Pacific Railway. Both the Platte and the canal are followed by a 450-mile trail system that forms the Denver Greenway Trails. Along with the mountain setting of Waterton Canyon, which is detailed above, you can follow interconnected routes through the Metro area. The maintained dirt trail that follows the canal can be picked up at hundreds of points along its meandering route. You will be amazed by the peaceful views, which, at times, place you in the middle of open-country settings, even though you are mere blocks from urban and suburban development. This is a resource that Denverites use often, but somehow it never seems too crowded. So hop onto your bike or slip in your comfy walking shoes and head out on this trail system. It will undoubtedly bring a sense of peace and well-being to your day. For a free map of the Denver Greenway Trail System, contact the Colorado Division of Outdoor Recreation at 303-866-3437. www.parks.state.co.us.

BEST Fun Times at a Reservoir
Lake Pueblo State Park (Pueblo)

Expectations don't exactly soar when you mention Pueblo, but over the years it has become a worthy destination. If you haven't been to the reservoir at Pueblo State Park, you'll first be impressed by its sheer size. Not that it competes with Lake Powell, but along the Front Range this is our favorite. Why? Lake Pueblo offers a variety of pleasant options for escaping the heat and a starkly beautiful, sixty-mile shoreline that snakes along the interior of this massive state park. It almost always finds ways to surprise and delight its increasing number of visitors.

Swimming, sailing, windsurfing, fishing, and motorboating are all excellent choices at the reservoir. Just below the dam you'll find the Rock Canyon Swim Beach (open Memorial Day to Labor Day), with a sandy waterfront, shady cottonwoods, and even a waterslide. Two marinas— north shore and south shore—provide mooring and boat rentals for those wanting to explore the 4,500-acre lake. Sailors love the constant buffeting wind at Lake Pueblo, especially in spring. Most motorcraft are used during the day to fish for walleye, large- and smallmouth bass, sunfish, catfish, and good-size trout. Windsurfing is permitted anywhere, but thanks to the snowmelt, beware of chilly water and arrive equipped with a wet suit through May. Windsurfers should check out the designated launch area on the north shore. If you aren't into plying the water, try hiking or biking on the many miles of marked trails inside the park. Below the dam, excellent wildlife-viewing opportunities can be found along the Arkansas River at the Greenway and Nature Center and the Raptor Center of Pueblo. The Greenway and Nature Center also hosts some excellent events, including the Rolling River Raft Race and one of the state's top bluegrass festivals.

Open year-round, Lake Pueblo State Park requires park passes and camping permits. Four hundred mostly cushy campsites (showers, hookups, and toilets) fill up on summer weekends, making reservations essential (800-678-2267 or 303-470-1144). For general information, contact the Park Headquarters and Visitors Center on the south shore. To get to the "Rez," drive west of town on CO Hwy. 96 until you see the signs. 640 Pueblo Reservoir Rd.; 719-561-9320; www.parks.state.co.us.

BEST Rock Climbing Close to the City
Eldorado Canyon (near Boulder)

Whether you are a climber yourself or one who likes to watch their death-defying antics, few earthly places match Eldorado Canyon. Climbers from around the world flock to the near-vertical 1,500-foot walls of ancient rock that line both sides of South Boulder Creek. If you already think of yourself as some kind of rock jock, there's no better place to entice you and your belay partner out of the climbing gym. The "Bastille" and various routes up 7,500-foot Shirt Tail Peak at the park's northern edge remain the most famous testing grounds for your climbing skills. Remember, though, this area requires proper training and equipment, so don't even think of scrambling up these rocks unless you are ready. Fixed bolts or pitons on the routes are not maintained, so please use caution.

If you are thinking about learning this sport, check in at the International Alpine School in Eldorado Springs. It has an excellent reputation and, thanks to its prime location, can help ensure your safety. The

Colorado Mountain Club and the City of Boulder also offer climbing instruction in the canyon. For additional climbing resources and detailed information about the many popular Eldorado routes, stop in at Neptune Mountaineering in Boulder, founded by Everest conqueror Gary Neptune.

Certainly one of the best attributes of this area lies just outside the state park. Ending your climbing day by slipping into the cool, clean waters at Eldorado Artesian Springs makes for a perfect finish (see page 21). No camping is allowed at Eldorado Canyon State Park. To get here, take CO Hwy. 93 (Broadway) south from Boulder for 5.5 miles. Turn right on Eldorado Springs Dr. and continue for three miles to the park entrance. Fee charged. 303-494-3943; www.parks.state.co.us.

BEST Footrace
Bolder Boulder

Thousands of runners take part in the annual Bolder Boulder footrace. PHOTO BY DOUG WHITEHEAD

Sneaker-clad feet by the tens of thousands run, plod, waddle, walk, shuffle, and fly. Bodies of every shape, height, width, and weight snake through the streets in a shimmering display and range of athletic ability. From serious wheelchair racers to families out for a 10K stroll; from weekend joggers to elite, world-class studs; from babes in strollers to eighty-something marvels, running aficionados celebrate this annual rite of spring known as the Bolder Boulder. It's a spectacle, a happening, a wonder unlike anything else in the world.

First off the start line every Memorial Day, inspiring handicapped athletes whir in their low-slung three-wheelers, arms pumping like well-oiled pistons, propelling themselves around the byways of Boulder. Next, wave after wave of citizen racers bolt at the crack of the starting gun, spreading out along the winding, rolling, sometimes-grueling 6.2-mile course, some running for a good time, others out for a good time. In this crazy crowd you might see Elvis gyrating in his blue suede shoes or Abe Lincoln lumbering in his top hat. Sauntering brides and grooms in gown and tux have been overheard saying "I do" to a backward-running parson. If that's not enough, spectators along the way are at least as entertaining as the main event. Belly dancers delight the passing drove, and rock bands keep a pulsing beat to run by.

On their way through residential portions of the course, overheated runners get welcome relief from garden hoses sprayed by obliging townsfolk in their front yards. When the streets finally clear, elite runners from Europe, Africa, and North and South America challenge the course, their strong strides broadcast live to a statewide television audience.

The University of Colorado's Folsom Field, filled with 35,000 well-wishers, provides the venue for the dramatic climax of this annual tradition. Loud cheers greet the first elite runners on their final push, circling the field in a last triumphant lap to the finish line. Jubilation reigns in this yearly festival called the Bolder Boulder. 303-444-RACE; www.bolder boulder.com.

BEST Statewide Event
Colorado State Fair (Pueblo)

The Colorado State Fair remains one of the state's favorite all-around special events. Beginning in mid-August, this action-packed two and a half weeks combine championship rodeo with hundreds of exhibits and a chance for visitors to see the requisite lambs, steers, hogs, horses, and other animals that journey to the fair. There's no better place for sales-people to hawk their wares, including food processors that dice, chop, and much, much more. Likewise, you can find any number of trinkets or some really nice Western wear, especially leather hats, coats, and belts.

But the real draw to the State Fair has always been its live entertainment. A free stage with local talent and regional acts remains a mainstay, but be sure to check the schedule to see who will be performing on the main stage. In past years, topflight musical entertainers have included Tom Jones, Bob Dylan, Mary Chapin Carpenter, and George Strait. Kids love the children's barnyard, carnival rides, and games, and adults enjoy wandering among the scores of free exhibit booths. Throughout the duration of the fair, more than a million people throng to the festival grounds, but each day is never too crowded to enjoy. To find out more about rubbing elbows with your fellow Coloradans at the fairgrounds, call the information line at 800-876-4567 or 719-561-8484; www. coloradosfair.com.

BEST Mingling with Offbeat Boulderites
Kinetic Conveyance Challenge

For two decades, the Boulder Reservoir has served as the site of an outrageous springtime race among comical, creative crafts crossing both land and water on nothing but human power (beer could be the other primary propulsion agent). Many conveyances feature engineering savvy with hundreds of moving parts; others simply manage to combine the sleek simplicity of a bike mounted on a kayak. Some 35,000 people gather each year on the shores of the reservoir for the massive party.

Every year the event embraces a silly outlook that overpowers any sense of serious drive to be the quickest to the finish line. Teams win in categories such as best newcomers, engineering, perseverance, sportsmanship, and looks. Ridiculous team names—such as the skunky Pepe Le Pew Eau de Parfum—match the sheer audacity of grown men and women sitting inside an oversized toilet or wearing special reservoir-tipped hats. The fastest teams arrive at the finish merely forty-five minutes after the start, whereas others straggle in three hours later. Some don't make it past the beach or a few yards into the water. One of the highlights has to be watching teams of participants climb out of the water and over the oozy mudflats.

Top bands play high-energy sets for the assembled throngs who attend this annual nonsense. Food and drink always come in bountiful supply. Be sure to bring your rain, wind, and sun gear, because the weather is almost as unpredictable as the contestants. Sponsored by KBCO (97.3 FM) radio station in early May; call 303-444-5600 for ticket and parking information. www.kbco.com.

BEST Scenery at a Golf Course
Arrowhead Golf Club (near Denver)

Only a handful of golf courses feature the kind of dramatic beauty that actually distracts from your play. Arrowhead Golf Club, near Roxborough State Park (see Best "Primitive" State Park on page 17), happens to be one of them. The winding fairways and manicured greens have found a spectacular home nestled amid jutting red-sandstone rocks that march along the eastern foothills of the Rocky Mountains. The red-rock backdrop is a geological kissing cousin to Garden of the Gods in Colorado Springs and Red Rocks Park and Amphitheater. That said, the management of this public course should spend more time and money maintaining this precious asset for all that it is worth.

Designed in 1970 by Robert Trent Jones Jr., the 6,682-yard, par-70 course brings tough elements into its undulating layout. Since surviving a series of financial starts and stops, Arrowhead has become a mainstay in *Golf Digest*'s top seventy-five public courses in America. It's an unforgettable golf experience, but be wary of areas of impassable scrub oak as well as seventy-six strategically placed sand traps and six lakes. The course looks deceptively open but plays rather tight.

Watch out for the 436-yard, par-4 fourth hole. "If you get out of here with a bogie, feel proud," says the pro. "The green alone can easily turn into a four putt." After a downhill tee shot, get within 200 yards of the fast, north-tilting, elevated green or you can almost be assured of a penalty stroke. Why? Consider the rocks and scrub oak to the left, a sand trap to the right, a gully on the left front, and, yes, water hazards on the right front. The back nine feature the prettiest holes, including hole thirteen, where you drive through two jutting red rocks and encounter a ninety-foot drop. *Golf Digest* calls hole fourteen "one of the most beautiful holes on the planet."

No doubt, you must be on your game to feel good about your score at Arrowhead, but even if you end up flogging the ball, you'll enjoy the scenery. You will likely spot some birds and animals (300 species inhabit the area), including nesting eagles and hawks as well as foxes and deer.

Stop in at the pro shop and recently renovated clubhouse restaurant. Tee times are rather pricey, but worth it. You can call seven days in advance. Please use spikeless golf shoes. Located forty-five minutes southwest of Denver at 10850 W. Sundown Trail. 303-973-9614.

BEST Scottish-Style Links
Riverdale Dunes (Brighton)

Brighton, best known for the Mile High Flea Market and barren agricultural and industrial development, can now be known as an excellent golf oasis. The area features two public courses: the Knolls and the newer, longer, Scottish-style Riverdale Dunes course. Designed in 1986 by the father-and-son team of Pete and Perry Dye, the Dunes features 7,027 yards of gently rolling fairways and difficult, fast greens along an alluvial plain next to the Platte River.

The course was completed by bringing in thousands of cubic meters of dirt. Its length is characterized, of course, by dunes, as well as rolling mounds, swales, and bunkers. With trees coming into play on only two holes, these wide-open links provide a unique set of challenges—the word "forgiving" will not enter your vocabulary often as you try to keep your score down. But the course has a high-country appeal with views of the majestic Rockies as a perfect backdrop to a day outside. Check out the award-winning pro shop and well-appointed restaurant and clubhouse. Reasonable green fees. 13300 Riverdale Rd.; 303-659-6700; www.riverdalegolf.com.

BEST Disk Golf Course
Edora Park (Fort Collins)

Forget the $100-plus fees and four hours it takes to play a round of golf. Pack up your favorite disk(s) and head out to our favorite course at Edora Park. You don't even have to abide by a strict dress code: go ahead and wear your cutoffs and T-shirt. Nobody will care. But that's not to say that people who play this course are lackadaisical about their sport. Though caddies are nowhere to be found and nobody's bragging about their new set of graphite clubs, you will see serious folfers (Frisbee golfers). They're the ones carrying special sets of disks of varying weights for driving, chipping, and, yes, putting. Many still like flinging their 165-gram standard Frisbee for the entire course.

The eighteen "holes" at this course can be found mounted on steel poles with dangling chains to guide the disks inward before dropping into a metal basket. You can pick up an official scorecard, which maps out the holes, at the Wright Life Store (800-321-8833) in town. A creek runs through the park, creating a decent water hazard on several holes. Watch for pedestrians who take their chances walking across your fairway. Have a most excellent time with your friends anytime between 6 A.M. and 11 P.M. The mature, beautifully landscaped park also features tennis courts, walking and biking paths, a BMX track, and horseshoe pits. To get to Edora Park, head to 1420 E. Stuart St. 970-221-6640; www.fcgov.com/parks.

BEST Zoo
Cheyenne Mountain Zoo (Colorado Springs)

Okay, so we really had only two contenders to choose from—Denver Zoo and Cheyenne Mountain Zoo—but it was still a difficult choice. When all things were considered, the dramatic mountainside setting of the Cheyenne Mountain Zoo set it apart. Just be sure to bring your walking shoes, unless you want to climb into one of the open-sided trolleys for a ride around the sloping roads that lead to the animal habitats. Being smallish, it doesn't take days to see all of the zoo's animal inhabitants. People, however, are lured back time and again by the richness of endangered species and the large, natural settings provided for the playful primates. Discover more than 650 zoo animals, including hungry giraffes, downcast vultures and proud birds of prey, snow leopards, lions, and black-footed ferrets.

An attraction near the zoo but at a higher elevation is the Shrine of the Sun, dedicated to famed American humorist Will Rogers. A drive up the mountain to the Shrine of the Sun is worthwhile for the sweeping views alone. Once there, you'll also hear a taped Will Rogers monologue and see photos of his life, which ended in a 1935 plane crash. The admission fee to the zoo includes the Shrine of the Sun.

Open daily 9 A.M. to 5 P.M. in summer, 9 A.M. to 4 P.M. in winter. From I-25, head south on Nevada Ave. Take a right on Lake Ave. and head to The Broadmoor. Turn right and up Mirada Rd., following signs to the zoo. 4250 Cheyenne Mountain Zoo Rd.; 719-633-9925; www.cmzoo.org.

Where to Eat, Drink, & Stay

expert pick

Top Five Colorado Brews
Eric Warner

Eric Warner, Lead Dog (a.k.a. Brewmaster) for Flying Dog Brewery, decided to spend his graduate school years in Munich at Weihenstephan University, which took his "beer game" to an entirely new level. He is one of only a few Americans to have ever completed the brewmaster program. He has authored a book, *German Wheat Beer* (Brewer's Publications, 1992), and has produced many award-winning beers during his career. Warner compares Colorado to the Napa Valley of beer because it is home to almost 100 breweries ranging from small brewpubs that make fifty gallons at a time to the world's largest brewing facility. He says being asked to pick the top five beers in the state is like being asked what your favorite movie or restaurant is. It depends on the mood:

Indeed, the seasons and climate in Colorado are so wildly varied that my taste preferences range from a light, golden ale on a summer day to a deep, dark, high-alcohol barley wine during a raging blizzard. Of course, I love all the beers we brew here at the Flying Dog Brewery, but here are five others that are also world-class:

▶▶ Having spent a few years in Germany, I have a huge place in my heart for lager beers, and that's why I love all of the lager and wheat beers at the **Sandlot Brewery**, adjacent to Coors Field. In particular, the Barmen Pilsner is as good as you'll find on this side of the Atlantic. Its beautiful, straw-golden color and dense, rocky head draw you in and the crisp, spicy hop finish delivers a memorable beer experience. Barmen is only available in a handful of bars and restaurants around Denver, including the Falling Rock, the Old Capitol Grill, and La Cueva.

▶▶ Known more for its big, hoppy beers, **White Rascal** from Avery Brewing in Boulder is a great example of a Belgian-style wheat beer. Brewed with coriander and orange peel, this unfiltered wheat beer looks as intriguing as it tastes. Avery beers are widely available in liquor stores and have some limited distribution in bars and restaurants in Colorado. www.averybrewing.com.

▶▶ If you like Belgian-style beers, then you can't miss with New Belgium Brewing's **Abbey Ale**. The beer geeks among us know that it is modeled after Belgian dubbel ale. To the lay drinker it is a dark, malty beer that has overtones of chocolate, coffee, and spice and finishes refreshingly sweet. If you're in Fort Collins, stop by the brewery, where you can sample the full range of the brewery's beers at their tasting room. The Abbey is also available in larger liquor stores throughout Colorado. www.newbelgium.com.

▸▸ The beer revolution in Colorado is synonymous with the brewpub, and one of the best ones in terms of grog and grub is **Gordon-Biersch**, in the Flatirons Mall in Broomfield. The brewery specializes in German-style beers. Brewmaster Tom Dargen is no slouch either, having brewed at the Wynkoop Brewery and consulted on numerous start-up brewpubs. My fave is the Marzen. It's a perfectly balanced, amber-colored beer that is rich enough to let you know you're drinking a real beer, but refreshing enough to go well with many of the spicier dishes at the brewery.

▸▸ American specialty beers are headed in the direction of bigger and bolder, and the **Bull and Bush** pub in Denver, if not on the cutting edge of this trend, has certainly embraced it. You'd never know it from the outside of the Bull and Bush, and once inside you feel like you've been thrown back in time to an old-school English pub. In addition to their regular lineup of beers, they've been known to experiment with oak-aged beers. My personal favorite is the "Man Beer," which is perhaps aptly named since it is a strong and aggressively hopped India Pale Ale–esque brew. www.bulland bush.com.

BEST Italian Ambience
Carmine's on Penn

Once you find Carmine's, tucked away on a Denver side street since 1994, you will never forget it. If loud and large is your style, then Carmine's will be a perfect dining fit for a casual and inexpensive night out. Loud, in that this is not the best place for intimate, quiet conversation among the often-large, sometimes-boisterous groups of family and friends. Large also in the size and vibrant flavors you will find in every meal. It feels like you are being invited to join a large, friendly Italian family, as waiters swirl around and get a little cozy with customers when describing the experience. Kids and adults seem to appreciate the ability to color on the butcher paper–covered tables as they wait for their meal while sampling the mouthwatering, garlic-imbued aromas. Be sure you hold back a bit when you order or you will be taking home food for the next week. Each entree is designed for sharing family style (two to three people per plate). Order the usual pasta variations with specialties such as gnocchi, cheesy baked ziti, and ravioli alla vodka. You may want to try a seafood, veal, or chicken pasta dish, which are expertly prepared by an experienced team in the kitchen. Fresh salads, soups, and bruschetta are perfect starters. Order a bottle from the Italian-only wine list or something from the bar and enjoy a cozy, even hip setting, which makes you feel just a little bit Soprano.

Open Tuesday through Sunday from 5:30 to 10:30 P.M. Make reservations in advance or you will never get in. Valet parking. 92 S. Pennsylvania; 303-777-6443.

BEST Sing-Along
The Golden Bee (Colorado Springs)

It might come as a surprise when you slip around behind the International Center at the world-class Broadmoor Resort and enter this authentic, nineteenth-century English pub. It seems out of place because it is. African mahogany figures adorn the pub as do intricate "gingerbread" carvings. Other striking accents include etched glass, a pressed-metal ceiling, antique prints from England, and gaslight-type fixtures. The entire interior of this intricate pub was shipped to the United States in crates from London in 1963. The time-travel effect on patrons is nothing short of incredible. Every evening, guests indulge in the merry sing-along with the ragtime piano player—songbooks are located on each table. No doubt, you and your friends will sound better when you are accompanied by yards of good, cold beer. Since most people stay for the evening, be sure to get here early, certainly by 7 P.M. or so.

The Golden Bee is open for lunch and dinner and offers good-quality, Old London–style pub food. Order Devonshire cheddar cheese soup, steak-and-potato pie, English "Ploughman's Lunch," or a hearty sandwich. The Golden Bee is open for walk-in dining from 11:30 A.M. to 1:30 A.M., offering lunch, dinner, and pub fare. Dress is casual. 1 Lake Cir., Colorado Springs; 719-577-5776.

BEST Casual Dining Experience
Austin's American Grill (Fort Collins)

When it comes to dining, Fort Collins is better known for Vern's Place, which serves giant cinnamon rolls, than about anything else. That assessment has changed over the years though, as downtown has become an excellent hub for dining, shopping, and nightlife. Locals will tell you that Austin's is the place they head for dining value and quality in a casual, historic setting. Who knows, you might like the setting so much you feel like proposing to the person across from you! The place has integrated historic photos, exposed brick, and contemporary lines into a seamless dining experience. A small patio with umbrella-covered tables on their prime corner location makes for great people watching. You can have a burger or a sandwich, but it is the entrees that really hit a home run: smoked rotisserie chicken, buffalo steak, prime rib, grilled salmon, and pork tenderloin. All are served with generous portions of vegetables and garlic-roasted mashed potatoes, and you can add a salad for a couple of bucks. They serve up some wonderful salads, including our favorite, with coconut shrimp. The small bar area is a nice place for a relaxing drink (nice selection of martinis and some single malts) along with friendly service.

Open daily for lunch and dinner. 100 W. Mountain Ave., Fort Collins; 970-224-9691. Austin's now has another location south of town at 2850 E. Harmony Rd. 970-267-6532.

BEST Historic Restaurant
Buckhorn Exchange (Denver)

For more than 100 years, this restaurant has been serving up an eclectic menu for its loyal patrons. If you are ready for an unforgettable historic atmosphere and some of the best-prepared wild game—elk, buffalo, rattlesnake, and alligator tail, to name a few—head to this unique spot. The dining room is marked by colorful red-checkered tablecloths, creaky floors, and a complete collection of taxidermied animal heads, including buffalo, mountain sheep, deer, moose, as well as many fowl. The extensive gun collection includes Colt .45s, Winchesters, derringers, flintlocks, smoothbores, repeating rifles, and even a palm pistol. This place embodies Colorado history, and you can almost imagine all these walls have seen. Theodore Roosevelt ate here before going hunting with owner Shorty Scout. Sitting Bull's nephew and a contingent of warriors from the Sioux and Blackfoot Tribes are said to have ceremoniously turned over the captured saber of General George Custer after the battle of Little Big Horn. Sit at the tables where former presidents Dwight Eisenhower, Jimmy Carter, and Ronald Reagan have eaten, as well as Bob Hope, Jimmy Cagney, and Princess Anne, among many others. Upstairs you can enjoy a drink at the white-oak bar, which was made in Essen, Germany, in 1857, or enjoy the rooftop patio on nice summer evenings. This is the home of the first liquor license ever issued in Colorado. Reasonably priced lunch menu. Expensive dinners. Located five minutes from downtown on the light-rail line. 1000 Osage St.; 303-534-9505.

BEST Brew Town
Fort Collins

In Fort Collins, the explosion of craft brewing can be seen in the shadow of a behemoth called Budweiser. This college town manages to hold its own against Denver with a delightful mix of micro-brewery and brewpub experiences alongside a fascinating glimpse at big-time corporate brewing. You can also attend the annual Colorado Brewers Festival (970-484-6500; www.down townfort-collins.com) on the last weekend in June, or you can head out to discover these brewery operations on your

The patio at Coopersmith's Pub draws in thirsty patrons in the heart of Old Town Fort Collins. PHOTO BY BRUCE CAUGHEY

own. Pick the experience to suit your mood or your taste buds.

Don't miss the low-key guided factory tour (on weekdays at 2 P.M. and 4 P.M.; Saturday tours run on the hour from 11 A.M. to 4 P.M.) where you'll see the factory in full action and sample the variety of excellent brews at New Belgium Brewing Company (500 Linden St.; 888-NBB-4044, 970-221-0524; www.newbelgium.com). Self-guided tours and tasting are available anytime the brewery is open. In the airy, well-appointed tasting room, the staff serves up platters of small goblets with a mouth-watering array of tastes, including the famous "Fat Tire" brand. With chairs and bar stools, this place seems to take its customers' comfort seriously. The state-of-the-art brewing facility prides itself on environmental friendliness. Employees swear this is the best place they've ever worked—after a year on the job, each employee is given a sturdy red bike similar to the one perched on their flagship brand's label. Here you can pick up a six-pack, a half-gallon "growler," or a keg.

Down the road, try out the up-and-coming Odell Brewing Company (800 E. Lincoln Ave.; 970-482-2881; www.odells.com). Their popular and hoppy-tasting 90 Shilling Ale finishes clean and instantly reminds us of Scotland with its hearty flavor.

For a night out with food and a game of pool, head straight to the long brick room at Coopersmith's Pub and Brewing Company (#5 Old Town Square; 970-498-0483; www.coopersmithspub.com).

The world's fastest-producing brewery, the massive Anheuser-Busch Brewery on the northern outskirts of town (at I-25 and Harmony Rd., exit 271), represents a totally different extreme. More than 2,000 cans per minute roll off the line; the well-organized tour takes an hour. At the hamlet, you get a close-up look at the groomed Clydesdales before retreating to the hospitality center to sample some of the product and buy a cap or key chain. 970-490-4500; www.budweisertours.com.

BEST Free Tour
Celestial Seasonings Tour of Tea (Boulder)

Poke your nose into the "mint room" at Celestial Seasonings in Boulder and you'll never forget the power of herbs. The strength of the aroma almost knocks you backward. During the rest of the fascinating thirty-five-minute tour you'll discover a wide range of wonderful scents. Include the rest of the large complex, where workers mix and bag an astonishing 1,000 bags of tea per minute, and an overview of all other Celestial operations, and you have the best free tour we can imagine.

The company was founded in 1969 when nineteen-year-old Mo Siegel started gathering herbs in Aspen. It has grown into an international success story. In addition to the free tour and tea tasting in the little gift shop, you can make a day of it by stopping for lunch at the Celestial Café. The factory floor gets pretty loud, so children under age five are not permitted for that part of the tour.

Guided tours are offered on the hour Monday through Saturday from 10 A.M. to 3 P.M. and Sunday from 11 A.M. to 3 P.M. From the Boulder Turnpike (U.S. Hwy. 36), take the Foothills Pkwy. exit and follow it north through Boulder; the road automatically feeds onto CO Hwy. 119 (the Diagonal) and continues northeast toward Longmont. Turn right, heading east, at Jay Rd. (stoplight) and drive east one mile to Spike Rd. Turn left and continue north for a half mile to the plant. 4600 Sleepytime Dr.; 303-581-1202; www.celestialseasonings.com.

BEST Chicago Cuisine in Colorado
Mustard's Last Stand (Denver and Boulder)

We tried to keep away from oxymorons in our "best of" titles ... really. But thinking of Chicago and cuisine in the same slightly acrid breath brings the image of a fully garnished hot dog complete with wedges of tomato, sweet relish, a fat slab of dill pickle, raw, chopped onions, mustard, and sauerkraut, all topped with a hot pepper. When you stop at Mustard's near the University of Colorado campus in Boulder or Mustard's II near the University of Denver campus, you'll conjure up a semblance of the Windy City, too. Especially if you order a red Vienna dog with the works and a side of perfectly cooked fries.

The stand's variations on a theme include Polish sausage, burgers, and even a tasty veggie dog made out of compressed tofu. "That gets the most complaints," says the guy behind the counter. "People think we gave 'em a real dog by mistake ... these tofu dogs are that good!"

If you want your hot dog done right, don't pressure the counter help to hurry or expect them to treat you with a subservient attitude, because this is just not the place. But when your name is called and you pick up your wax paper–wrapped creation, you are about to enter a Chicago dimension. Check out the photo wall of official vendors of Vienna Beef products from as far away as Hawaii. Take one of just a few seats inside, or, better yet, find a shaded outdoor table and watch the university students hurry by. Located in Denver near the corner of Evans and University Blvd. at 2801 S. University. 303-722-7936. In Boulder: 1719 Broadway; 303-444-5841.

BEST Beans with Breakfast
Lucile's (Boulder)

Let the slow cooking of red beans at Lucile's set a leisurely breakfast pace for you and a special friend. If an opening exists, nab a table on the front porch on a warm summer morning, and then settle in for some chicory coffee and delicious beignets. If you head inside the old restored house, you'll find tables decorated with faded calico napkins nestled throughout the home's small, intimate rooms. As the coffee begins to warm you up, settle in on your breakfast entree. Lots of egg dishes entice, but nothing hits your belly better than the kitchen's special Cajun Breakfast—a hearty serving of red beans alongside poached eggs and hollandaise sauce, all served with grits or potatoes and a fresh buttermilk biscuit. You might also consider the wonderful eggs *sardu*. Around lunch the menu includes spicy gumbo, shrimp Creole, crawfish étouffée, and blackened red snapper. You just can't miss with this reasonably priced Boulder mainstay.

You can find Lucile's on a side street just off the Boulder Mall. For more than a decade, it has attracted locals to its unobtrusive location, so expect a wait, especially on weekends. 2124 14th St.; 303-442-4743.

BEST Nightlife District
LoDo (Denver)

In the late 1980s, LoDo could have been called NoDo. It simply didn't exist. That is, except in the minds of modern-day pioneers who had a vision of refurbishing Lower Downtown's (hence, the name LoDo) turn-of-the-century brick warehouses into something unique to Denver. In an era of sameness, the LoDo area, bordered by 14th and 22nd Sts. between Larimer St. and the tracks, brings a unique vibrancy to downtown Denver. Thousands have moved into the area's lofts, so, unlike most downtown areas, the streets don't roll up at night. Quite the contrary; on many nights you'll see crowds down here until the bars close at 2 A.M.

During eighty regular-season games each year, the Colorado Rockies bring hordes of nightlife seekers downtown. Most games will find corner ticket sellers offering discounted tickets to the games. Depending on your perspective, you might decide to come down here during a Rockies' game or avoid it at all costs. After scoring a parking place, you have your choice, ranging from dozens of sports bars and several brewpubs to dance clubs, wine or martini bars, and live jazz and blues clubs. Here are our top picks for a week of nightlife:

▸▸ **Monday: El Chapultepec**—A good night to pull up a Naugahyde bar stool and listen to some cool, live, traditional jazz at this Denver institution. 1962 Market St.; 303-295-9126.

▸▸ **Tuesday: Denver Chop House and Brewery**—In the shadow of Coors Field, this rather dark but luxurious place serves good handcrafted beer and high-quality food. 1735 19th St.; 303-296-0800.

▸▸ **Wednesday: Wynkoop Brewpub**—The true original, this outstanding brewpub serves up a selection of ales and features a second-floor pool hall. 1634 18th St.; 303-297-2700.

▸▸ **Thursday: Jackson's All American Grille**—If sports pulses through your veins and you just aren't happy without TVs blaring minute-by-minute scores, dis is da place! 1520 20th St.; 303-298-7625.

▸▸ **Friday: LoDo Bar and Grille**—A tidal wave of people head here before and immediately after Rockies games. Wander through the crowds inside and head straight to the rooftop on a summer night. 1946 Market St.; 303-293-8555.

▸▸ **Saturday: Soiled Dove**—Even if you're in the back row of high-back chairs at Denver's top live-music nightspot, you'll only be forty-five feet from the stage. The excellent sounds of top local and national names in rock, jazz, blues, and folk music fill the room. 1949 Market St.; 303-299-0100.

▸▸ **Sunday: Cruise Room at the Oxford Hotel**—This classy, restored art-deco bar opened in the 1930s and remains the place for a perfectly shaken martini. 1600 17th St.; 303-628-5400.

BEST Exotic Teahouse
Boulder Dushanbe Tea House

The decorative, multicolored elements of this teahouse can be attributed to the hard work of more than forty artisans from Tajikistan. They toiled for some dozen years in their homeland creating hand-carved, distinctly painted elements for this extraordinarily detailed building. Crate by crate, thousands of pieces were shipped to Boulder as a gift before being reconstructed as what we see today. All of this effort celebrates the two towns' special sister-city relationship. We never did hear what gift Boulder sent in return, but suspect a truckload of Boulder's own Celestial Seasonings tea would not quite suffice.

Dushanbe's (Doo-shawn-bay) unparalleled craftsmanship can be seen in its tables, stools, and columns as well as the ceiling and exterior ceramic panels. The instant you look up at the brightly colored, elaborate, rectangular structure from its well-kept garden courtyard and outdoor-seating area, you know a special experience awaits. But without the Himalayas looming more than 24,000 feet above in the background, you'll have to use your imagination before you can actually see yourself traveling along the Silk Route to this destination.

The teahouse features a carefully selected menu for lunch, teatime, dinner, and weekend brunch. The worldly selections borrow from cuisines ranging from Indian to Mediterranean to Mexican. Dinner entrees include Persian lamb kabobs, stew, and Thai curry noodles. At other times, you'll see tofu, egg dishes, pasta, unique salads, and even an excellent breakfast burrito. Depending on your mealtime, these choices are complemented by beer, wine, juices, coffee, and, of course, an excellent variety of teas. The strong black teas range from classic Earl Grey to Darjeeling from India. Or try the mild tastes of the low-caffeine green teas, with delicate flavors emerging from almost-clear liquid. For a caffeine buzz from tea that is equivalent to coffee, try the Matta Latte. In nice weather, retreat to the tables alongside bubbling Boulder Creek. Otherwise, the inside beckons with a unique sensory experience even before you taste the food. 1770 13th St.; 303-442-4993; www.boulder teahouse.com.

BEST Pool Hall
Wynkoop Brewing Company (Denver)

When John Hickenlooper opened the first brewpub in Colorado since Prohibition ended—on the outskirts of downtown Denver in the 1980s— people thought he was crazy. Yeah, crazy as a fox. The out-of-work-geologist-turned-legendary-marketer-and-populist-Denver-mayor jumped ahead of the pack by a few years, and the Wynkoop now enjoys one of downtown's best locations. Thanks to Coors Field and the rash of development around Lower Downtown (see Best Nightlife District on page 35), the Wynkoop continues to draw crowds. Hickenlooper's brewpub spawned other business ideas, but none is better than a terrific second-floor pool hall featuring the same great beer and atmosphere as the popular downstairs restaurant/pub.

So take a cue and head upstairs to the high-quality slate tables, which rent by the hour. You will find twenty-two full-size billiard tables, five dart lanes, shuffleboard, and a full bar. They are spaced so you won't get jabbed often, and the upbeat crowd makes the whole experience uplifting, in contrast to the dark, dank pool halls we have all tried at one time or another. If you get there between 3 and 6 P.M., you can enjoy happy-hour prices on pints of fresh beer (our favorite is the St. Charles E.S.B.) and a relatively quiet game of pool. When the downtown office buildings let out, people stream to this place, and long waits for tables become common. For a truly special event, reserve one of the private billiards rooms. Located at 1634 18th St. 303-297-2700; www.wynkoop.com.

BEST Fried Chicken
Castle Café (Castle Rock)

In these days of endless salads, tofu burgers, and protein drinks, we all look for the perfect place to backslide a bit to the simpler days when we didn't know better. For family-style food, especially fried chicken done to perfection—crispy on the outside, tender and juicy on the inside—there's no better place we've found than the Castle Café. The owners gutted a historic, rundown stone building on Castle Rock's main street (Wilcox) and created a casual atmosphere with a focus on heaping servings of home-style food. The building used to cater to local quarry workers, ranchers, and travelers back in 1890, and the place was wild enough that an extra deputy was scheduled to work nearby on paydays. Slide into a comfortable booth, order a heavy mug of beer or an icy margarita, and settle in for a meal of complete and utter decadence.

Those not in the mood for chicken might try a steak, prime rib, or fish dish. The side dishes appeal almost as much as the entrees. Along with its fried-chicken specialty, the Castle Café has become known for its buttery mashed potatoes, rich, brown cracklin' gravy, tasty slaw, and hot rolls. As you lick your fingers clean, you'll keep thinking, "Dang, this is good!" If, for some reason, you don't get enough to eat, top off your meal with a massive serving of four-layer dark-chocolate cake or perhaps "Truckstop" bread pudding with vanilla cream. For a similar atmosphere with good bar food, you might wander over to the Bar Next Door, which, as you may have guessed, is adjacent to the Castle Café.

Open nightly for dinner starting at 4:30 P.M. and Sundays from 11:30 A.M. to 8 P.M. 403 Wilcox; 303-814-2716; www.castlecafe.com.

BEST Mexican Food
La Cueva (Denver)

Now that we have sampled burritos, enchiladas, and, yes, margaritas across the Front Range, we can honestly say you won't be disappointed by La Cueva. Set along a stretch of East Colfax surrounded by pawnshops lies a hidden gem called "The Cave" that has flourished for more than two decades. The Nuñoz family insists on fixing food from scratch with the freshest ingredients available, using recipes from their native home of Guanajuato, Mexico. Actually, "Papa" does the cooking and "Mama" greets the customers. "I don't cook a bean!" she laughs when asked about the food preparation. "But I promise, everything is homemade."

Regular customers told us they cannot remember one bad experience at La Cueva. If your Spanish is rusty, you may need to play a little charades to communicate with the prompt, polite servers. You will be delighted by the service and care you receive, even as you are waiting for a table to free up—which happens a lot, especially on weekends.

From the moment a black crock of fresh, spicy salsa arrives, you know you're in for a treat. The light, almost-greaseless *flautas* topped with guacamole and sour cream are out of this world. The chicken mole and tacos *al carbón* remain perennial favorites, and the chile rellenos couldn't be more appealing (unless you like 'em crispy). The beef and chicken melt in your mouth; the marinated and slow-baked meat is moist, tender, and almost greaseless. A side of beans doesn't mean a side of lard here, so go ahead and chow down. Sometimes the best item on a menu is the simplest: green chile smothers the burritos or comes in a bowl with warm tortillas. End your meal with a sopaipilla, flan, or an empanada, and you will be back here whenever you think of dining Mexican. Located in Aurora at 9742 E. Colfax Ave. 303-367-1422.

BEST Bed-and-Breakfast
Abriendo Inn (Pueblo)

Whether you are a business traveler or are just visiting the Pueblo area, you will appreciate the homey ambiance of this lovely and well-run bed-and-breakfast. Since 1989, when the restoration of this mammoth foursquare 1906 Victorian was complete, guests have been returning year after year, often filling the home to capacity. Why do people love this place? It might be because of the decadent morning meals or possibly it's Kerrelyn McCafferty Trent, the friendly owner. The garden setting in central Pueblo, only a couple of blocks from the Union Ave. historic district, offers another reason to stay, as does the sheer elegance of the common areas combined with the practical amenities of the rooms.

You shouldn't come to the Abriendo to get completely away from modern features; each room has them, including televisions and telephones and recently added data ports to better serve business clients. You will also discover a decorator charm, careful craftsmanship, and imaginative use of space unknown to most hotels. The inn offers ten clean, comfortable bedrooms with private bathrooms. The common areas truly inspire the friendly interaction of the guests. As lace curtains filter the sunlight, guests gather in the living room for lingering moments of relaxation. On a warm afternoon, find a wicker chair on the wide veranda and enjoy the garden setting and large trees. Help yourself to a complimentary cup of tea or rummage through the fridge for a chilled soda or bottled water as you settle in and enjoy this historic home. During the holidays, each room has a Christmas tree and individually themed decorations; an eighteen-foot-tall tree decorated in Victorian-style silver and lace can be found in the living room during the season.

The sunny dining room and back patio provide a backdrop for a full breakfast. When we visited, guests walked into the dining room for freshly brewed coffee before diving into their meal of stuffed ham-and-cheddar French toast as well as oatmeal coffee cake with a coconut topping. The next day's offering: a breakfast enchilada with seafood.

The inn discourages guests from bringing young children; pets are not allowed. No smoking. A range of reasonable rates for various-size rooms. 300 W. Abriendo Ave.; 719-544-2703; www.abriendoinn.com.

The Cliff House has been transformed into the crown jewel of Manitou Springs. PHOTO BY BRUCE CAUGHEY

BEST Inn
Cliff House (Manitou Springs)

The many transformations of the Cliff House have resulted in a very beautiful final stage. The smashing overhaul of this 126-year-old structure will transport you in many ways, most notably off the somewhat funky, somewhat hit-and-miss action on the streets of Manitou Springs. In short, the Cliff House appears a bit out of place. This majestic building, with its stunning interior rehab, deserves several hundred acres of gardens surrounding it—with some horse stables, a burbling creek full of hungry trout, and a serene place to watch the sunrise.

Instead the Cliff House is crushed between a hillside of houses and the busy trinket shops and arcades that give

Manitou its no-snobs-allowed charm. An enchanting setting? That's a stretch. But you still need to stay here. It's a perfect spot for getting away if you don't have all day to get somewhere. It's intimate, homelike, and welcoming. The rooms are beautifully appointed; indeed, the deluxe suites practically insist that you relax. Your room fee includes afternoon tea, a satisfying complimentary breakfast, and travel tips from the staff. The restaurant offers a fine assortment of creative dishes, fine wines, and friendly Colorado service—sincere but not too much.

This structure has endured floods, fire, and multiple attempts to revive it. This time, barring a disaster, the latest incarnation of the Cliff House should be here for a long, long time. 306 Canon Ave.; 888-212-7000 or 719-685-3000; www.thecliffhouse.com.

BEST Historic Hotel
Brown Palace (Denver)

Since 1892, the Brown Palace has served as a tangible monument to the ingenuity and core beliefs of this ever-optimistic city. Now dwarfed by imposing steel-and-glass office buildings, the nine-story Brown Palace, designed by Frank Edbrooke, still deserves respect and admiration from passersby at its prime downtown location. Built of native red granite and Arizona sandstone, the unusual triangular shape and Victorian architecture leave a distinctive mark on this most famous of Colorado hotels. Inside, six tiers of cast-iron balconies

The imposing Brown Palace in downtown Denver dwarfs Emma Whitehead. PHOTO BY DOUG WHITEHEAD

lead upward to a magnificent Tiffany stained-glass ceiling some eighty feet above. The lobby's Mexican onyx walls and white marble floor lend the hotel an elegant permanence that today's buildings rarely capture.

Now entering its second century of operation, the hotel manages to reinvent itself without forgetting the past. Comfortable furnishings can be found throughout the 230 guest rooms (and twenty-five spacious suites), which come replete with brass beds, TVs hidden inside armoires, down comforters, linen duvets, and private bathrooms with brass fixtures. Rooms come decorated in an art-deco style, a more traditional Victorian style, and even a kind of Western baroque. Famous guests of the Brown include The Beatles, who stayed here in 1964 when they performed at Red Rocks. Dwight D. "Ike" Eisenhower based his 1952 presidential campaign from the hotel and maintained the "Western White House" here during his presidency.

The beautifully adorned, comfortable lobby sets the tone for the hotel. Polished tunes from a grand piano waft by as guests enjoy high tea or perhaps an evening cocktail. The hotel never forgets its Western roots; every January it still proudly displays the prize bull from the National Western Stock Show in the lobby. Around the perimeter of the atrium lobby, guests may choose to dine at the ultrafancy Palace Arms, the classy Ellyngton's (great brunch), or the steady Ship Tavern nestled in the narrow prow of the building.

Rest assured that the well-trained staff at the Brown Palace will make your entire stay comfortable and relaxed. Expensive. 321 17th St.; 303-296-6666; www.brownpalace.com.

BEST Exclusive Night's Stay
The Broadmoor (Colorado Springs)

Feel like royalty by checking into The Broadmoor, an exceptional historic resort set at the base of Cheyenne Mountain in Colorado Springs. Much more than a hotel, this sprawling collection of buildings, situated around a large lake, conjures up images of Europe. As you drive toward the entrance, your view shifts from beautiful landscaped gardens to the rose hues of impeccably maintained Italian Renaissance–style buildings. The Mediterranean feel of The Broadmoor sets the tone for the entire complex, and you feel like you have transitioned back to a timeless age— one where unhurried hospitality remains something of an art form. Sure, it's expensive, but flawless service is everywhere. That happens when you have the equivalent of two staff for each single guest room.

Built in 1918 by Spencer Penrose, a mining magnate, The Broadmoor's opulent surroundings include marble staircases, sparkling chandeliers, and a fabulous collection of original art and antiques. Penrose and his wife traveled the world to find just the right mix of fine art, tapestries, sculptures, and furnishings. Spacious, luxurious guest rooms include the finest toiletries, plush towels and robes, and, of course, room service. Three eighteen-hole golf courses sweep in and around the complex, or you can try one of the sixteen tennis courts, three heated pools, biking and hiking trails, equestrian courses, or trap, skeet, and rifle shooting ranges. Check out one of the nine restaurants, ranging from the Charles Court, an elegant English country manor, to raucous sing-alongs at the Golden Bee pub (see page 31 for more information). 1 Lake Ave.; 800-634-7711 or 719-577-5775; www.broadmoor.com.

NORTHWEST

It was a great, wild country.
In the creek bottoms there were a good many ranches;
but we only occasionally passed by these on our way to
our hunting grounds in the wilderness along the edge of the snow-
line. The mountains crowded close together
in chain, peak and tableland. . . .

—THEODORE ROOSEVELT,
FROM *A Colorado Bear Hunt*

From Grand Mesa, North America's largest flattop mountain, to the desolate river canyons of Dinosaur National Monument and natural rock archways of Rattlesnake Canyon, the beautiful northwest portion of Colorado resembles facets on a gemstone. The eye-popping beauty of some areas, however, seems impossible to imagine in others. Massive in scope and relatively unpopulated, this area has long stretches of open road distinct from the obvious resort highlights of Steamboat Springs, Aspen, and Vail. Stark buttes and cliffs are interspersed among a quilt of national forestlands, soaring mountain passes, pretty river canyons, and remote alpine lakes.

Once the domain of Ute Indians, the northwest portion of present-day Colorado gradually became an appealing draw to miners, ranchers, and recreationists. As inroads and transportation networks pushed into the area, the Utes found themselves displaced to reservations in extreme southwest Colorado and across the Utah border. The Meeker Massacre in 1879 became the final blow to the nomadic tribes of American Indians who had lived here for generations.

With a forty-year period of extensive oil and uranium production behind it, much of northwestern Colorado now has become a hunters' mecca. Lower elevations and warmer climates encompass excellent cherry and peach orchards and vineyards around the base of Grand Mesa. Stopping at roadside fruit stands in late summer and pausing to sample Palisade's fermented produce, in the form of wine, should be on your list of things to do. Located in the fertile Grand Valley, the town of Grand Junction feels about as Midwestern as it gets, but, within a basin of weirdly eroded plateaus, offers nearly unlimited recreation possibilities.

Skiing and snowboarding the wooded glades at Steamboat Springs, sampling the ritzy nightlife and art galleries of Aspen, or soaking in the "world's largest" hot-springs pools at Glenwood Springs are just a few of the experiences you should seek out. Above all, with thousands of acres of Routt and White River National Forests awaiting, we suggest packing up your camping gear, mountain bike, and fishing pole and heading into nature. Ice fishing in the frozen expanse of North Park brings its own appeal. The many contrasts of northwestern Colorado make it difficult to describe in sweeping terms—but its differences contribute to this region's intrigue as a logical destination for curious travelers.

Cultural & Historical

BEST Remembrance of Fallen Firefighters
Storm King Mountain Memorial Trail
(Glenwood Springs)

On July 6, 1994, in one of the saddest chapters in Colorado's history, fourteen firefighters lost their lives on the top of Storm King Mountain while battling the South Canyon Fire. During late afternoon on that fateful day, a sudden change in the weather caused the forest fire to blow up, trapping the wildland firefighters on the side of the steep mountain. Unable to escape the massive fire as it raced up the sheer mountainside, four women and ten men perished, making the ultimate sacrifice doing what they loved.

As a tribute to those brave men and women, as well as firefighters everywhere, volunteers created the Storm King Mountain Memorial Trail, a steep, narrow path that takes visitors up to an observation point overlooking the site of the 1994 tragedy on Storm King Mountain. The trail is a bit tough, rising 700 vertical feet during its one-mile course to the top. Markers along the way explain that the trail is meant to be difficult to show the hardships wildland firefighters endure while battling a brutal forest fire.

The Storm King Mountain Memorial Trail began as a footpath worn into the side of the mountain by firefighters, family members, and others hiking up to pay tribute to the brave firefighters who died. Blackened, lifeless stumps and gnarled, scarred trees beside the trail are eerie reminders of the deadly power that ravaged the mountain. Despite its bleak surroundings, the memorial at the top is a beautiful place of quiet solitude, broken only by gentle sounds of the birds and insects that have returned to Storm King Mountain as nature begins to reclaim the bleak landscape. On the hillside where the men and women died, small stone crosses blend with grass and small bushes that force their way into the desolation as if to demonstrate the power of life over death.

From the memorial, these small crosses are not clearly visible without binoculars, but there is a small, treacherous footpath along the side of Storm King Mountain up to the sites where the firefighters died. This trail, which is not maintained and only vaguely marked by rock cairns, can be dangerous, especially in inclement weather.

The Storm King Mountain Trail is a tough climb on a mountain known for rapid and intense weather changes, so be sure to bring plenty of water, sturdy footwear, and clothing for all types of weather.

To get to the trail from Glenwood Springs, take I-70 west to the Canyon Creek exit (109), then turn right and head east on the frontage road, which ends at the trailhead.

BEST Chronicle of Ski History
Colorado Ski Museum and
Colorado Ski Hall of Fame (Vail)

The only place to see the complete history of the state's ski industry is Vail, home of the Colorado Ski Museum and Colorado Ski Hall of Fame. This small museum is packed with ski memorabilia and antique equipment covering the 144-year history of the state's oldest sport. You'll see skis, boots, and poles spanning more than 100 years, including wooden skis with leather lace-up bindings used by ministers and mailmen to reach the isolated miners during the long winter months of the late 1800s, metal skis popular in the 1960s, and modern fiberglass designs used today. Some of the most interesting items are the various bindings used over the years, beginning with leather straps, moving on to metal clamps attached to springs, and evolving into state-of-the-art modern bindings. And, of course, there's an entire section devoted to the evolution of snowboards, from their humble beginnings as a carpet-covered plank of wood with metal sheeting on the bottom and pieces of bike inner tubes for bindings, to the snurfboard, which combined the best designs of skis and surfboards. They even have one on display that was used in a James Bond film.

The museum's walls are covered with photos of Colorado's ski history and some of the state's pioneers in the sport. You'll see how skiing in Colorado changed from a mode of transportation to a multimillion-dollar industry and, along the way, produced many of the sport's champions. Photos, memorabilia, equipment, and medals from Colorado's most famous skiers are on display, from the first Winter Olympic Games in Chamonix, France to the most recent in Salt Lake City.

Take a peek at turn-of-the-century ski fashions and how these dramatically changed from drab coats and pants created to keep out the cold to trendy designer outfits created to make a fashion statement. Watch the famous Warren Miller movies that helped popularize the sport of skiing. Meander through the 10th Mountain Division section, a room filled with photos, equipment, and video testimonials from veteran soldiers on skis whose heroic deeds in the mountains of Europe during World War II brought glory to the sport of skiing, increasing its popularity and giving birth to a new era of mega ski resorts worldwide.

Located off I-70 at exit 176 in Vail. 970-476-1876; www.vailsoft. com/museum. Small admission fee for adults. Call ahead. Closed in mud season.

BEST Place to Get Sweaty
Yampah Spa and Salon Hot Springs Vapor Caves
(Glenwood Springs)

The only place in North America you can take a natural vapor bath inside a cave is right here in Colorado. Referred to as the Palace in Hell and Hygienic Hades, the Glenwood Springs Vapor Caves are an eerie, spiritual way to take a healthy sauna. Powered by Mother Nature, the vapor caves get their high-intensity steam from the natural hot springs that gave the town its name. Underneath the cave floor, hot mineral waters flow through at a sizzling 125° F. Over millions of years, steaming water made its way from the bowels of the Earth to the surface, creating underground caves filled with mineral-laden steam. They were prized for their health virtues by the Ute Indians long before white settlers in the late 1800s discovered the natural spa.

The Utes guarded their miraculous waters and claimed the hot springs and vapor caves could "heal all aches of man and beast," which is exactly why the caves have remained popular for more than 100 years—despite feeling a tad dark as you walk down the steep stairway. It's a bit like descending into Dante's Inferno, but for those who love a good, hot steam bath, there is nothing quite like the natural surroundings of the caves.

Commercial use of the Glenwood Springs Vapor Caves dates back to 1883, when the Defiance Town and Land Company allowed bathers to crawl through a narrow tunnel to the underground caves. Due to Victorian conventions at the time, men and women were not permitted to use the caves at the same time and often wore heavy linen bags with drawstring necks to hide their bodies. Today, men and women visit the caves together wearing swimsuits, allowing their bodies to breathe amidst the stifling heat. While retaining their natural ruggedness, the caves have been transformed into a full spa, with services that include massage therapy, body mud wraps, salt glow rubs, a full-service salon, and a wide variety of spa amenities to help you soothe both body and soul.

The Yampah Spa and Vapor Caves, located just east of the Hot Springs Lodge and Pool complex at 709 E. 6th St. in Glenwood Springs, is open year-round. 970-945-0667; www.yampahspa.com.

BEST Local Arts Scene
Aspen Music Festival and School

In an effort to fill a void created by the country's wracking emotional pain in the years following World War II, a group of artists and intellectuals formed a gathering in Aspen to celebrate human goodness—and nearly 2,000 people showed up! The Goethe Bicentennial Convocation and Music Festival in 1949 included visits by humanitarian Albert Schweitzer and conductor and pianist Arthur Rubinstein. This effort at human renewal signaled the birth of the Aspen Music Festival and School, which still flourishes today.

The festival lasts two months, from late June to late August, and brings some of the finest musicians in the world to this mountain Shangri-la. Promising students play, practice, and learn from musical masters—you get the sense from their sheer determination that many will come back someday as acclaimed artists themselves, perpetuating this worthy cycle. The town takes on a unique aura as you see bulky string instrument cases at bus stops, hear sounds of arpeggios escaping from open windows, and listen to concert perfection at the renowned music tent. But the mostly classical concerts represent only one way to enjoy the music. Be sure to visit during the rehearsals, attend a workshop, or stop and pause to hear the unusually talented sidewalk musicians. Even if you cannot afford tickets to the concerts, you can always find a perch on the grassy expanse outside the tent to hear the sounds.

During the Music Festival, the Aspen Walking Mall often attracts world-class musicians to the street scene. PHOTO BY BURNHAM ARNDT, ASPEN CHAMBER RESORT ASSOCIATION

Aspen and the arts come together with a historical depth and creative breadth that no other mountain town can touch. Here galleries, theater, music, and dance are as much a part of the environment as the ever-present aspen tree. Give yourself pause, and remember how it all began five decades ago. 970-925-9042; www.aspenmusicfestival.com.

BEST Place to Experience Colorado as It Once Was
North Park

Ute Indians who came here in the 1800s following buffalo and other game called it the "Bullpen." Now it is known as North Park. No matter at what point you drop into the immense North Park basin, you find your eyes drawn across the broad plain to the surrounding mountain vistas. Massive peaks comprising several distinct mountain chains—the Never Summer and Rabbit Ears Ranges to the south, the Park Range to the west, and the Medicine Bows to the east—were created through buckling and movement of bedrock. The high valley floor shifted downward from the mountain peaks in North Park just as it did in Colorado's Middle Park, South Park, and San Luis Valley. Driving across the arid plain, the views open, you get a sense of Colorado as it once was, without the resort developments so common in other parts of the state. Thousands of acres of public lands, including the Arapaho National Wildlife Refuge area, make this an appealing destination.

In North Park during harvest season, stacks of hay are gathered up in advance of the long winter. PHOTO BY BRUCE CAUGHEY

After the Utes came stalwart pioneers searching for fur-bearing animals and eventually gold, but those who stayed based their livelihoods on ranching. Hikers who want remote destinations enjoy the beautiful and secluded trails that enter the Mount Zirkel Wilderness and Routt National Forest. Fishing success can be found year-round on area streams, lakes, and ponds; North Park continues to be a popular ice-fishing destination. Scores of hunters set out from North Park with one of the area's many outfitters. As you drive through North Park, take some side routes and you'll see just how much of the place remains open range. North Park has been extensively logged, but much of its forest area has healthy secondary forests coming into their own. Along the beaver ponds on Illinois Creek, near Rand, a moose reintroduction program now has the herd numbering more than 600.

Visitors interested in history should wander among the ruins of Teller City, a town that in 1879 claimed 1,300 residents. One cabin has been rebuilt, and about twenty others in tumbledown condition can be seen on a short loop hike into the woods. The most interesting ruin may be of the Yates Hotel, which once boasted forty rooms and furnishings such as Persian rugs and a grand piano in its well-appointed lobby. For a complete overview of North Park's history, check out the guns, antiques, tools, and historic photos at the North Park Pioneer Museum (small fee). For more information, call 970-723-4344. www.northpark.org.

BEST Canyon Passageway
I-70 through Glenwood Canyon

It took millions of years of steady erosion, massive uplifting, and geologic chaos to create the gorgeous, almost-vertical 2,000-foot-high rock walls of Glenwood Canyon. Today, the canyon remains a wonderful resource with easy access to drivers, bicyclists, in-line skaters, kayakers, hikers, and picnickers. In recent history, the canyon had remained impassable; even the Utes forsook the area for easier routes. Eventually the pull of gold and the pleasure of natural hot springs in Glenwood Springs (formerly Grand Springs) proved to be the impetus for pathways to be built through the canyon.

The first Denver and Rio Grande tracks pushed through the canyon in 1887 (thanks to the audacity of David Moffat), and today trains still make frequent runs on the opposite bank. The development culminated in the completion of a four-lane highway (I-70) in 1992—truly an engineering feat that should count as a Wonder of the World.

Though early opponents of the highway expansion cited environmental and aesthetic concerns, almost everyone agrees that the twelve-mile link successfully achieved a balanced outcome. The stretch of smooth concrete represents a magnificent engineering marvel with countless attractive recreational opportunities for the public to use and enjoy.

From Glenwood Springs, drive east on I-70 and the canyon begins almost immediately. The Hanging Lake trailhead (see write-up on page 54) can be found ten miles up the canyon. From Denver, Glenwood Canyon can be reached easily by heading west on I-70 for 140 miles.

BEST View from a Cave System
Glenwood Caverns Adventure Park

What used to be an out-of-the way trip up a winding dirt road has been transformed into a destination with many activities for you and your family. Thankfully, the addition of six-passenger tram cars allows visitors to this burgeoning destination to bypass the bumpy dirt road and enjoy incredible views over the wide and many-layered red-sandstone valley basin, formed over millions of years by the Colorado and Roaring Fork Rivers. Because there are only a few cars on the cable at any one time, this new access system does not drastically increase the visitor capacity; so even when it is busy, there are not going to be throngs of people visiting the caves at any one time. Guided tours leave regularly into the Caverns and Historic Fairy Caves, which, until recently, had been closed to the public since 1917.

The wonders of this reopened cave system are on display, including the mind-warping formations in Kings Row and long strands of oddly shaped cave bacon. Like looking up into puffy cumulus clouds on a summer afternoon, you will begin to make these oddly shaped formations mean something to you: there is a rabbit or a camel over there, perhaps the Michelin man or a bride and groom. Rarefied crystals have developed in the vapor-locked confines of this cave system Adventurous spirits who are in decent shape may want to slither through tight gaps on the three- to four-hour headlamp-lighted Wild Tour. At the top of the tramway, a little tourist village is being constructed with a wooden sluice for the kids to enjoy panning for gemstones from bags of purchased sand (fake but fun), a climbing wall, and a human-size gyroscope contraption. Can minigolf be far behind?

At this point, the owners are trying to balance the demand for activities and a hefty payment for their investment in the tramway with the need to maintain a natural environment. The balance is tipping a bit dangerously toward the tacky. That said, the cave system is incredible and impeccably maintained, and the good-natured guides are knowledgeable about the geology and history of the area. And, the Exclamation Point Restaurant offers reasonably priced and good-quality food with incredible views. Without a doubt, this is one of the best places in Colorado to enjoy a sunset.

A young visitor enjoys fanciful views from deep within an underground system of caves. COURTESY OF GLENWOOD CAVERNS ADVENTURE PARK

Open daily, except on Thanksgiving and Christmas days. Hours vary for the tram and the restaurant. 51000 Two Rivers Plaza Rd.; 800-530-1635; www.glenwoodcaverns.com.

BEST Ghost Town
Ashcroft

Back in 1879, three mining camps were quickly established in the area to accommodate the silver-mining boom: Ashcroft, Ute City (later Aspen), and Independence, which is located high up the Roaring Fork Valley toward the famous pass of the same name. Ashcroft was named for its founder (T. E. Ashcraft, but pronounced "Ashcroft"), who had a knack for promotion. He laid out his site along Castle Creek at an elevation of 9,000 feet about a dozen miles from Ute City. Within two years, the camp had 500 residents, and throughout the early 1880s, Ashcroft rivaled Aspen in importance as miners pulled tons of silver ore from the surrounding mountains. But, as fate would have it, Aspen triumphed while Ashcroft withered away. In 1887, the Denver and Rio Grande Railroad puffed into Aspen, dooming tough-to-reach Ashcroft to its current fate as a ghost town.

In 1949, Muriel Sibell Wolle wrote in her classic book, *Stampede to Timberline*, "Store after store lines the principal street, each in a different state of disintegration. The roof of one is caved in; the false front of another is stripped of its cornice and presents a bare upthrust palisade of boards; a third has shuttered windows, through whose cracks the interior with its counters and shelves can be seen; and a fourth has succumbed to wind and snow, and lies a pile of jumbled lumber." The passage of time has taken away much more in the past half century, but you can still see many remnants of better days.

As you walk, bike, or ski past Ashcroft's remaining shells of weathered wooden buildings, try to imagine a peak population of 2,500, two bustling main streets, three hotels, a jail, and a newspaper office. If you're lucky, you'll meet the ghost of Ashcroft, a helper from the Aspen Historical Society who can help you interpret what you are seeing. However, you won't have to imagine the gorgeous views of the surrounding Elk Mountains. To get to Ashcroft from Aspen, drive west on CO Hwy. 82 to Castle Creek Rd. Turn left and continue twelve miles along Castle Creek Rd. to Ashcroft. During summer, experienced four-wheel-drive enthusiasts can continue up and over 12,705-foot Pearl Pass and down into Crested Butte on the other side.

Outdoor Activities & Events

expert pick

Colorado's Best Mountain-Bike Ride
Troy Rarick

As the founder and general manager of Over the Edge Sports in Fruita, Troy Rarick often finds himself dispensing advice as well as new tubes, bikes, and miscellaneous supplies. We asked about his favorite ride and he put together, in his own words, the following description of Kokopelli's Trail. For more information, stop in and say hi to Troy at Over The Edge Sports, 202 E. Aspen Ave., Fruita; 970-858-7220; www.otesports.com.

There are many loop trails in the Kokopelli's Trail system, but the Kokopelli itself is a continuous 142-mile route from the Loma parking lot to the town of Moab, Utah. A single-track route begins near Fruita but continues on mostly double-track jeep roads into Utah. The trail roughly follows the Colorado River and its red-sandstone canyons. At times you're riding a single-track along the cliffs of the Colorado River, Ruby Canyon, and Horsethief Canyon. Other times the route heads across high-desert plateaus with sandstone-rock towers next to the trail and views for fifty miles. Nearer to Moab the route heads up to the base of the LaSalle Mountains reaching more than 7,000 feet and into a pine forest before dropping past Slickrock Trail to its finish at the mountain-bike mecca of Moab.

For the day rider, the loop system of the Kokopelli's Trail just off I-70 near Fruita is the ticket. Several single-track loops offer perfect day trips for both beginner and advanced riders. Eight different looping trails keep a rider busy for any duration from an hour to a full weekend. Advice on these trails is available at the local bike shop and in the area guidebook *The Fruita Fat Tire Guide* by Troy Rarick (2000).

By their very nature, the popular loop trails are the best one-day rides and therefore attract many more riders. But for a multiday camping trip on the bike, the longer Kokopelli offers fantastic scenery from desert to mountain and a pleasingly remote setting. You probably wouldn't want to take a rank beginner on the Kokopelli's Trail—except to drive the sag vehicle and make sure the beer is chilled—but for most moderately experienced mountain bikers, it is certainly manageable. Many people even complete the trail pulling there own gear in MTB trailers, although that includes a few chunks of walking for sure.

The draw of the Kokopelli's Trail is the opportunity to spend three to five days on your mountain bike in a spectacular desert setting. During your ride, you are unlikely to see other riders except when you find yourself near Moab and Fruita. Riding all day, camping under the stars with a cold beer, and spending time outdoors with a bunch of good friends—these are the memories I have of the Kokopelli.

BEST Monument to Nature
Colorado National Monument

Eons of wind and water have created the beautiful rock monoliths of Colorado National Monument. PHOTO BY BRUCE CAUGHEY

For millions of years, the forces of nature slowly carved and sculpted the wild, desolate plateau southwest of Grand Junction into a surrealistic landscape of molded rock spires, towering rock monoliths, and steep, terraced canyons. Known as the Colorado National Monument, it undoubtedly remains one of the best places in the state to see the Earth's geologic history. Say thanks to the Civilian Conservation Corps, the Depression-era workers who built the twenty-three-mile-long Rim Rock Drive along the Uncompahgre Plateau's rim to the visitors center. Look out your window at a virtual feast of rock formations and intricate geologic patterns as you tour the one-hour detour between Grand Junction and Fruita.

The view demonstrates Mother Nature's intense power to shape and mold the land, and the valley below unfolds before you with acres of rich orchards, towns, and farmland. It is amazing to imagine the erosive powers of wind and water in carving deep canyons into the rock, revealing the area's natural history in layers of the Earth. The panorama from the visitors center and Rim Rock Dr. gives you a firsthand glimpse at the geologic chapters of our planet.

In addition to these wonders of nature, Colorado National Monument has an abundance of trails, both easy and challenging, taking hikers and bikers across mesa tops or into backcountry canyons. These forays off the main road offer breathtaking views of some of the state's most amazing rock creations. Stone skyscrapers, such as Independence Monument, the Kissing Hands, and Sentinel Spire, rise out of the canyon floor like rocky fingers reaching for the clouds.

The west entrance to Colorado National Monument is twelve miles west of Grand Junction on CO Hwy. 340. The east entrance is four miles west of Grand Junction on Monument Rd. 970-858-3617; www.nps.gov/colm.

BEST Chopped-Off Peaks
Flat Tops Wilderness Area

Between Meeker and Steamboat Springs in the northwest corner of the state, a distinct group of mountains creates a Colorado anomaly. Colorado, known for its towering peaks, has a section where the tops have been flattened and named accordingly. Visiting the Flat Tops Wilderness Area opens up rugged and majestic vistas, as long as you can get used to gazing up at sheared-off summits. They are beautiful yet strange, and worth the drive to see them.

CR 8 heads right into the heart of the Flat Tops Wilderness Area. We begin the route near historic Meeker—named for Indian agent Nathan Meeker, who met an untimely demise when he tried to convert nomadic Ute Indians into farmers with disastrous results—with rolling, green hills dotted by farms and cattle ranches. The winding route cuts through dense, deciduous forests, hillsides flush with aspens and pine trees, gorgeous rivers and streams, and, of course, the famous flattop mountains before it drops you off in Yampa on the eastern side of the wilderness. Every autumn, hunters from all over the United States migrate to the Flat Tops Wilderness for a chance to bag elk, deer, moose, or pheasants, many of which you may see along the road. The area is also full of trails and campgrounds, but a huge forest fire in 2002 decimated some of the higher regions, particularly around Trapper's Lake. However, the land adjacent to the lake was spared, leaving the lake and its campgrounds as beautiful as they were before the fire. If you decide to head up to Trapper's Lake, don't let the bleak, macabre landscape deter you; you'll discover the enigmatic nature of forest fires that can burn one spot and yet leave another completely untouched. The massive rock formation behind the lake, called the amphitheater, represents a scene of tremendous beauty—marred by the utter devastation—and surrounded by the totally natural cycle of fire and rebirth. This dichotomy of the natural world makes the Flat Tops Wilderness Area worth a detour on your next road trip to this part of Colorado.

BEST Treasure at the End of the Trail
Hanging Lake

Misty waterfalls and a translucent lake provide a welcome reward at the end of the Hanging Lake Trail. PHOTO BY BRUCE CAUGHEY

As its name suggests, Hanging Lake is precariously perched on a high ledge between two sheer rock walls and seems to be literally hanging from the side of a mountain. This is truly one of the most magnificent feats of nature you'll ever see—if you survive the hike up, that is. Though Hanging Lake is tiny—more of a pond, actually—its emerald and turquoise water gives it a jewel-like quality that is enhanced by the surrounding colorful cliffs and aptly named waterfall, Bridal Veil Falls. Delicate plants hang over the edge, giving the appearance of a woman's veil. The unique combination of the falls and Hanging Lake has inspired many artists and photographers to make the steep one-mile climb to capture this hidden treasure.

And it is a steep climb from the trailhead to the lake. This trail rises 1,020 feet in one mile from beginning to end, so be prepared for a workout. You'll encounter several places where you'll have to clamber over rocks and small boulders, especially at the top where the trail morphs into stairs. Bring plenty of water and sturdy shoes, but don't let our description scare you off. The Hanging Lake Trail is gorgeous as it winds its way along Dead Horse Creek. The sights awaiting you at the top are worth every upward step.

While at the top, don't miss a visit to Spouting Rock, one of the coolest waterfalls you'll ever see. As you start toward Hanging Lake on the boardwalk, look to your left and you'll see a small sign that says "Spouting Rock" with an arrow (the arrow is hard to see but it's there). Crawl over the boulder field behind the sign and you'll come to a trail that will take you a short distance to a waterfall spouting directly out of a rock wall. It's amazing and unlike anything we've seen before, almost as if someone turned on a water faucet.

It's important to note that fishing and swimming are not allowed in Hanging Lake and no pets are allowed on the trail. Also, getting to the trailhead parking lot can be tricky if you're traveling west on I-70. Westbound travelers must take the Grizzly Creek exit and double back in the eastbound lane of I-70 to the Hanging Lake exit. Eastbound travelers can go directly to the Hanging Lake exit.

BEST Unexpected Tropics
Rifle Falls State Park

Believe it or not, the lush tropics can be found right here in Colorado. Rifle Falls is a beautiful oddity in the Rocky Mountains because spray from the three cascading waterfalls keeps the area moist, creating the perfect condition for plants not usually associated with the Colorado high country. During summer, the thundering water creates a misty world of mossy rocks and lush vegetation at the base of the falls, where you'll find reeds, delicate aquatic plants, dense grasses, and many other types of riparian foliage. The top of each waterfall

Three separate waterfalls cascade down over a unique ecosystem at Rifle Falls State Park. PHOTO BY TAMRA MONAHAN

is thick with moss and a variety of tropical-looking plants that drape themselves across the falls. Moss can also be found on the rocks, trees, bushes, and just about everything else surrounding Rifle Falls.

Be sure to check out the eerie limestone caves to the right of the falls. These are spectacular formations whose dark depths can easily be explored. Most of the caves have enough natural light for your spelunking adventures, though you may find a flashlight helpful. The dense, deciduous forest throughout Rifle Falls State Park makes it a gorgeous place to visit in the autumn when the scenery explodes with color. The short hike to the falls and limestone caves is very easy and even accessible during the winter, when the triple waterfall transforms into a fantastic natural ice sculpture with icicles reaching almost to the bottom.

A riparian zone above Rifle Falls is another unique natural phenomenon that you have to see to believe. Limestone deposits have formed small ledges in Rifle Creek creating a series of tiny, mossy waterfalls and ponds teeming with small aquatic plants and reeds. With its surrounding dense forest full of snails and ferns, this area looks more like Oregon than Colorado and is a fantastic spot for photography. To get there, take a right out of the Rifle State Park parking lot and go two-tenths of a mile to a sign on the right that says "Riparian Zone" (the sign sits back from the road so watch for it carefully). Walk across the old metal bridge and follow the trail to the left until you see the waterfalls on your left.

To get to Rifle Falls, take CO Hwy. 325 north from Rifle toward Meeker. Watch for a sign on the right about six miles out of Rifle directing you to the Rifle Falls State Park. Follow the road around the reservoir and continue another five miles to the park. 0050 CR 219; 970-625-1607; www.parks.state.co.us.

BEST Rock Formations for Climbing
Rifle Mountain Park

The magnificent rock formations and sheer, steep walls of Rifle Mountain Park are not only splendid to look at but also offer Colorado's best limestone sport climbing. In fact, many climbing enthusiasts rate Rifle Mountain Park as the best limestone sport climbing in North America, especially for 5.12 grades and up. Climbing routes here are generally long and complex and range from slightly overhanging to very overhanging. A lot of climbers believe Rifle Mountain Park has the largest concentration of 5.13 to 5.14 sport routes in America. Ice climbing during the winter can be fantastic on frozen waterfalls, but summer and fall are the best seasons for rock climbing. Spring can be treacherous, since much of the rock is slippery from water seeping through it.

This narrow, 2.5-mile canyon is not just a climbing utopia. It's also a fantastic place to camp, fish, hike, or take a scenic drive to see the limestone caves and surrealistic color patterns covering the steep canyon walls. In winter, the park has a very distinctive look, combining clear-blue ice, stark-white snow, and black-streaked reddish brown rock walls. Autumn presents another colorful time in the park, when it is full of deciduous trees that create a blaze of color in September and the first part of October.

Rifle Mountain Park is owned and operated by the city of Rifle, and there is an entrance fee to access the park. To get there, take I-70 to the Rifle exit, then go north on CO Hwy. 13 for three miles. Turn right at the bowling alley onto CO Hwy. 325. Drive 9.8 miles through Rifle Gap, over the dam and past the reservoir, past Rifle Falls State Park, and when the road turns from pavement to dirt, you're there. 970-625-2151; www.rifleco.org.

BEST Smooth High-Altitude Riding
Vail Pass/Tenmile Canyon National Recreational Trail

If you're up to the challenge, you can ride your bike from Breckenridge to Vail on a well-maintained paved bike path that combines easy sections with heart-pumping steep climbs. This thirty-three-mile trail is actually three connected trails. From Breckenridge through Frisco to Copper Mountain it's the Blue River Bikeway; from Copper to Vail Pass it's the Tenmile Canyon National Recreation Trail; and from Vail Pass to Vail it's known as the Vail Pass Trail.

For most of its length, the Vail Pass/Tenmile Canyon National Recreational Trail follows I-70; however, a large portion of it is secluded from the highway. Though you can hear the traffic on I-70, you won't see much of it during your ride. The trail alternates between stretches running parallel to the highway and sections meandering through forests and picturesque alpine meadows. Parts of it are more challenging than others, so for an easier ride, hop on the trail in Breckenridge at the northern edge of town along the Blue River; in Frisco at the trailhead parking lot located at the end of Main St. (you can also get to the parking lot by taking exit 201 on I-70 and heading into Frisco—the lot will be immediately on your right); or in Copper Mountain at the Wheeler Flats trailhead. The trail gets steeper and more difficult as you head west from Copper Mountain toward the Vail Pass summit. The toughest section lies on the trail's west side going from Vail (Gore Creek Campground trailhead) to the top of Vail Pass, where the trail rises 1,872 feet in 9.7 miles with grades ranging from 5 to 7 percent. If you'd like the easiest ride possible, drive or take a shuttle to the top of Vail Pass and head down west to Vail or east to Copper Mountain and beyond. This is a great way to experience the magnificent scenery along the trail without enduring a killer bike ride. Once you get to Vail, you can connect with the Gore Creek Trail and continue your ride through the Vail Valley.

Shuttles to the summit are available for a per-person charge at locations throughout Summit County. Call the Chamber of Commerce at 866-433-2244 for more information.

BEST Short Hike
Fish Creek Falls (near Steamboat Springs)

Where else but in Colorado could you see two magnificent waterfalls on one hike? The popular Fish Creek Falls Trail is not about a wilderness getaway, but rather a short hike to a large waterfall. The trail leads through lush aspen groves and gorgeous fields of wildflowers and ferns to a smaller waterfall above. The first section of the trail to the lower waterfall is wide and smooth, but not very scenic until you get to the bridge over Fish

Creek. From here, you'll get a spectacular view of the first waterfall, which is about 280 feet high. Be sure to head across the bridge and follow the trail two miles to the upper falls. The sunlight filters through the trees and highlights the dense green foliage covering the ground as gnarled tree roots snake their way through the shadows like something out of *The Hobbit*. Just beware of what lies around the next corner, because virtually everyone in Steamboat seems to like hiking with an unleashed dog, which can be a bit surprising, especially if they have a Great Dane!

A short hike up to Fish Creek Falls yields a spectacular view. Hike a bit farther to reach a second, smaller waterfall. PHOTO BY TAMRA MONAHAN

Once at the top, you'll discover a somewhat smaller but no less magnificent waterfall and a pool where you can cool your toes or your whole body if you dare. The water is glacially cold, even in the summer, so you may want to think twice before jumping in. The hike to the upper falls is moderately difficult with some steep parts and a few places where you'll have to climb over rocks, but the scenery along the way and the waterfall at the end is well worth the trek. The Fish Creek Falls Trail can be crowded, so to avoid the crush, hike early in the morning or later in the afternoon.

To get to Fish Creek Falls from Steamboat, take Lincoln Ave. to 3rd St. Go east to Fish Creek Falls Rd. and follow this to the trailhead and parking lot.

BEST Fly-Fishing
Fryingpan River (Basalt)

If you haven't heard about the great fishing on the Fryingpan, you're not listening. Regular insect hatches, big fish, and long stretches of public water make this fly-fishing heaven. Unfortunately, any place so highly regarded becomes crowded, so you may want to consider some off-peak times to visit the stretch of free-flowing water that joins the Roaring Fork River at Basalt. Besides, the water flows clear and relatively low in early spring and late winter. And the scenery, with high, reddish bluffs, forested hillsides, and mountain views, could hardly be more beautiful.

The prime area is the mile below Reudi Reservoir, which features massive trout in the eight- to ten-pound range, thanks to the Mysis shrimp that flourish in the reservoir and tend to inhabit the waters below the release. You are likely to catch good-size brown, brook, and cutthroat trout in addition to lunker rainbows in this Gold Medal–designated stream.

To match the shrimp and drive the trout wild, try a Burton or Dorsey pattern in a fourteen to eighteen at the end of your (5–6X) tippet. March and April bring midges, mayflies, and blue-winged olives. For almost-guaranteed success, get to the river in July or August for the green drake hatch. A road runs beside the fourteen-mile length of river below the dam with numerous pullouts for easy access. A couple of good shops in Basalt can answer your questions and fill your fishing vest with all of the essentials. For a quick status check on the river and what flies are working, check www.fryingpananglers.com.

BEST Mountain Golf Course
Steamboat Sheraton (Steamboat Springs)

Robert Trent Jr. designed this highly regarded mountain course, which has been open since 1974. At 7,000 feet in elevation, the fairly low-lying course offers more playing days (mid-May through late October) than most mountain courses. Yet you still get to enjoy incredible mountain vistas and gentle bluegrass fairways lined by groves of fluttering aspen and sturdy pine trees. The real reason to play here remains the big views up to the ski mountain as well as down the valley. Fish Creek winds through seven of the eighteen holes, and seventy-seven sand traps lie in wait, making for ample challenges on the 6,902-yard course.

The Sheraton offers value packages all season long, with some of the best early- and late-season deals around. One of our favorites is the weekday "Golf 'Til You Drop" package, which includes hotel accommodations and greens fees for up to thirty-six holes per day. There is even a suggestive-sounding "Swinger's Weekend." The resort complex of the Sheraton features three restaurants, condo units, and nearly 300 hotel rooms. As a place to stay, the first-class rooms are pretty standard, but the setting at the base of the ski mountain is anything but. If you don't have a hotel reservation, you can walk on seven days a week or make reservations twenty-four hours in advance—but be prepared to pay for the privilege. Clubhouse, rentals, and instruction are available. 970-879-2220; www.starwood.com/sheraton.

BEST Land o' Lakes
Grand Mesa

One of the world's largest flattop mountains, Grand Mesa lures travelers with its high-alpine vegetation and thick forests dotted with more than 300 lakes and reservoirs. At an average elevation of 10,000 feet, Grand Mesa soars above the surrounding valleys and provides sweeping views from its perimeter edges. It remains a most spectacular place to take in the view in the early and late hours of the day, especially if a storm looms nearby. The mesa lies sandwiched between the orchards of Palisade to the west and Cedaredge to the east. Formed millions of years ago by volcanic activity, the fifty-three-square-mile mesa is situated atop a deep lava bed. The passage of geologic time with massive glaciers, steady erosion, and violent uplift has created wide variations of terrain for backcountry enthusiasts.

Before the 1880s, this area was a Ute hunting ground. The Utes called the region Thigunawat, or "home of departed spirits," and a story recounted in the *WPA Guide to 1930s Colorado* tells how the Utes saw the formation of so many lakes. The story goes that the north rim of the mesa was home to great eagles that feasted on deer and antelope and sometimes carried off Ute children. One day the chief's son was taken away to the eagle's nest and the vengeful father climbed up, pulled out young eaglets, and threw them down the hill to a giant serpent that lived at the base of the cliff. When the eagles returned, they were full of rage and suspected only the serpent. They carried it high up in the air by their talons and tore it to shreds. The dismembered body of the serpent fell to the earth with such force that it formed deep pits that later turned into lakes. Okay, so it's a bit of a logical stretch, but it's a fascinating tale steeped in the oral tradition of the Utes.

Fishing continues to be a major draw on the mesa, and the lakes and streams get stocked each year. The lakes, with easy access, draw many visitors and can be a drag for those interested in isolation. Hikers can head out on a ten-mile circular trail providing sweeping views of the entire southwestern corner of Colorado and into Utah from high on an undulating spine on the mesa top. The seventy-eight-mile (one-way) Grand Mesa Scenic and Historic Byway and the memorable Land's End Rd. provide added enticements for motor travelers. For information, contact the Grand Junction Ranger District Office by calling 970-242-8211 or the Grand Mesa Visitor's Center at 970-856-4153.

BEST In-Town Rafting
Yampa River (Steamboat Springs)

Okay, several Colorado destinations allow you to raft, kayak, and tube right through town. But the Yampa River, which flows right through the middle of Steamboat Springs, is the only one where you can pull your watercraft to the side and warm your fanny in a natural riverside hot spring. Several excellent put-ins lie along the five miles of river that flow right through town, and a bike trail also traces the river's route. The shallow but nice natural hot springs lie right across the street in a parklike setting, from Steamboat Health and Recreation (the developed hot springs can be found at 136 Lincoln St., with a covered waterslide and various-temperature pools; call 970-879-1828 for information). You will see a nook of rocks from the Yampa where the hot water emerges to mix with the cold river water. Sit back and enjoy the perfect temperature—but please be sure to maintain your modesty here, unlike down the road at Strawberry Park Hot Springs (see Best Hot Springs on page 63).

For those who enjoy fly-fishing, this stretch of water can be productive, but all trout must be returned, and please restrict your tackle to flies and lures. It's best before 11 A.M. and after 6 P.M. in summer because of the hordes of tubers that scare the living daylights out of the fish. For more information, contact the Steamboat Chamber of Commerce at 800-922-2722. www.steamboat-chamber.com.

There is no admission fee for this hot springs pool in Steamboat's Yampa River.
PHOTO BY BRUCE CAUGHEY

BEST Place to See Moose
Colorado State Forest

The Colorado State Forest comprises a 72,000-acre swath of remote backcountry just north of Rocky Mountain National Park, about two hours west of Fort Collins. Its rugged beauty is complemented by views of rocky peaks, and the land encompasses a natural area with alpine lakes, trails, campgrounds, and fewer visitors than you might expect. One major attraction: this is one of the few locations where moose can be found in Colorado (another is along the Illinois River in North Park). You might also see raptors, deer, elk, and other smaller four-legged creatures. The Colorado State Parks' excellent Web site offers some interesting facts about the lovable moose. For example, did you know:

It's best to see moose early in the morning at Colorado State Forest. COURTESY OF WINTER PARK RESORT

▸▸ Moose are actually deer, and an adult male can weigh 1,200 pounds and stand six feet at the shoulders?

▶▶ The hairy flap that hangs from a moose's neck is called a "bell" or "dewlap"? Biologists are not sure of its purpose, if any. During cold winters, it may freeze and fall off.

▶▶ Moose are excellent swimmers and spend much of their time in or near the water? They like to feed on aquatic plants and have been known to dive to eighteen feet to feed on them.

▶▶ Moose can live up to twenty years in the wild?

Some thirty-six moose were introduced into the state forest between 1978 and 1987; today, the Division of Wildlife estimates the herd at 500. A recommended stop is the moose-viewing platform, which is located on CR 41 about seven miles into the state forest. Although there are no guarantees of sightings, the platform overlooks prime moose habitat. The lumbering creatures can often be spotted best in the low light at dawn or dusk. Look closely for any kind of motion, because moose blend in extremely well with their environment. Even if you don't see one, check for evidence in the unusual scrape marks on bark from their front teeth and antlers.

The State Park Visitors Center provides an excellent introduction to all the wildlife in the area—you'll know you're at the right place when you spot a seven-foot-tall barbed-wire moose replica near the park entrance on CO Hwy. 14. Stop in for a look at the interactive displays and shop for T-shirts, posters, postcards, and more. Contact the State Forest Park Office for more information at 970-723-8366. www.parks.state.co.us.

BEST Rock Arches
Rattlesnake Canyon (west of Grand Junction)

Colorado's natural character remains a primary reason why many of us choose to live here and is the pull for visitors who return year after year. Thanks to the turbulent geologic past that formed Colorado's mountains, plateaus, and valleys, we also have a stunning, little-known collection of natural rock archways just west of Colorado National Monument near Grand Junction. When thinking of arches, most people immediately think either of McDonald's or Arches National Park in Utah. But don't forget our own obscure local collection—the second-highest natural concentration in the world—in an out-of-the-way location on Bureau of Land Management (BLM) land called Rattlesnake Canyon.

You'll need a high-clearance SUV, a good map, and plenty of gas and water to safely enjoy this beautiful area. Amid weirdly eroded Entrada sandstone canyons, hardy explorers can four-wheel, hike, or bike into

Rattlesnake Canyon to find twelve natural rock arches. The largest, Rainbow Bridge, spans some 100 feet, providing a compelling sight. All of the archways reach new photogenic heights during the soft, shadow-lengthening light just before dusk. The rocks, canyon walls, and archways take on even redder hues against the azure Colorado sky as sunset approaches. But because of Rattlesnake Canyon's difficult-to-reach location and intimidating name, this beautiful place has never achieved any true acclaim. Overnight camping is prohibited in and around the arches. You just won't ever find a crowd here. For more information, contact the BLM office in Grand Junction at 970-244-3000. www.co.blm.gov/colocanyons.

BEST Hot Springs
Strawberry Park Hot Springs (Steamboat Springs)

Since the late 1970s, this privately owned hot springs, located seven miles north of Steamboat Springs, has managed to escape resort development and cushy spa amenities, remaining something of an inexpensive hangout at the end of a rough road. Many will remember the teepee changing room, which provides only a modicum of privacy. Kids love the place but should be supervised, as Strawberry Park tries to be a "rest and relaxation" center, not a splash playland. And, yes, after darkness falls, children are asked to leave so adults can shed their suits if they please.

Strawberry Park Hot Springs provides a relaxing retreat in summer or winter. PHOTO BY BRUCE CAUGHEY

Unlike the old days, the three large, clearly defined pools, ranging from 70° 106° F, are now surrounded by rock terraces and sculpted gardens. In summer, the place employs two full-time gardeners— and it shows! In winter, the backdrop changes as snow piles up on the surrounding trees, never sticking to the source waterfall that emerges at a piping-hot 135° F. No matter the season, the mineral water doesn't smell and it feels clean against your skin. You can also slip away to a private room and enjoy a leisurely massage or enter the pools with a trained Watsu expert who will massage you in the buoyancy and heat of the natural springs. The place stays open 365 days a year. Consider taking a tour from town or skiing into Strawberry Park in winter because the road can become treacherous, and if you slide off you may be subject to a $500 fine.

To stay overnight in one of the five rustic cabins or to reserve a tent site nearby, you'll need to mail a deposit for your stay. No pets, no

smoking. Call 970-879-0342 or check out www.strawberryhot
springs.com for information.

BEST Dog-Lovers' Spectacle
Meeker Classic Sheepdog Championship Trials

It takes only seconds for the sheep to assess the dog. If the border collie
shows no power, no control, the woolly mutton scoffs and pays no heed.
Come to North America's largest sheepdog trials and witness the brilliance, patience, and tenacity of canines bred for centuries and trained for
years to herd large flocks of sheep on the open range. Here in Meeker,
organizers of this event could never have guessed that what they started
in 1987 would eventually draw as many as 12,000 onlookers to this small
town of 2,000 people.

"There is no good flock without a good Shepherd and there is no
good Shepherd without a good Dog." This ancient motto of the International Sheep Dog Society reflects the tone of the five-day trials. The han-
dler's whistle commands his dog to approach a group of six sheep 450
yards distant. Onlookers in the stands sit captivated, groaning or booing
at a wrong move by sheep or dog or cheering a job well done. Under the
keen eye of the judge, the winning pair works in concert, directing the
flock through a series of gates within time constraints, demonstrating
supreme skill and control.

Even before nationwide interest was spawned by the success of the
movie *Babe*, in which a pig performs a sheepdog's job, the Meeker Classic
had begun to grow. By 1999, 126 entrants took part in the trials, repre-
senting at least seventeen states from California to Virginia and even
Alberta, Canada.

The Meeker Classic Sheepdog Championship Trials take place
every September on the weekend after Labor Day. For information, call
Gus Halandras at 970-878-5483 or the Chamber of Commerce at 970-
878-5510. Or write to the organizers at P.O. Box 225, Meeker, CO
81641. www.meekerchamber.com.

BEST Multiday Raft Trip
Dinosaur National Monument

If dam builders had had their way in the 1950s, the river-canyon country
within Dinosaur National Monument would now be a standing reservoir.
Fortunately, the dams were never built, and you can still experience the
richness and variety of wilderness while floating the Green and Yampa
Rivers. The marks of man are nonetheless present, but in the form of
ancient rock art that depicts the game they hunted as well as primitive
rituals and ceremonies. Go back much farther in time, 140 million years to

the Jurassic period, and you will begin to understand the netherworld of massive prehistoric beasts that used to roam the land. Combine this with a sometimes-wild, sometimes-calm river passage and you have all the makings of a great multi-day river trip.

Beginning at the popular and imposing Gates of Lodore, most rafters put into the flat, calm waters with a heightened sense of discovery. You cannot see beyond the bend; two massive rock gates mark your entry point. The first foolhardy boaters who navigated this area in 1825 as a kind of shortcut to the western gold mines took massive risks and were lucky to walk away alive. In 1869, the famous one-armed explorer, Major John Wesley Powell, kept journal entries and created

Behind the Gates of Lodore, rafters may encounter Jurassic-era dinosaur remains in a unique natural world along the Utah–Colorado border. PHOTO BY BRUCE CAUGHEY

detailed maps during his daring adventures down the Green and Yampa. He managed to name many of the prominent landforms, including Echo Park and Steamboat Rock.

The waters can still be treacherous, but with solid equipment, good maps, and 150 years of experience, it has become a fairly safe voyage. Be sure that if you take the trip during spring runoff you'll have your share of white water. So hire a good outfitter and head into the great unknown. Lean back on your raft while crossing calm water and just listen to your remote surroundings. When emerging at the Dinosaur Quarry in Utah three days later, you again see the trappings of modern life but will be fascinated by the paleontology of the area. Getting away from it all takes on a new perspective while eating, drinking, and sleeping in a free-flowing river canyon. 970-374-3000; www.nps.gov/dino.

BEST Dogsledding
Krablooniks (Snowmass)

The approach to Krablooniks, with its chorus of yapping huskies, gets you in the mood for what's to come. And when is the last time you visited a place named for "bushy eyebrows," as *krablooniks* means in Eskimo? But for a select few, dogsledding happens to be one of those "once-in-a-lifetime" adventures. You will gather at the restaurant before settling into your wood sled, covered in warm blankets for a gorgeous ride up-valley from Old Snowmass. The musher stands behind you barking orders to his troops, getting enthusiastic barks in response and a strong team pull. And you're off on a half-day ride that includes homemade food in a gorgeous setting. You feel a bit guilty chowing down as the huskies huff and puff out steam in the cold mountain air, but soon realize they are enjoying the day almost as much as you are—it's as if they were built for this task.

Even if you cannot spare the rather expensive fee for dogsledding, be sure to visit Krablooniks for lunch or dinner. The five-star restaurant features some of the finest game dishes you'll ever taste. Absolutely, no matter what, try a bowl of the rich wild mushroom soup—it's incredibly good. You can get to Krablooniks by car or cross-country skis. Reservations necessary for dogsledding or dinner. 970-923-3953.

BEST Hut System
10th Mountain Division Hut System

No question, really: the finest hut skiing (mountain biking or hiking) in Colorado can be found along the 350 miles of trails in the scenic mountain area between Leadville, Vail, and Aspen. Named for the famous World War II ski troops who trained in the area before going overseas, the 10th Mountain Division Hut System has grown to include twenty-nine overnight accommodations with interconnected trails. Each hut comes provisioned with the basic necessities, including a wood-burning stove, firewood, electric lights, cookstoves, and cookware. Outhouse facilities and sleeping quarters with mattresses make for comfortable stays, and some even feature an opportunity to sweat in a sauna.

Although the word "hut" implies a small building, most are surprisingly large, with an attractive two-story wood-frame design that sleeps sixteen people; a couple of privately run lodging options also fit into the trail system. The absolutely stunning views will bring you back again and again, with standouts being the Shrine Mountain Inn and Fowler/Hilliard huts.

Originally built for skiing, this extensive hut system now entices guests year-round who hike or ski into these backcountry destinations. Well-marked, well-used trails follow recommended routes to the huts, but a maze of side routes veer away and surround the basic trail system, providing unlimited opportunities for discovery. Just be prepared and stay within your experience level. Very reasonable costs (this system is managed as a nonprofit), but reserve your huts early to avoid disappointment. To reserve, call 970-925-5775. www.huts.com.

BEST Ski Town
Aspen

Despite all the hot air ski resorts create about their on-mountain experiences, we'd like to highlight another aspect: the town. The ultimate ski town can be found in the Roaring Fork Valley, thriving 120 years after it was founded during the silver-mining boom. Yes, its reputation conjures up all sorts of images, some fond, others full of bile, but the fact remains that no other place truly compares.

The town has maintained its cultural, historical roots better than most places on the planet. And despite endless controversies over development, transit, and furs, Aspen residents do have a real town, and they care deeply about it. It may not feel that way when you walk among upscale galleries and boutiques and realize the average house costs more than you are likely to make in a lifetime of working. But the heart of a real town beats strongly, and the sheer beauty of the surroundings at this true destination more than make up for petty comments on its shortcomings.

Visitors get to take in a slice of it just by showing up. Plus, in winter, they can choose from four different on-mountain experiences: Aspen Mountain, Aspen Highlands, Buttermilk, and Snowmass. For convenience, visitors should head straight to Snowmass for a range of ski-in, ski-out condos. But for the joy of wandering around, taking in a play, browsing the racks of a good bookstore, checking out a restaurant, or partying all night, stay right in the town of Aspen. The accommodations and dining tend to be expensive, but certain places do cater to the non–Gold Card set. And many activities rely on community property: the surrounding White River National Forest brings out people who like to hike, mountain bike, and fish for endless outdoor fun. In summer, you can even camp overnight not too far from town. For information on lodging, start with Aspen Central Reservations, 888-290-1325. For more information on Aspen Skiing Company, try their Web site at www.ski aspen.com.

BEST Bowl Skiing and Boarding
Vail

Wide vistas of white powder stretch out in front of you in a space so vast, no adequate comparisons can be made. You become conscious of your own labored breathing as you look down at the snow crystals sparkling on the slope, watching as they fall quickly downward, away from the intense-blue sky above. You've worked hard to be ready for this frozen moment of pure pleasure in Colorado's best wide-open ski and snowboard experience. With 87 percent of its back bowls classified as expert terrain, but much of it suitable for strong intermediates, you'd better have your legs under you before setting out. Nothing compares to the adventure of the nearly 4,000 acres of Vail's back bowls on a powder day.

Locals know each of the seven back bowls has its own distinct personality and times of day when it shines. Sun Down and Sun Up bowls make it obvious when to delve into their delights. But to really get to know the bowls, you need to venture out to China, Siberia, Inner Mongolia, Outer Mongolia, and Tea Cup. Nothing in North America comes close to the mostly ungroomed experience of this terrain. Not that it's always picture-perfect. The conditions can vary widely from chopped blocks of half-melted crust on the fringe to big bumps down the spine of the ridge. Find a powder day, and you'll never want to go anyplace else. Boarders love carving fat turns on the open sides of the mountain, swinging from wall to wall.

The sheer scale combined with the stunning mountain backdrop makes it seem more reminiscent of Europe than of North America. So even if you are not totally taken by the nouveau Bavarian village of Vail below, this back side of the mountain is sure to satisfy. And even if you stay for a week, you'll not finish exploring the rest of this massive area, with its complex range of peaks, valleys, glades, and chutes, all served by thirty-one lifts. Great ski school, too. For more information, contact 970-476-5601 or refer to www.vail.snow.com.

BEST Family Ski Area
Sunlight Mountain Resort (near Glenwood Springs)

Only ten miles from Glenwood Springs, Sunlight Mountain Resort appeals to families in need of mostly mellow slopes and affordable lift-ticket prices. With few lifts and a map that an eight-year-old can read, you can all go skiing or snowboarding on 2,010 vertical feet of mostly beginner and intermediate trails. You won't find high-speed, detachable quad chairlifts, but you will find an unpretentious, friendly environment. And the lift-ticket prices have held for years. (Sunlight provides all the necessary amenities, despite its small size, but if you want a truly memorable night's stay in the area, check out the write-up on the Four Mile Creek Bed-and-Breakfast on page 75.) Call Sunlight Mountain Resort for information at 800-445-7931.

After a chilly day on the slopes, nothing feels better than slipping through a veil of steam into the 104° F hydrotherapy pool at the hot springs in downtown Glenwood, especially on a snowy night. However, tiptoeing across the frozen concrete from the lockers can be a shock to one's system! Kids absolutely love the mystical experience of swimming outdoors in winter and will beg you to come back every night you stay in town. Fee charged. 970-945-6571; www.sunlightmtn.com.

BEST Tree Skiing
Steamboat Springs

When the light filters through the bare aspen trees, nothing compares to dodging in and out of a forested, pick-your-own slalom course. Tree skiing takes a certain amount of raw nerve, quick, reflexive timing, and skill. Here at Steamboat, because of the generous spacing between immovable tree trunks and ample snowfall, skiers can practice their moves and build some confidence. Without lower branches, aspen glades provide the perfect venue. With nearly 3,000 acres of runs at the massive resort, including 1,149 acres of skiable/ridable glades, Steamboat remains the king of tree skiing. The best tree runs in our book have long been Shadows and Twilight in the gorgeous Priest Creek area. In addition to planned runs, the area features 1,790 acres of in-bounds timber bashing for adventuresome souls. Nothing could possibly make you smile more than making turns here on a perfect powder day. For complete skiing information on Steamboat, call 970-879-6111. www.steamboat.com.

Where to Eat, Drink, & Stay

expert pick

Top Five Colorado Restaurants
Noel Cunningham

Since Strings opened its doors back in 1986 in a perfect uptown location in Denver, it has been the restaurant of choice for those people who enjoy fine dining in a smart, contemporary ambience. The restaurant is often the setting for raucous cast parties on the final night of performances at the Auditorium Theatre. Noel Cunningham often finds himself in the middle of the energy in the restaurant, greeting guests and making sure every detail is attended to with grace and experienced ease. Noel cares for the finer appetites in town, without ever being pretentious. He used to do a lot more cooking, but now he has a chef who runs the kitchen who has a great knack for creating combinations and flavors. Cunningham also owns 240 Union Restaurant in Lakewood, which he describes as "casually sophisticated."

In addition to his restaurants, Cunningham devotes considerable time and energy to care for those less fortunate. He has established a foundation to help support Ethiopians who are on the brink of existence when it comes to basics such as food, clothing, and access to education. He works tirelessly with students around the Metro area to donate small sums of money, in quarter denominations, to bring a better life to people who truly need it.

We asked Cunningham about his favorite Colorado restaurants and he fired back with his favorite top five:

▸▸ **Sweet Basil (Vail)**—They are always on the cutting edge, and this restaurant is a source of inspiration for me. The tastes are clean and crisp and the atmosphere is first rate. 193 Gore Creek Dr.; 970-426-0125.

▸▸ **Mizuna (Denver)**—Frank Bonanno, who runs this small restaurant, pays attention to each detail of the dining experience. The bold flavors explode, and they are anything but froufrou. This intimate place reminds me of Italy. 225 E. 7th Ave.; 303-832-4778.

▸▸ **Frasca (Boulder)**—Getting a reservation at this new Italian restaurant is like winning the lotto. Run by former French Laundry (one of the best restaurants in the whole world) chef Lachlan MacKinnon-Patterson, this nicely understated, contemporary restaurant will awaken your senses. Great flavors and combinations. 1738 Pearl St.; 303-442-6966.

▸▸ **Montagna at Little Nell (Aspen)**—For a very posh meal, this is elegance at its best. This place reminds me of Europe, and it remains a great choice: the menu changes when it should, the chef changes when it should, and the carpet is replaced six months before it should. 675 E. Durant; 970-925-5882.

▸▸ **Steakhouse 10 (Englewood)**—The Kallas family inject supercharged Greek energy into this casual steak place, which used to be known as Sparks Steakhouse. Why come here? Steaks, of course, but a small glass of ouzo after dessert is a nice touch! 3517 S. Elati St.; 303-789-0911.

BEST Place to Stay and Soak
Hotel Colorado (Glenwood Springs)

During its 110-year history, the Hotel Colorado in Glenwood Springs has hosted presidents, silver barons, society's elite, movie stars, debutantes, and gangsters, and it continues to be the hotel of choice—partly due to its rich history and partly due to a prime location just behind the large and wondrous hot-springs pool.

In the early 1900s, the Hotel Colorado was known as the "Little White House of the United States" when presidents Taft and Roosevelt used it as their headquarters during visits to Colorado. Guests who stay in the Roosevelt Suite have access to the balcony where both presidents gave speeches to crowds of local citizens standing in the hotel's historic courtyard.

Later, in the 1920s and 1930s, the Hotel Colorado was home to two of America's most notorious gangsters, who used the secluded, luxurious hotel as a hideaway. Surreptitiously slipping in and out of the hotel via a secret tunnel, Diamond Jack Alterie was the first nefarious character to discover this jewel in the Rockies, which he introduced to his pal Al Capone.

Although the entire 126-room hotel has been completely renovated to offer guests the most modern con-

The storied Hotel Colorado towers over Glenwood's famous hot springs. PHOTO BY TAMRA MONAHAN

veniences, the Hotel Colorado's rich history has been maintained throughout the lobby, restaurants, and rooms. You can choose from a variety of themed suites, each decorated with Victorian-era furnishings that reveal Colorado's notorious past. The most historic place to stay, besides the Roosevelt Suite, is the Molly Brown Suite. Located high in one of the hotel's two bell towers, this suite of rooms contains artifacts donated by Molly Brown's great-granddaughter chronicling the legendary Colorado woman's life as the wife of a silver baron and the survivor of the legendary *Titanic* disaster.

The largest and most luxurious suite is named for the hotel's first owner, Walter Devereux, who, in 1893, built the Hotel Colorado next to the famous hot-springs pool as a luxury spa that catered to America's wealthiest clientele. Although the hot-springs pool is no longer affiliated with the hotel, guests have easy access to the pool and Glenwood's legendary vapor caves (see more about the vapor caves on page 46).

From I-70, the Hotel Colorado is located one block north and one block east of the Glenwood Springs exit. For more information, call 800-544-3998. www.hotelcolorado.com.

BEST Steaks
Juicy Lucy's Steakhouse (Glenwood Springs)

When David and C. C. Zumwinkle opened their steak house in Glenwood Springs, they wanted to name the restaurant for their daughter and let people know they serve the best steaks in town. Hence, the name Juicy Lucy's—Lucy for their daughter and Juicy for the steaks—and locals agree this is the top spot in Glenwood Springs for steak and seafood. Juicy Lucy's specialties include elk sirloin, New York strip, fresh-

72

You may never find a better steak than in
the comfortable setting at Juicy Lucy's.
PHOTO BY TAMRA MONAHAN

fish specialties, Seventh Street salad, and
the restaurant's signature dish, Lucy's au
gratin potatoes, which are unlike any au
gratin potatoes you've ever had before.
Thinly sliced potatoes are layered two
inches high in a round, deep dish and
cooked with just the right amount of
cheese and cream, then served as a
wedge, much like a piece of pie. The
effect is as extraordinary as the taste.

Juicy Lucy's also has an extensive,
award-winning wine list featuring Colorado's own Western Slope wines as well
as vintages from all over the world,
including Germany, France, Australia,
Chile, Argentina, South Africa, Portugal,
New Zealand, Italy, and Spain. But it's
not just the great food and wine that
keep locals coming back to this steak
house. It's also the atmosphere. Juicy Lucy's has the look and feel of old-
time Glenwood Springs with original lights and stamped-ceiling details
dating back to the 1930s, along with rustic chairs and tables, and coat
hooks on the walls made from bullhorns.

Whether you belly up to the bar or sidle into a booth to enjoy your
juicy steak and famous au gratin potatoes, Juicy Lucy's is one restaurant not
to be missed when you visit Glenwood Springs. 308 7th St.; 970-945-4619.

BEST Throwback to the '50s
Sleepy Cat Ranch (Meeker)

Sleepy Cat Ranch, eighteen miles east of Meeker, is a great place to get
away from it all, whether your "it" is work, kids, or a demanding boss.
Sleepy Cat offers peaceful serenity because the cabins have no telephone,
television, or Internet access, which means the world will have a tough
time intruding on your vacation. Staying at the Sleepy Cat Ranch will
bring reminiscences of when life was simpler and family vacations meant
piling everyone (including the dog) into the station wagon and heading
out on the open highway. Most of the cabins were built in the 1950s and
still look much the same. Outside they look like Lincoln Log homes, and
inside they have a distinctive Roy Rogers and Dale Evans's feel, from the
cowboy-style couch and lampshades to the pine cabinets and vintage
appliances in the kitchenettes. It won't be long before your kids can't
help but end up playing Marshall Dillon roaming the ranch looking for
cattle rustlers.

Staying at Sleepy Cat makes a great base camp for hunting and fishing trips to the Flat Tops Wilderness Area. The ranch sits right next to the White River (and, unfortunately, a bit close to the road), so you can rise with the sun and walk to your favorite spot for a little fly-fishing before breakfast.

Every cabin comes equipped with a bathroom, fireplace, and small kitchen for doing your own cooking. If, on the other hand, you're the type who wants to be waited on during your vacation, then walk over to the Sleepy Cat Lodge, which is open for breakfast, lunch, and dinner. The bar is open in the evenings, and this joint is swinging on Friday and Saturday nights, when you may need a reservation.

Well-behaved pets are allowed in the cabins. During October and November (hunting season), a five-night minimum stay is required. And for those of you who can't stand to be away from civilization, there is a television and Internet access in the lodge and one TV/VCR for rent. 970-878-4413 or 970-878-5432; www.sleepycatguestranch.com.

BEST Place to Wear Lederhosen
Sonnenalp Resort of Vail

For a taste of old Bavaria combined with superior modern amenities, the Sonnenalp Resort of Vail is your best bet. This luxurious resort is privately owned and operated by the Fassler family, who began their tradition of *gemutlichkeit*—warm, friendly hospitality—nearly a century ago high in the Bavarian Alps with the original Sonnenalp Hotel, which is still one of Germany's premier hotels. The name *Sonnenalp* means, "Sun on the Alps," and although the Vail resort sits adjacent to Gore Creek, it embodies the Old World charm reminiscent of a Bavarian inn. Burled-wood banisters and doors adorned with heavy iron hinges, hand-carved beamed ceilings, a stone archway at the entrance, and window boxes bursting with flowers all combine to give guests the feeling of staying at the Fasslers' alpine home, not some huge hotel. This cozy atmosphere was intentional, but don't be misled into believing that Vail's Sonnenalp is anything but a grand resort with all the upscale luxuries guests crave. A heated indoor-outdoor pool allows guests to plunge in year-round, either inside the warmth of the hotel or outside with a glorious Rocky Mountain backdrop. The Sonnenalp's world-class spa offers guests a massage, facial, pedicure, manicure, steam bath, or just about anything else they might need to help them relax and enjoy their stay.

The 178 rooms are spread out among three "houses": the Sonnenalp, the Austria Haus and Club, and the Swiss Hotel and Spa. All of the rooms feature plush feather comforters and handcrafted German imported furniture. Two of the hotel's best features are the library and Ludwig's restaurant. On the main floor next to the lobby, the Fasslers have provided a cozy library where the walls are lined with heavy wooden shelves laden with books of all types. Here guests can read by a roaring fire or exercise their minds with a game of chess or backgammon. Afterward, they can stroll over to the Sonnenalp's premier European-style restaurant, Ludwig's, for some of Vail's finest European cuisine.

The Sonnenalp Resort is the best way to experience the Alps in the Rocky Mountains, but the place is expensive and you'll need to book far in advance during peak seasons. 970-476-5656; www.sonnenalp.com.

BEST Luxury Ranches
Vista Verde and Home Ranch (Clark)

Just outside Steamboat Springs near the town of Clark, two plush guest ranches made it impossible to decide which one to include as the best. Our solution: give them shared billing as the best guest ranches. Vista Verde Ranch and Home Ranch offer many of the same luxurious Colorado-cowboy amenities, but there are subtle differences between the two. At both ranches you can ride horses, learn to rope and herd cattle, fish on the many scenic rivers in the Yampa Valley, hike and bike in the mountains, cross-country ski, and generally enjoy the life of an outdoorsman or cowboy without sacrificing any comforts. After a day in the wilderness, whether in a saddle on a horse or on a bike, you'll be pampered back home at the ranches with gourmet cuisine, luxurious cabins, and friendly people who cater to your every need.

So what's the difference between the two ranches? It comes down to what you want from your ranch-style vacation. Vista Verde is a bit more family oriented and prides itself on a wide variety of activities that are tailor-made for every guest. This convenience is great for families because they can participate in any program at any time instead of being tied to a set schedule that may not fit their needs. The atmosphere at Vista Verde is full of bustling activity, from people riding mountain bikes to fishermen taking fly-fishing lessons from expert guides to guests learning how to drive a team of horses. Home Ranch, on the other hand, offers most of the same activities but with a little more emphasis on subdued comfort. If your idea of a rustic ranch vacation in the Colorado Rockies includes a bit less activity and bit more lounging in comfort around a beautifully appointed pool, then Home Ranch may be more suited to your style.

Both ranches are open in the summer from June through September and in winter from December through March and require a minimum stay of a week. Vista Verde allows shorter vacations during the winter season, however. Vista Verde: 800-526-7433; www.vistaverde.com. Home Ranch: 970-879-1780; www.homeranch.com.

BEST Decadent Large Hotel
Bachelor's Gulch Ritz Carlton (Beaver Creek)

This one hotel comprises what is basically a little Colorado mountain village of its own, reminiscent of the grand lodges in our favorite national parks, except this place comes with a 21,000-square-foot spa and fitness center, including a heated outdoor pool. The hotel has expansive common areas and 237 wonderfully appointed guest rooms, most with fireplaces. Constructed of indigenous wood and stone, this massive hotel somehow retains a scale of personalized service. It has all the 24-hour amenities you could wish for from its well-trained staff. Thanks to a perfect setting near upscale Beaver Creek, you can enjoy luxury within the lap of luxury. The setting provides easy winter access to Beaver Creek Mountain, a top ski and snowboard area, right from its back door. During warmer seasons, guests can check out Bachelor, the lodge's in-residence Labrador retriever. Unlike in neighboring Beaver Creek, dogs are welcome here. The rooms feature feather beds, heavy terry cloth robes, a marble bathroom with a deep soaking tub, and glass shower. Oh, and three telephones, high-speed Internet access, and a fully stocked minibar. Nothing, though, compares to the spectacular mountain or valley views that you will enjoy from almost every room. Staying at the Ritz is expensive and worth it. Enjoy indoor or seasonal outdoor dining at Remingtons or head to the Daybreak Deli or Mountainside Terrace. You never have to leave this place once you check in. Located at 0130 Daybreak Ridge. 800-241-3333; www.ritzcarlton.com.

BEST Cabin Getaway with Breakfast
Four Mile Creek Bed-and-Breakfast (Glenwood Springs)

You cannot miss the imposing, weathered red barn as you round a bend in the road 6.5 miles south of Glenwood Springs. Located in a quiet meadow with massive shade trees on Four Mile Creek, this original 1885 homestead features a mix of bed-and-breakfast comfort and comfortable cabin rentals. Depending on your preference, you can reserve one of two rooms in the main house or find yourself cozily ensconced in one of two newly constructed cabins with heavy wood beams and private kitchens. One is located right on the creek and the other has a front porch that looks out over the peaceful garden. Friendly owners Sharill and Jim Hawkins know the area well and have put their hearts and souls into this place. You can even climb up into their barn and enjoy the company of a resident cat or explore the continuous flea market of historic "junk" that Jim cannot seem to help but collect. Wander out onto the grounds, enjoy the small apple orchard, feed the resident llamas and goats, or just sit back and lapse into a simpler, unhurried time. In winter, you are close to the family-friendly slopes of Sunlight ski area, and, in summer, you can wander around Glenwood Springs or easily head up to Redstone or Marble for the day. Stay for a night or two or enjoy a week, and you will not regret a moment. Inside the main house, over a complete hot breakfast, take some time to enjoy the synchronicity of the art and collectibles displayed in the home. Former art-gallery owner Sharill has a decorating sensibility that is unique and pleasing. Reserve in advance, especially on weekends. 6471 CR 117; 970-945-4004; www.fourmilecreek.com.

BEST Brunch
Redstone Inn (near Carbondale)

The Tudor clock tower at the Redstone Inn creates a focal point at the end of the town's quaint main street. PHOTO BY BRUCE CAUGHEY

It seems an unusual sight as you reach the south end of Redstone, a coal-mining town turned artisans' community. There lies a distinctive Tudor-style inn with a square clock tower modeled after a Dutch inn. Back in 1902, John Osgood, a paternalistic coal-mining baron who ruled the town with a velvet glove, built this place for his unmarried coal workers as part of a model industrial village. It has long since been transformed into luxury accommodations, just like Osgood's former house, a true castle situated on the Crystal River two miles up-valley. Even if you can't stay overnight, don't miss a chance to enjoy the Redstone Inn's classic Sunday brunch.

With bold colors, the inn and its well-regarded restaurant preserve Old European charm for its guests. Here you'll find attention to detail, from the friendly waitstaff to the carefully folded linen napkins and tasteful place settings. A cold buffet offers beautifully presented fresh fruits, baked goods (including cherry croissants on our visit), salmon mousse, and fresh tomato slices topped with fresh basil and mozzarella. Hot entrees ordered from the menu include eggs Benedict, ricotta crepes, and potato tatin layered with prosciutto. People from miles around make a special trip here to enjoy the setting and the food.

Redstone is located about seventeen miles south of Carbondale on CO Hwy. 133. For information and reservations, call 970-963-2526. www.redstoneinn.com.

BEST Unusual Dining Experience
Pine Creek Cookhouse (Ashcroft)

As the moon slowly rises from the east, a gathering of thirty to forty people gets a demonstration of how their cross-country ski bindings and headlamps work at the base area for the Ashcroft Ski Touring Center. The center maintains thirty-eight kilometers of cross-country trails for day use, but, unlike most touring centers, it receives an influx of guests as the sun sets. Outside the ghost town of Ashcroft (see Best Ghost Town on page 50), the activity reminds you of an era past. Now you are about to ski to dinner. It's common to hear languages from several different countries and feel a natural camaraderie among the group. A 1.5-mile trail leads gently uphill to the Pine Creek Cookhouse, a backcountry restaurant where soft candlelight, a roaring fire, and a gourmet-dining experience await.

Once there, your ski guide transforms into your food server, taking orders from the full bar (remember, you've got to ski back down!) to start off your meal. Enjoy a good glass of wine before turning your attention to your feast of salmon, chicken, or wild game cooked up in a creative Colorado style. For nonskiers, a horse-drawn sleigh also makes the leisurely trek to the cookhouse. This unique restaurant also serves lunch, but dinner remains the most special excursion. This is the kind of place you visit once and remember for a lifetime. It's also open June through October for drive- and hike-in guests. For reservations, call 970-925-1044.

BEST Wine Tasting
Palisade

Few people realize that in northwest Colorado you have your choice of wine-tasting rooms. Yes, it's a long way from Napa Valley, but when you find yourself amid the hundreds of acres of vineyards in Palisade, near Grand Junction, it feels like a special discovery. And, most likely, you won't be intimidated by snooty, swirling, sniffing wine aficionados or haughty attitudes from the local vintners. What you will find are a half dozen relaxed places to enjoy award-winning locally produced wines. With its hot days to build sugar in the grapes and cool nights to provide a distinctive crispness, the Grand Valley

Enjoy a taste of Colorado's finest wines at many Palisade vineyards. PHOTO BY BRUCE CAUGHEY

along the Colorado River serves as a perfect location for growing and harvesting many varieties of grapes. So hop into your car or grab your bike and tour the green, carefully tended Palisade vineyards surrounded by the reddish cliffs and arid mesas.

Vineyards started in this area before the turn of the century but were squashed in 1920 when Prohibition came into effect and the vines were ripped out by authorities. It's taken a long time to rebound, but the industry has boomed in the past decade. Palisade has long been a destination for people who love its flavorful peaches, but today the area's rising star has become the grape. Slowly but surely, winemakers have expanded their varieties from the ever-popular Chardonnay and Merlot varieties to more exotic Syrah, Sangiovese, and Viognier strains. They have also added drip irrigation, high-tech monitoring equipment, and comfortable tasting rooms for visitors. In our view, the top three Palisade vineyards to visit are as follows:

▸▸ **Plum Creek Cellars**—Since 1984, the owners of Plum Creek have been producing some of the state's most consistent Chardonnay and Merlot wines. Nice tasting room, store, and outdoor picnic area. 970-464-7586.

▸▸ **Grand River Vineyards**—The airy interior of the facilities here allows the vintners to stack casks of wine in the back storeroom. You will find many varieties, including the distinctive Meritage red and Barrel Select Chardonnay. The tasting room, store, and picnic area make a great stop just off I-70. 970-464-5867.

▸▸ **Carlson Vineyards**—Parker and Mary Carlson push the humor limits with whimsical wine names such as Tyrannosaurus Red, Prairie Dog Blush, and Pearadactal. With colorful labels and these offbeat names, you might be tempted to buy this wine just to surprise and amaze your friends. It tastes great, too! 970-464-5554.

▸▸ During harvesttime in mid-September, try to attend the **Colorado Mountain Winefest**. Tour the area's wineries, sample the wines, and kick back for some music and appetizers. No tickets necessary. 800-704-3667; www.colorado wine.com.

BEST Cinnamon Roll
Winona's (Steamboat Springs)

Some travel writer proclaimed that Johnson's Corner near Fort Collins had the best cinnamon rolls in the country, but they must have missed stopping off at Winona's restaurant in Steamboat Springs. This small, well-appointed place on Lincoln Ave. attracts a mix of locals and tourists for its delicious selection of pastries. Full breakfasts include eggs Benedict, lox omelets, a killer breakfast burrito, and fluffy pancakes. Still, the cinnamon roll remains the menu's standout with its soft swirls of buttery cinnamon pleasure finished with a calorie-laden honey-and-cream cheese frosting. *Bon Appetit* magazine calls it a "Plump, perfect cinnamon roll," and we're not going to argue. More than a decade ago, Winona started this restaurant with her favorite recipes, and the small restaurant has been sustained by strong business ever since. During high season, you are pretty much guaranteed a wait for breakfast, although lunch and dinner are not quite as packed. 617 Cincola Ave.; 970-879-2483.

BEST Historic Hotel
Hotel Jerome (Aspen)

When you visit Aspen, the town's history becomes paramount to your experience, so let it guide your selection of a place to stay. The Hotel Jerome maintains a stately Victorian elegance as the three-story brick anchor of the town's silver-mining past. The hotel opened on Thanksgiving Day in 1889, after mining magnate and former Macy's president Jerome B. Wheeler decided to pour his time and funds into making this hotel one of the best of its day. Since that time, it has had some ups and downs, but a massive renovation in 1989, when the hotel was 100 years old, recaptured the hotel's splendor. The original building houses twenty-seven luxurious rooms, and a new wing, seamlessly built behind the hotel, offers an additional sixty-seven guest rooms.

Each spacious room features period floral wallpaper, antique brass and cast-iron beds, and Eastlake armoires in a way that blends comfort with convenience. Modern touches have been gracefully added, including robes, telephones, televisions, and even hair dryers in the oversized bathrooms. The pool on the west side of the hotel, with patio seating at umbrella tables, can be quite a scene in summer. Room service, valet parking, and a ski concierge round out the services, though the staff can sometimes seem aloof to requests. Even if you don't splurge on a room at the Jerome, spend some time plopped comfortably on a sofa in the historic lobby with its high glass ceiling or stop in for a drink at the always popular J-Bar. Expensive. 330 E. Main St.; 800-331-7213; www.hotel jerome.com.

BEST Chain Hotel
Hyatt Regency (Beaver Creek)

As you drive up to the horseshoe-shaped entrance, with its heated brick pavers, the realization comes over you that this hotel—no, this entire village—represents a carefully crafted departure from your day-to-day existence. You just don't see anything unless it's tasteful and upscale, and the Hyatt represents the best of the best. So suspend your view of the world, get into vacation mode, and enjoy this European-style hotel for all that it offers: convenience, style, romance, warmth, and Old World charm. It doesn't feel anything like a chain, and that's why we selected it. Its sandstone and rough-hewn wood interior in tasteful combinations, numerous wood-burning fireplaces—some with massive, wall-size mantels (in winter, the hotel retains a full-time fire tender)—and plenty of little nooks and alcoves invite intimate conversation. Oh, and something magical comes over you as you sit back in the large outdoor hot tub filled by a steaming cascade of water coming down a rocky slope.

In summer or winter—or in between with some great package deals—the Hyatt remains a very special hotel, one that looks out for your every need. From the coffeemaker in the bathroom to the fluffy bedcoverings to the logic and convenience of the design, the 276 guest rooms assume a masterful decadence. Speaking of which, the ski concierge's assurance that your gear is ready and waiting takes a lot of hassle away from the sport, as does the convenient slope-side location. The peaceful feng shui ambiance of the on-site Allagria spa with its full-service salon, massage, wraps, and body scrubs can be a perfect time-out from strenuous outdoor activities. Pamper yourself a bit before you need to return home, preserving your time here as a memory.

Camp Hyatt will take care of your kids at times, so you can all enjoy the vacation. Children (two under eighteen years of age) may stay in their parents' room free of charge or, if available, in an adjoining room at half price. Three on-site restaurants. 970-949-1234; www.beaver creek.hyatt.com.

BEST Dude Ranch
Latigo Ranch (North Park)

Sit back, close your eyes, and imagine a true Western experience: you and your family are being transported to an isolated ranch in a beautiful forest setting, and you have your very own horse to ride each day. You feel comfortable in jeans and boots, and you make lasting friendships over hearty meals. Your kids run and play with others their age, yet you still share many wonderful times with them. Snap out of it! It's not a dream, it's Latigo Ranch, which accommodates a small number of guests (about thirty-five) in its tailored, year-round vacation programs.

Over the years, the two families who own and run Latigo have been pleasing guests with their attention to detail. With the help of a well-trained and caring staff, they have found a way to strike a balance between a ranch experience and vacation comfort. Their low-key approach without intrusiveness helps you enjoy simple, memorable times without daily hassles. Small duplex cabins tucked into the woods bring a welcome degree of comfort without being overly plush. After spending all day building your appetite, you'll truly enjoy sitting down for gourmet food in the common dining room. You won't go away hungry.

In summer, the ranch focuses on horseback riding, with wranglers who manage to match your riding skills with one of their sixty horses. Be sure to try a breakfast or sunset ride sometime during your stay; experienced riders should inquire about going on an actual cattle roundup. Other summer activities include fishing, white-water rafting, hay rides, and nature walks; however, guests are not railroaded into participating if they'd rather just hang out by the pool and enjoy the setting. In winter, cross-country skiing on thirty-five kilometers of groomed trails and snowshoeing on backcountry trails remain the most popular activities. A special photo workshop and other programs are available. 800-227-9655 or 970-724-9008; www.latigotrails.com.

NORTH-CENTRAL

For it was here on May 6, 1859,
that John H. Gregory's discovery of a rich vein
of gold-bearing quartz gave the state its first real rush.
Other strikes followed quickly, and within a few months
Gregory Gulch was swarming with thousands of
frenzied gold seekers.

—KENT RUTH, FROM *Colorado Vacations,*
REGARDING THE FAMOUS GOLD STRIKE ON CLEAR CREEK
NEAR CENTRAL CITY

High mountain passes, jagged peaks, and vast stretches of open space come to mind when one thinks about the diverse landscape in the northern middle of the state. This rich area started out as a haven for miners and loggers in the mid-1800s and eventually transitioned into an enmeshed collection of nature preserves, mountain vistas, and booming resort communities. Stretching south from the Wyoming border to the vast spaces of North Park to the foothills beside the eastern plains, the region's above-timberline centerpiece is Rocky Mountain National Park. Containing some seventy peaks more than 12,000 feet tall and providing a perfect habitat for an abundance of wildlife, this national treasure embodies the best attributes of an already remarkable region.

Consider the range of year-round outdoor experiences you can have in north-central Colorado. You won't be disappointed by visiting the awesome landscape while traveling among the communities of Estes Park, Grand Lake, Summit County, and Central City. The forty miles of free-flowing water in the often-raging Cache la Poudre River provide excellent grounds for fishing and kayaking. The excellent snow and friendly mentality of Winter Park, a laid-back Colorado resort stalwart, has been a major draw since the T-Bar first brought skiers up the mountain in 1940. The three-mile tracks of the Georgetown Loop Railroad and belching black smoke of the restored railway still recall the engineering tenacity it took to bring ore down from the mines above Silver Plume. The Central City Opera brings out our common cultural heritage and stands as true historic preservation in the midst of gaming and massive development.

Much of this part of the state—especially those rounded, heavily forested mountains that lie just north of Rocky Mountain National Park—remains undisturbed and relatively unknown. So, depending on the season, break out your hiking boots, mountain bike, or cross-country skis and find the beauty and isolation of this scenic area. If heart-pumping outdoor activities are not your thing, then hop in your car and tour some of the places that served as the impetus for the settlement of the West.

Cultural & Historical

BEST Place to Satisfy Your Sweet Tooth
Georgetown Valley Candy Company

Nestled on a corner of Georgetown's historic 6th St., there's a place that takes you back to your childhood the minute you walk inside. The sweet aroma of chocolate, colorful array of brightly wrapped candy, and other sweet delights seductively bring back memories of visiting candy stores when you were a kid. This is the magic of the Georgetown Valley Candy Company, a wonderful little shop where owners Nina and Rube Goeringer make candy and ice cream from scratch. The candy store is one of the most popular places in Georgetown, and the secret to its success is a combination of good, old-fashioned ingredients and small-town friendliness. Nina has been making candy all

Children participate in the Santa Lucia pageant, a Scandinavian tradition at Georgetown's famous Christmas market.
PHOTO BY RUTH ROSENFELD, HISTORIC GEORGETOWN

of her life, learning many of her famous recipes from her mother back in Arkansas. Nina and her son Scott, a master chef who returned to the family business after years cooking in fine restaurants, make the huge assortment of candy at the store. Behind antique glass cases you'll discover Nina's fabulous creations, from caramel and chocolate turtles to English toffee to fudge that'll make you swoon. Almost any kind of chocolate treat imaginable is there for you to indulge yourself in and be a kid again.

Over the years she perfected her craft and branched out into making ice cream after discovering that she and Rube could make a better-quality ice cream than anything available. Made from rich, decadent ingredients, this ice cream, with its one-of-a-kind flavors, is only surpassed by Rube's famous singing as he scoops the creamy treat into a sugar cone. The Old Goat, as he's known locally, began singing softly years ago as a way to keep himself entertained while making candy and ice cream. Eventually people asked him to sing louder, and over the years his crooning has become legendary in the town and adds to the store's charm, especially at Christmas. The Georgetown Valley Candy Company is located on the corner of 6th St. and Taos St. in historic Georgetown. 303-569-2778.

BEST Summer Drive in a Convertible
Guanella Pass

One of Colorado's best scenic and historic byways lies a mere forty-five miles west of Denver and offers visitors a unique view of disparate ecological systems without the need for a four-wheel-drive Hummer. In fact, this easy, year-round route rises to 11,669 feet between historic Georgetown and Grant and is a spectacular, scenic passage. Visitors will find limitless opportunities for hiking, camping, and cross-country skiing and easy access to the Mount Evans Wilderness Area. Rising more than 3,000 feet, Guanella Pass winds through a succession of distinct environments.

At the lower elevations, you'll find groves of pine, aspen, fir, and spruce trees lining the road, and in mid-September, Guanella Pass is a fabulous place to view autumn's fiery colors as gently quaking aspens create golden waves along this picturesque highway. Or, head out in springtime to the road's higher elevations, where wildflowers of all colors and sizes dot landscapes characterized by alpine meadows and streams meandering through the trees. Beaver dams have produced a series of ponds on Geneva Creek, providing another welcome distraction along this route.

Guanella Pass is the perfect outdoor classroom. At the summit, visitors are greeted by a stunning display of fragile tundra, small flowers, and plants barely peeking out above ground level during the brief summer weather. Majestic peaks tower above this tundralike landscape, surrounding visitors on all sides with spectacular views of some of Colorado's most famous mountains. The summit of Guanella Pass provides hiking access to two of Colorado's Fourteeners—Mount Evans and Mount Bierstadt—as well as a variety of shorter hikes for those less inclined to scale the adjacent lofty peaks.

Originally a wagon trail used by miners traveling between Grant and Georgetown, Guanella Pass is now an easy way for people to escape from the city for a day to experience Colorado's varied natural wonders. To get to Guanella Pass, take U.S. Hwy. 285 west from Denver to Grant. Turn right on CR 62 and travel approximately 13.5 miles to Guanella Pass Rd. You can also catch this route by taking the Georgetown exit off I-70 and following the signs in town.

BEST Operatic Experience
Central City Opera

We heartily recommend the Central City Opera House in the foothills west of Denver. The understandable (in English), witty, vibrant operas have always drawn crowds, and the vintage-1878 opera house remains a stable Victorian-era anchor in a town that has been transformed by gambling over the past decade. Serious opera aficionados should check out Opera Colorado, but for most of us the Central City experience fits the bill. During the hall's construction, the *Rocky Mountain News* declared it "the most beautiful auditorium to be found between Chicago and San Francisco." In this small setting you can actually catch the nuance of voice and expression of the performers, making the experience memorable even for those who are not fans of opera. With the new, padded theater-style seats, it's a complete experience (the seats used to be on a par with the cold metal benches in the south stands at Mile High Stadium).

The nation's longest-running summer opera has been performing shows annually since 1932, and here's why: the high-powered talent, popular productions, and a tasteful, intimate setting. The talent runs the gamut from regional stars to Sylvia McNair, one of the world's finest lyric sopranos, who performed a 1999 concert of the music of George Gershwin. You feel as if you have been transported back to the town's mining-era heyday, for operagoers still tend to get gussied up for the show. Feeling the energy of the crowd in this historic opera house also seems to propel the performers to new artistic heights. In addition to full operas, visitors can reserve tickets for opera dinners, salon recitals, and shortened, à la carte performances. Children under six are not allowed. Each show tends to sell out early, so be sure to call in advance to reserve seats for the summer season program. 800-851-8175 or 303-292-6700; www.centralcityopera.org.

BEST Place to Celebrate a Dead Hero
Buffalo Bill Museum and Grave (near Golden)

In his day, William Frederick Cody (a.k.a. Buffalo Bill) managed to achieve folk-hero status in distant parts of the world, thanks largely to the spectacle of his traveling Wild West Show. But before turning into a famous frontier personality, "Bill" rode for the Pony Express, served as a scout in the army, and killed far more buffalo than he should have—including 4,280 buffalo in one eight-month period. The mythology of his persona can be difficult to sort out from the reality, but nobody questions that Buffalo Bill captured the imagination of millions.

In the narrow shadows of radio transmitter towers on Lookout

Mountain above Golden, Buffalo Bill and his wife are buried under a rock marker. Sweeping views east to the plains mesmerize visitors, and from lower down the trail, an equally expansive mountain view lies to the west. A small museum commemorates the man and the myth. A huge gift shop sells the usual mix of everything from fake tomahawks to shot glasses.

Inside the museum, be sure to catch the video on Buffalo Bill and his life, which began in 1846 and ended in 1917. Displays capture some of what made him famous, including a collection of shotguns, lots of buckskin clothing, and some Native American artifacts. Reflection brings into question Buffalo Bill's hero status in terms of his relationship with the people who were here first. Did he kill many or was he "kind and decent to Indians" as the video claims? The truth, no doubt, lies somewhere in between; with the benefit of the passage of time, we can all be the judge.

Small admission fee. Located off I-70 and Lookout Mountain Rd. Follow the signs. Take your picnic lunch next door to the tables set up in sixty-six-acre Lookout Mountain Park. 303-526-0747; www.buffalobill.org.

B E S T Way into the Mountains without Driving
The Ski Train from Denver to Winter Park

Leave the driving to a train conductor. The trip into the mountains becomes even more of an adventure when you hear the whistle blow while departing Denver's Union Station. For nearly sixty years, Denver residents and visitors have enjoyed this direct route to the slopes of Winter Park, which bypasses Berthoud Pass on U.S. Hwy. 40 and crosses the Continental Divide via the 6.2-mile-long Moffat Tunnel. Winter Park is the only resort in the United States with direct train service. The Ski Train takes about two hours each way and runs every Saturday and Sunday from mid-December to mid-April and Fridays in February and March. Service has recently been expanded to include weekends in other seasons too— especially during festivals and for fall foliage tours. For information on the train, call 303-296-4754. www.skitrain.com.

On the Ski Train, head through the 6.2-mile-long Moffat Tunnel on the way from Denver to Winter Park. PHOTO BY BYRON HETZLER, WINTER PARK RESORT

BEST Short Railroad Trip
Georgetown Loop Railroad

Even though there is a new company operating the train, passengers still have about the same experience. You load into open-air cars, some covered, some not, for a brief ride into the past. On narrow-gauge track, which is more than a foot narrower than today's standard rails, the train begins its trip from the well-preserved Victorian confines of Georgetown with a loud blast of its whistle. The route begins by crossing a curving span of steel called Devil's Gate as the train chugs its way up the steep grade. It travels past the Lebanon Mine, where riders can disembark for a mine tour, on a steadily winding route to Silver Plume. The six-mile round-trip takes only slightly more than an hour, just as it did when the route was completed in 1884.

Along the way, the railcars cross the roily white water of Clear Creek four times. The slow but powerful steam train could never have made the trip if it were not for the engineering effort to overcome the impossible 6 percent gradient between the towns. By building the winding track with a series of curves—hence the name Georgetown Loop—the grade was sufficiently reduced. In another feat of human tenacity, the entire route was rebuilt in 1984 with help from the Colorado Historical Society; the original tracks were sold for scrap in 1939.

Now riders can catch the train at the Georgetown or Silver Plume depots many times daily throughout the warmer months. Keep your eyes peeled for the bighorn sheep that inhabit the rocky crags adjacent to I-70. Since the train was retrofitted to burn oil instead of coal, passengers need not worry about cinders, but the primary engine still belches huge blasts of smoke along the route. Be sure to bring jackets, gloves, and rain gear, as even seemingly clear summer mornings can turn rainy, windy, and cold in a Rocky Mountain minute. For information and reservations, call 303-866-3682. www.coloradohistory.com.

Outdoor Activities & Events

expert pick

Top Five Dog-Friendly Places
Cindy Hirschfeld

You love to travel, but hate to leave your best friend behind. Cindy Hirschfeld and her dog, Clover, have the scoop on where the "No Dogs Allowed" signs have been taken down all over the state. From her book *Canine Colorado: Where to Go and What to Do with Your Dog* (Fulcrum Publishing, 2001), you'll be surprised at the fancy hotels that welcome Fido and the trails where Spot can run off-leash. Cindy's "Top Five Dog-Friendly Places" are just the tip of the iceberg.

▸▸ For pure puppy pampering (we're not talking dogs on a budget here), it's a tie between Denver's Hotel Teatro and The Little Nell in Aspen. Both hotels have luxurious furnishings and impeccable service for dogs and humans alike, including staffers who will graciously take Rover out for a pee break in your absence. The Teatro welcomes dogs with a collar tag inscribed with the hotel's name and address, chew toys, food and water bowls, and bottled Fiji water. The Nell provides a collar tag, bowls, bed, home-baked biscuits, and room-service pet menu. Will it be the city or the country this weekend, Fido? Hotel Teatro: 1100 14th St., Denver; 888-727-1200; www.hotelteatro.com; The Little Nell: 675 E. Durant; 970-920-4600; www.thelittlenell.com.

▸▸ At Colorado Canines in Boulder, one of the state's first pet-specialty stores, Rover can browse for hours among the impressive selection of toys, treats, gear for the active dog, and natural food. The store also offers classes and demonstrations on health- and nutrition-related topics and even runs adventure trips—rafting on the Arkansas, say, or hiking in Steamboat Springs—for dogs and their people. 1738 Pearl St., Boulder; 303-449-5069; www.coloradocanines.com.

▸▸ Every April, the weekend after the lifts close at Aspen's Buttermilk ski area, dogs in the know gather for the K-9 Uphill, a 2,000-vertical-foot snowshoe or ski climb from the base of the mountain to the summit. It's the one time you want your dog to pull you! And it's easy to win a prize in the extensive raffle afterward. Organized by Aspenite Erik Skarvan, the event raises money for local animal shelters. SunDog Athletics: 970-925-1069.

▸▸ Since dogs aren't allowed on any trails in Rocky Mountain National Park, you'll have to look elsewhere for a place to enjoy the scenery together. On the east side (near Estes Park), it's Crosier Mountain Trail, which includes a vast, wildflower-filled meadow and a spectacular vista of the peaks in the park. On the west side (outside of Grand Lake), the Baker Gulch Trail actually starts inside the park and then tops out among the peaks of the Never Summer Range. U.S. Forest Service offices, Estes Park: 161 2nd St.; 970-586-3440; Granby: 9 Ten Mile Dr.; 970-887-4100.

▸ The Piney Creek Nordic Center, located at the top of Tennessee Pass outside Leadville, allows skiers and snowshoers to bring their dogs on all twenty-five kilometers of groomed trails, the most extensive trail network open to "powderhounds" in the state. You'll have to buy a trail pass, but Fido skis free and off-leash to boot. 719-486-1750; www.tennesseepass.com.

BEST Devilish Good Times
Devil's Thumb Ranch (Fraser)

Despite its slightly checkered past, this ranch is an excellent destination for year-round adventures, thanks to the current owners. Located in the beautiful Ranch Creek Valley of Grand County, not far from the downhill slopes of Winter Park, Devil's Thumb Ranch is perfectly situated to offer its guests miles of first-class Nordic ski trails in the winter and prime fly-fishing water in the summer. Devil's Thumb provides luxurious accommodations in a variety of private cabins or in the main lodge, with excellent Nordic and snowshoe trails right at your doorstep. Devil's Thumb also offers a range of summer outdoor activities including fly-fishing, kayaking, and horseback riding. Year-round you can find an excellent place to get a bite to eat at the Ranch Restaurant.

You can park your car and leave it for your entire winter vacation because Devil's Thumb has more than 3,700 acres of land, including 100 kilometers of groomed trails for classic and skate skiing as well as twenty kilometers of marked snowshoe trails. On many of the trails you can bring your dog for a day of skijoring, which is cross-country skiing while tethered to your pooch (see page 92). In addition, Devil's Thumb has sleigh rides and an outdoor ice-skating rink for more wintertime fun.

Summer transforms the ranch into a fly-fishing frontier, all without the hassle of driving to different spots. Park your car, grab your gear, and head out to the superb fly-fishing waters surrounding Devil's Thumb. If you don't have your own equipment or are new to the sport, no worries. Everything you need, from rods and reels to waders to instructors, is available at the Orvis-approved Devil's Thumb Fly-Fishing Adventure Center. When you're not casting on the river, take a guided raft trip, a trail ride, or a hike on one of the ranch's scenic trails. Late summer and early fall, when the autumn leaves are at their colorful peak, are great times to visit Devil's Thumb.

Devil's Thumb Ranch is located between the towns of Fraser and Tabernash in Grand County. Take I-70 to exit 232. Head west on U.S. Hwy. 40, about two miles past Fraser, then take a right on CR 83. Follow the signs and keep right at the fork on your way to the ranch. 970-726-5632; www.devilsthumbranch.com.

BEST Cross-Country Skiing Destination
Grand County

If you love winter sports, such as cross-country skiing, snowshoeing, ski-joring, and even dogsledding, you should head out to a snowy paradise just outside of Denver where the trails go on for miles. Grand County is legendary for its snow and wide-open spaces, perfect for every type of winter pastime. Its unique location on the western slope of the Continental Divide creates ideal weather for plentiful snow. Here are some of the best places:

▸▸ **Devil's Thumb Ranch**—Tucked into the Ranch Creek Valley between the towns of Fraser and Tabernash, Devil's Thumb Ranch has 125 kilometers of groomed trails and skating tracks, including some lighted trails. The entire property encompasses an astonishing 4,000 acres of secluded meadows and hills, with challenges for every level of skier. Devil's Thumb also offers excellent places to stay the night and a spa for recovering from any outdoor activity. We consider the Ranch House Restaurant the area's top spot for fine dining in a rustic vintage-1937 homestead atmosphere. 970-726-8231; www.devilsthumbranch.com.

▸▸ **Snow Mountain Ranch**—This top Nordic destination, which is part of the YMCA of the Rockies facility near Granby, has 100 kilometers of groomed tracks (including a lighted trail for night skiing) and trails through pine forest, wide meadows, and along Pole Creek. Other "Y" activities include snowshoeing, a biathlon range, and skijoring, a technique in which you ski while harnessed to your dog. Snow Mountain Nordic is also the home of one of the country's premier Nordic events, the Subaru Snow Mountain Stampede, each spring. Family-style lodgings and meals are also available on the extensive YMCA campus. 970-887-2152; www.ymcarockies.org.

▸▸ **SolVista Basin at Granby Ranch**—Also near Granby, SolVista offers Nordic skiers one of the best bargains in the area atop the downhill area at the Quick Draw lift. Pick up a free trail pass or buy a lift ticket that takes you right to the head of twenty-five kilometers of uncrowded, groomed trails that wind through the forest bordering two alpine ski hills. The ski shop rents both classic and skate skis. 970-887-3384; www.solvista.com.

▸▸ **Grand Lake Touring Center**—During the summer, this is one of Grand County's best golf courses, but after the snow falls, skis replace clubs. Find thirty kilometers of groomed and tracked trails, as well as skating trails that wander over the gentle hills of the golf course and into the nearby forest. The center also serves as the trailhead for many more challenging backcountry trails that stretch out into public lands that border the property. 970-627-8008; www.grandlake colorado.com/touringcenter/.

▸▸ **Winter Park**—Better known for its long history of alpine skiing in Colorado, Winter Park and the Fraser Valley are becoming increasingly recognized for their wealth of options for Nordic skiers and snowshoers. From groomed resort tracks to pristine backcountry trails, the choices are outstanding. 970-726-5514; www.skiwinterpark.com.

▸▸ **Latigo Ranch**—On the far western side of the county near the town of Kremmling, you'll get great guest-ranch hospitality and prime Nordic skiing with sixty kilometers of groomed track and many more backcountry and telemark trails branching out into the surrounding 200 square miles of national forest. 800-227-9655; www.latigotrails.com.

▸▸ **Public Land**—Hard-core backcountry skiers know that some of the best touring is through the many thousands of acres of public lands. Local Nordic centers, retail shops, and ski clubs are staffed with experienced skiers who can provide valuable information about permits and accessing these remote areas, which include Rocky Mountain National Park, Arapaho National Forest and Recreation Area, Medicine Bow/Routt National Forest, and the Vasquez Peak, Byers Peak, Never Summer, and Indian Peaks Wilderness Areas.

In Grand County, skijoring has become a popular pastime for dog owners. COURTESY OF THE WINTER PARK AND FRASER VALLEY CHAMBER OF COMMERCE

BEST Wintry Day with Your Dog
Skijoring in Grand County

A sport that's becoming popular in Colorado, especially in the pristine snow country of Grand County, is skijoring. Basically, this is cross-country skiing attached to a dog, and Grand County is one of the best places to tether yourself to your four-legged friend and hit the trails. Most people ski with their dogs as companions, but if your dog is big enough, you can relax and let canine enthusiasm pull you along the trail. *Skijoring*, which is Norwegian for "ski driving," originated in Scandinavia and was brought to the United States when Scandinavian prospectors rushed to the Yukon for gold. Although it died out for many years, recently skijoring has caught on as a great way to combine Nordic skiing and quality time with man's best friend. However, not all cross-country ski areas allow skijoring, so be sure to check before you take your dog on the trails. The best places can be found in Grand County, including Devil's Thumb Ranch, Snow Mountain Ranch, and the Grand Lake Touring Center.

MOST LIKELY Place to Hear Bagpipes
Longs Peak Scottish/Irish Highland Festival (Estes Park)

Kilts are common at the Longs Peak Scottish/Irish Highland Festival. PHOTO BY TAMRA MONAHAN

Men and women dressed in kilts? Drum and bagpipe music in the air? It must be the Longs Peak Scottish/Irish Highland Festival in Estes Park, an annual event that brings kilted clansmen from all over the United States to the Rocky Mountains. The festival takes place every year at Estes Park's Stanley Fairgrounds the weekend after Labor Day, and it's the best place to experience a bit of the Scottish Highlands in our own highlands. For three days, clansmen gather to compete in traditional Highland Games, such as the caber toss (picture throwing a telephone pole like a toothpick), hammer throw, and sheaf toss. These events, just like the traditional Irish and Scottish dances, go back hundreds of years and are carried on today by Celtic men and women, girls and boys who take pride in their heritage.

A walk through the Scottish/Irish Festival is like stepping across the big pond to the British Isles. Sample Celtic cuisine, such as bangers and mash, haggis (don't ask what's in it!), scones, or Scottish meat pies. Then wash it down with a hearty glass of Guinness, Irish ale, or Scotch whiskey. Watch sheepdogs work their magic herding reluctant sheep into pens. Check out the clan tent where you might discover something about your ancestry. And don't forget to visit the merchandise tent where you can buy almost anything Celtic, Scottish, Irish, or any combination thereof. You'll find beautiful jewelry, belt buckles, clothing, ornamental swords, Celtic music, and, of course, kilts in an assortment of plaids and styles. Before buying one, you may want to find out what your clan's ancestral plaid is to be true to your Scottish roots.

One of the greatest aspects of this festival is the array of traditional Scottish and Irish outfits people wear, which go far beyond the basic kilt. From head to toe, people dress themselves in their Celtic best, including kilts, hand-tooled leather shields and drums, kilt sashes and pins, ghillie brogues (shoes), and sporrans (like a pouch or purse worn in front of the kilt). If it's Scottish or Irish, you'll see it at the Longs Peak Scottish/Irish Highland Festival. Please note that pets are not allowed at the festival, so be sure to leave Fido home; the dogs you see at the festival are competitors or show dogs. Tickets can be purchased in advance online or at the festival's main gate. www.scotfest.com.

BEST Sailing
Lake Dillon

Surrounded by three mountain ranges and with constantly shifting wind directions, the huge body of water called Lake Dillon has always been a challenge to sailors. "You can be sitting on the lake when it's as flat as glass," says hard-core sailing aficionado Roy Burley. "Then five minutes later, forty-knot winds kick up and can rip your headsail off!" Sailors come here mostly because of the pristine environment and terrific views. "If you can sail here, you can sail anyplace in the world," says Bob Evans, harbormaster of the Dillon Marina.

Because the reservoir serves as a main water source for Denver, the deep, cold waters are off-limits to swimming, waterskiing, jet skiing, and other immersion activities. You can, however, head out on a charter cruise, pontoon, or motorized fishing vessel if you don't want to count totally on wind power. No matter what you choose to get you around the lake, you'll be amazed by the panoramic views and the beauty of countless small side channels. If your craft has running lights, you'll get to enjoy midnight sailing at its absolute best.

With its unpredictable winds, however, the reservoir does not cater to novices. Afternoon brings about rapid changes in wind direction, including some breezes that seemingly sweep straight down off the surrounding mountains. On a warm day the water remains a chilly 40° F, and it's 200 to 300 feet deep in places. "Bodies and boats lie at the bottom of this reservoir," Burley confides with a serious tone. "If you don't know what you're doing, get off the lake before the afternoon winds invariably kick up."

Two marinas serve the boating population and provide rentals. Dillon Marina (970-468-5100; www.dillonmarina.com) on the northeast shore remains the best; it sponsors regular competitive regattas on the lake and even a sunset cruise with a five-course gourmet dinner. To the west, Frisco Bay Marina (970-668-5573; www.ospreyadventuresusa.com) provides services, boat rentals (including canoes), and boat-launching ramps.

BEST Public Golf Course
Pole Creek (near Fraser)

"Verging on holy" was the way Kim Anders, longtime pro at Pole Creek Golf Course, described the vistas from his favorite tee box on hole number nine. Here the green, rolling fairway drops 130 feet and sweeping views of the Continental Divide distract from the stated reason you're here: getting that small white ball in the hole in as few strokes as possible.

At an elevation of 8,600 feet, the ball flies 12 percent farther than at sea level, according to Anders. That advantage disappears when you try to find a level lie in this undulating environment and you begin to learn that the ball tends to break toward Pole Creek, which runs right through the middle of the course. *Golf Digest* just loves this place and has named it the number-one "place to play" in Colorado, among other accolades, over the years. If you want to beware of any one hole, watch out for the 570-yard hole number seven. "You need three well-placed shots in a row to have any hope," says Anders.

The eighteen-hole course just expanded to include nine new holes. Course architect Dennis Griffith, who was inspecting his work when we visited, says this new area is "a wonderful palette." He worked hard to match the landforms surrounding the greens to the strikingly beautiful mountain horizon. Thanks to the thick woods, he says, "golfers feel a simultaneous sense of openness and isolation." Griffith's care to blend the course into the environment while building memorable holes must be working, because golfers are lining up tee times earlier each year, making it harder to get last-minute slots. For a fee, golfers can reserve choice times a month or more in advance. Pole Creek features a

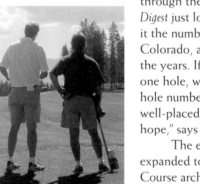

Golf professional Kim Anders surveys the view to the Indian Peaks from Pole Creek Golf Course. PHOTO BY BRUCE CAUGHEY

well-positioned clubhouse (great deck), putting green, driving range, and pro shop. Though fees do not compete with the big resorts, they're not cheap either. Located eleven miles northwest of the town of Fraser on U.S. Hwy. 40. Call 800-511-5076 or 970-887-9195 for information; www.polecreekgolf.com.

BEST Destination to Bag Four Fourteeners
Mounts Democrat, Cameron, Lincoln, and Bross

A peak-bagger who wants to get a head start on capturing all fifty-four 14,000-foot peaks in Colorado may well want to begin with a full day in the Tenmile and Mosquito Ranges. There, Mounts Democrat, Cameron, Lincoln, and Bross can be found towering just above the tiny burg of Alma in South Park. In addition to being interlaced with trails that rise and fall with the mountains' saddles, in effect shortening each hike, these routes to the summits are fairly gentle. Nonetheless, any travel by foot in high elevations requires stamina and knowledge. These popular peaks require no technical mountaineering skills, but hikers should be prepared for all sorts of elements and beware of the altitude. Get an early start to avoid the storms and give yourself some leeway—oh, and have fun, too!

Several approaches and combinations of routes may be taken to bag these four nearby peaks. The easiest and most popular route begins at Kite Lake and completes the ultimate up-and-down cirque to each of the high summits. A popular route begins up the east ridge to the 14,148-foot summit of Mount Democrat before descending east to the saddle between it and Mount Cameron. Hike up the top of 14,238-foot Cameron before heading northeast to Mount Lincoln (14,286 feet) and then back to the saddle between Lincoln and Cameron. The final leg begins here up the gentle southeast slope to the flat summit of 14,172-foot Mount Bross. This aerobic outing will put your Stairmaster workouts to shame. Keep your eyes peeled for well-adapted mountain goats, and be nice to the other humans who have decided to make this same popular trip. For more detailed route information, check out the excellent second-edition guidebook *Colorado's Fourteeners* by Gerry Roach (Fulcrum Publishing, 1999). (For Gerry's top five mountains to climb, see page 148.)

BEST Mountain-Biking System
Winter Park and Fraser

Who wouldn't love the adrenaline rush and intense focus that comes over you when powering your bike up and down single-track trails, darting around obstacles, and splattering through the mud? You feel like a kid again, maneuvering your bike with balance and dexterity, building your confidence and speed as the day wears on. Hopefully you haven't been a couch potato lately, because this sport requires muscle and stamina. Also, though you may be able to negotiate your old Schwinn most anywhere, you'll appreciate the gadgetry—including clip-in shoes and front shock absorbers—of modern mountain bicycles as well as tried-and-tested accessories such as fingerless bike gloves and padded shorts (a must!).

Since debuting its on-mountain trails in 1991, Winter Park Resort has continued to expand its marked trails to accommodate all skill levels—although first-timers should stick to the valley floor. Riders take their bikes up the ski lift (for a reasonable fee) and then get to skip most of the thigh-burning uphills. Stop in for an energy-boosting lunch and glorious views from 10,700 feet at the massive log-hewn Sunspot Lodge. In addition to the downhill experience at the ski mountain, riders can

Fat tire bike enthusiasts flock to the Winter Park Area and hundreds of miles of trails.
PHOTO BY ROD WALKER, WINTER PARK RESORT

access more than 600 miles of marked, mapped trails throughout the valley. A couple of favorites: the mellow six-mile Northwest Passage and the more difficult twelve-mile Zoom Loop. Families tend to migrate to the area's miles of dirt roads and the paved Fraser River Trail, which winds along for five mostly forested miles between Winter Park Resort and Fraser. Thousands of additional miles of unmarked trails and dirt roads, most of which started out as logging roads, get frequent use by in-the-know locals.

The annual Fat Tire Classic in late June remains one of the top fund-raising events (for the American Red Cross) anywhere. Winter Park is also a regular stop on the National Off-Road Biking Association (NORBA) series. For information and updates on trail conditions, contact 800-903-7275. www.skiwinterpark.com.

BEST Place to Make Your Relatives Gasp
Mount Evans Rd.

Coloradans sometimes take for granted that we have fifty-four mountains topping 14,000 feet in elevation right in our backyard. Instead of just gazing up at them, pack up a picnic lunch, hop into your car, and journey up to the top of 14,264-foot Mount Evans, enjoying incredible views along the way. Aunt Edna and Uncle Bert and all the little cousins will need to acclimate for a few days before you whisk them into oxygen dep-

rivation at nearly three miles high. This famed Scenic and Historic Byway also captures the prize as the highest paved automobile route in North America. Please share the road with countless road bikers huffing their way to the summit.

As the dominant peak dwarfing the Denver skyline, Evans provides memorable sights, including an ancient bristlecone pine forest, scenic vistas, and ample wildlife. You can also veer off the road to explore more than 100 miles of hiking trails. The first stop on the driving route is beautiful Echo Lake, with its roadside fishing, campsites, and picnic tables. After Echo Lake, pay your entrance fee and get ready for countless "oohs" and "aahs" the rest of the way. Keep your eyes peeled for yellow-bellied marmots (also called whis-

Bikers wend their way up to the top of Mount Evans under the watchful eye of resident mountain goats. PHOTO BY BRUCE CAUGHEY

tle pigs because of their distinctive call), bighorn sheep, pikas, and mountain goats. Volunteers from the Division of Wildlife set up an interpretive stand during summer weekends at Summit Lake. The parking lot leaves a quarter-mile hike to the mountaintop, where you'll enjoy an unparalleled panorama below. The Clear Creek Ranger District operates a visitors center in Idaho Springs that offers publications, including a Junior Ranger Adventure program as well as an excellent taped audio tour. For more information, call 303-567-2901. www.mountevans.com.

BEST Wildlife Viewing
Rocky Mountain National Park

The eerie bugle of elk in the fall and the sight of a little pika scampering about the rocky tundra represent two vastly different wildlife experiences. Add agile bighorn sheep and the bulbous-nosed moose, along with an entire range of other mammals and birds (from ptarmigan to large birds of prey), and this 415-mile wilderness becomes the best wildlife viewing location in the state. More than sixty peaks above 12,000 feet and the massive slopes of Longs Peak (14,255 feet) dominate the park. It encompasses a glorious natural area with lakes, waterfalls, grassy meadows, and vast stretches of above–tree line terrain. Even with 3 million annual visitors, Rocky Mountain National Park brings an important, accessible slice of nature to those who seek it out.

Many area residents drive to the park in late September and early

October each year to see herds of elk and watch as the bulls put on quite a show for a bevy of cows. They sometimes fight, locking racks in mock battle, but mostly they strut their up-to-1,100-pound frames among the herd and emit a loud bugle (which ranges from a distinctive, low roar to a high-pitched squeal) in a fascinating mating ritual. People bring out their lawn chairs to sit, watch, and listen to this natural phenomenon, which occurs most often at dawn and dusk. The elk can be counted on to congregate in Horseshoe Park, Moraine Park, Kawuneeche Valley, and Upper Beaver. Just minutes from the busy main street of Estes Park, you can enjoy the wildlife experience of a lifetime. For more information, contact the National Park Service at 970-586-1206. www.national parks.org.

BEST Roadside Stop
Trail Ridge Rd. Gift Shop

High above timberline in a place known more for treacherous weather conditions and bighorn sheep, you can find fabulous shopping at this gem of a gift shop. Dads tend to cringe when the kids get all excited about stopping at a gift shop, but The Trail Ridge Store at the top of Trail Ridge Rd. in Rocky Mountain National Park is not your ordinary roadside tourist trap. This store has an amazing assortment of gifts, jewelry, clothing, and Native American arts and crafts; there's no junk here. The Trail Ridge Store carries unique handmade items for your home that could easily sell in some of the nicest stores in Denver. Ceramic pottery with delicate leaf designs, hand-turned vases, and candleholders made from fallen aspen trees, as well as a collection of handcrafted wooden kitchen items, clocks, candles, and Christmas decorations fill the store, along with a good selection of outdoor clothing. In addition, The Trail Ridge Store is well-known for its Gallery of American Western Arts, which contains a wide assortment of Native American handmade gifts and artwork, as well as renderings of life in the Old West.

The Trail Ridge Store sits adjacent to the Alpine Visitor Center at the top of Trail Ridge Rd., which is the highest continuous motorway in the United States, with more than eight miles above 11,000 feet. Because of its high altitude, the store is only open from Memorial Day to Columbus Day, weather permitting. One of the best times to take the scenic drive on Trail Ridge Rd. to the top is in mid-September, when the colors of the autumn leaves are at their best and brightest. The store also has a pretty good snack bar with an awesome view of the Continental Divide. Built in 1936, it is one of the oldest roadside gift and snack shops in Colorado. Although it's been expanded twice since then, the original building still contains the entire store except for the snack bar. If you are traveling in the area, definitely make this a stop on your high-altitude road trip.

BEST Place to Pretend It's the '60s
Rocky Grass Festival (Lyons)

In late July, time traveling backward into the tie-dye haze of the 1960s becomes easy in Lyons, even if the participants seem to sport more gray hair each year. Next to the St. Vrain River, a permanent stage brings nationally acclaimed bluegrass musicians together for three days of jamming in a superb outdoor setting. The rapid strains of traditional music fit perfectly in this natural setting at the base of a high rock cliff. Throw down your blanket and your low-slung chair and settle in for a dynamic mix of music and the best people watching anywhere.

At Lyons' Rocky Grass Festival, one of many musical groups entertains the crowd. PHOTO BY ERIC ABRAMSON

The river flows along one side of the concert green, enticing audience members to head in for a little wading or tubing; many take the flagstone rocks from the river bottom to create impressive rock pylons as the day wears on. Others prefer to laze in a hammock and listen to the live music under the shade trees at river's edge. At the back of the concert green, twenty or more pairs of gyrating hips attempt to keep hula hoops aloft in rhythm to the music.

A veritable marketplace springs up with international food sellers and arts and crafts. There's no better place to buy a toe ring, micro beer, or veggie wrap. The sweet kettle popcorn entices customers by its scent and is served delightfully warm. Concertgoers can reserve a three-day pass (or just a day at a time) and a nearby campsite. Just be sure you call early to buy tickets because this show is limited to 3,500 and it sells out earlier each year. Kids under twelve are free. 303-823-0848; www.blue grass.com.

BEST Wild River
Poudre River

The ancient granite walls of spectacular Cache la Poudre Canyon have been cut over time by the powerful passage of water rushing down from the Continental Divide. Thankfully, one of the last free-flowing rivers along the Front Range, just west of Fort Collins, has never been dammed (some bumper stickers still scream, "Don't Damn the Poudre"), and thanks to its Wild and Scenic status, it is likely to stay that way. The river crashes downhill from the high reaches of Rocky Mountain National

Park, through the canyon toward the plains, mellowing in the flatlands before becoming subsumed by the South Platte. The Poudre's journey has formed a historical and geological thread that creates understanding and appreciation of the entire area. And because the river is paralleled much of the way by CO Hwy. 14, you can easily enjoy the canyon and river from many scenic vantage points. Numerous excellent campgrounds and picnic areas lie along its forty-mile length. The small Cache la Poudre Wilderness Area caters to those who want to explore the more peaceful higher reaches of the canyon.

The unusual name, meaning "hide the powder," came in the mid-1800s when some French trappers didn't want to continue carrying heavy barrels of gunpowder—so they stashed them at the river's edge. For many years, the river represented a shared route into the mountains by both Indians and trappers, but when gold hunters flooded the state, they never really made any significant discoveries here. Over the years, the area became a popular tourist and transportation route. The river proves an excellent fishing destination (for smallish browns and rainbows), including some stretches of designated wild trout water. It has also become a magnet for thrill-seeking kayakers and rafters. The variety of courses and put-ins provide water to suit various skill levels, but all enthusiasts should beware: you can't just float here and hope to come out the other end of these sometimes-dangerous waterfalls, eddies, drops, and rapids that grind you through huge rocks, boulders, and other dangers. So hire an experienced guide, go with people who know the river, or just be supercautious in your planning.

Kayakers enjoy white water along the Poudre River, the last free-flowing river on the Front Range. PHOTO BY BRUCE CAUGHEY

BEST Program for the Disabled
National Sports Center for the Disabled (Winter Park)

"A feeling of freedom so profound I can't begin to describe," wrote one participant about the National Sports Center for the Disabled at Winter Park. You can see confidence and joy spreading across the face of a blind skier or the sheer determination of a man paralyzed from the waist down making turns on a specially equipped mono-ski. Since its inception in 1970 with twenty-three amputee children from Children's Hospital in Denver, this program has taught 45,000 students with physical and mental disabilities. Tens of thousands of volunteer hours are logged annually as area residents reach out to make a difference in someone's life.

The popular winter program includes skiing (downhill and cross-country), snowboarding, and snowshoeing. Hal O'Leary, founder of the program, has been singled out as one of "the best 100 things to happen to skiing" by *Ski* magazine. The successful competitive program offers regional, national, and international experiences that were once reserved for a select few athletes to those with disabilities.

Of late, the winter program has been expanded to offer a range of year-round recreational opportunities. Summer programs include rafting, therapeutic horseback riding, hand-crank and tandem biking, camping, rock climbing, and sailing. In addition to the sports center programs, casual physically challenged visitors appreciate the area's wheelchair-accessible trails. The Bonfils Stanton Trail, located across from the Winter Park Resort entrance, features a boardwalk that winds into nature and strategically placed picnic tables along the way. The Fraser River Trail offers five miles of "champagne pavement" winding through the forest between the town of Fraser and the ski resort. For more information on disabled recreational opportunities, contact the center at 970-726-1540. www.nscd.org.

BEST Sledding
Winter Park and Fraser

Sledding and tubing are guaranteed to bring on smiles at two premier Winter Park locations. COURTESY OF WINTER PARK RESORT

As you drive up and over Berthoud Pass, the treacherous vertical landscape makes sledding seem nearly impossible. But once you settle into the valley floor, many places seem perfectly suited to that new wood toboggan, odd-shaped inner tube, or molded-plastic sled. One of the prime sledding hills for all ages lies about a half mile beyond the entrance to Mary Jane on the right side (or about four miles south of Winter Park Resort on the left side). This slope, about the size of a horizontally situated football field, has various setting-off points—it features longer, hair-raising runs as well as much mellower runs better suited to younger kids. The entire hill features a perfectly flat landing, and there's ample parking, so you can run back to your vehicle to stock up on hot chocolate between runs. So hike up and enjoy the ride down.

If you are not much into hiking uphill, consider taking a shuttle to Fraser to try snow tubing at the Fraser Tubing Hill. At this commercial operation you can fly down the fairly steep, snow-covered slope on a rental tube and enjoy the ride back up to the top by a primitive but effective rope tow. The warming house atop the hill has a fire in its hearth and a snack bar ready to get you and the kids buzzed on sugar before heading back into the cold. 970-726-5954.

BEST Outdoor Ice-Skating
Evergreen Lake

Like the small town of Evergreen, with its wooden sidewalks and false-fronted shops, ice-skating on Evergreen Lake evokes memories of simpler days. Denver families make the traditional twenty-eight-mile trip up to this popular winter activity. Evergreen Lake's uneven ice may not compare to an indoor arena, but the uplifting mood can't be beat. On the recent 50° F day we visited, the place was packed with laughing kids and adults all enjoying the Colorado sun and pretty, if not spectacular, mountain views.

Families with infant children skate in tight knots with small plastic sleds in tow or even bring strollers onto the ice. Young kids spread their coats to catch the breeze so that it propels them across the frozen expanse. Couples circle the immense skating area holding hands while groups of adolescents play hockey on adjacent makeshift rinks. Grandparents and others watch from the deck of the impressive log Lakehouse. Evergreen Lake helps you forget about everyday stresses of city life and zero in on what's truly important.

Small admission fee. Snack bar and hearth can be found inside the Lakehouse; rental skates available by the hour with a picture I.D. (expect a long wait on weekends, especially during nice weather). Occasional closures due to bad ice and weather conditions. Call the hotline at 303-512-9300 before heading out. www.evergreenlakehouse.com.

BEST Bump Skiing
Mary Jane (Winter Park)

So you want to batter your body by tackling deep, well-carved bumps, some the size of Volkswagens? There's no better place than "the Jane," with its steep pitches of moguls that seemingly go on forever. As one of four interconnected ski mountains at Winter Park Resort, Mary Jane challenges the best skiers and thrashes the rest. Opened in 1939, Winter Park remains the oldest continuously operated resort in the country, and Mary Jane has steadfastly hung onto its mantle as the state's bump heaven.

With 60 percent of its slopes classified as "most difficult" and only 3 per-cent beginner terrain, you won't run into many newbies on these long runs, which stretch to 4.5 miles in length.

Mary Jane's generous 2,610-foot vertical drop and separate base area lie five miles away from all the new residential development at Win-ter Park's base area. Another good stop for experts who want to explore a variety of terrain besides mogul fields can be found in the ungroomed, off-piste conditions of Vasquez Cirque. A complex at the Mary Jane base features cafeteria food and full-service dining (outstanding mud pie at the Club Car restaurant), rentals, and tickets. If the bumps beat you up, con-sider signing up for a coaching session with an expert bump skier; the more skiers who sign up, the more time you get for your money. For snow conditions, call 970-SNOW, or from Denver, 303-572-SNOW. www.skiwinterpark.com.

BEST Late-Season Snow
Arapahoe Basin

Always a rebel in terms of its outlook, Arapahoe Basin takes full advan-tage of its high-alpine perch near the Continental Divide on the west side of Loveland Pass. So what if it's the smallest area in Summit County? A-Basin remains one of the state's best places to challenge your skills. A low-key but demanding day area, A-Basin's slopes provide 90 percent intermediate and expert terrain, so beginners beware. Thanks to the country's highest summit, at 13,050 feet, and 360 inches of annual snow-fall, skiers and boarders can ride here much later in the season than any-place else in Colorado—sometimes past the Fourth of July! Due to A-Basin's astonishing summit elevation, lowlanders should give them-selves a few days to acclimate before tackling this area.

Without a condo anywhere nearby, Arapahoe offers views of a more natural environment and access to some of the finest steeps and above-timberline skiing anyplace. The spring snow isn't usually reminis-cent of February powder days, and the 490 skiable acres tend to dwindle as the days get longer, but with fantastic views, pushing turns through morning crust, and afternoon mashed potatoes, it still adds up to a great day on the slopes. So cop an attitude, lather up with sunscreen, and don some strange attire—on nice days, a bikini top for the ladies or Hawaiian shirt for the guys is perfectly acceptable. Come a bit early and snag a slope-side parking slot, set up your hibachi grill, and enjoy the lunch and après ski party with a low-key Colorado style.

Rentals, child care, and a cafeteria are offered. Located several miles east of Keystone on U.S. Hwy. 6 on the western slopes of Loveland Pass. 970-496-7077. www.arapahoebasin.com.

BEST Collection of Ski Areas
Summit County

Named Summit County for a reason, the spectacular landscape just west of the Continental Divide, conveniently located off I-70, features some of the finest skiing and snowboarding anywhere—lots of it! Arapahoe Basin, Breckenridge, Keystone, and Copper Mountain comprise the four separate Summit County resorts, each with a distinct personality. In a nutshell:

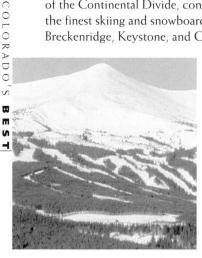

Breckridge ski area in the distance. PHOTO BY
BOB WINSETT, THE VILLAGE AT BRECKENRIDGE

▸▸ **Arapahoe Basin**—Geared toward expert and strong intermediate skills, this rather small day-use area attracts a younger, more aggressive crowd of boarders and skiers. The snow here tends to pile up faster and stay longer, thanks to its extreme, 13,050-foot summit elevation and majority of above-timberline terrain. 970-496-7077; www.arapahoe basin.com. (See entry above for more information.)

▸▸ **Breckenridge Ski Area**—With a quaint Victorian mining town at its base and a range of modern condos and hotels for destination travelers, Breckenridge lays a strong claim to full resort status. A mix of slopes on a quartet of interconnected peaks attracts a broad range of skiers and boarders to its 1,600 acres of terrain. Advanced skiers enjoy the double–black diamond challenges—such as the forbidding pitch of Devil's Crotch on Peak 9—while beginner and intermediate skiers find enjoyment gliding down other areas. 970-453-5000; www.breckenridge.com.

▸▸ **Keystone Resort**—The consummate learning area, Keystone has continually improved its stature by adding steeper terrain at North Peak and the rollicking ungroomed slopes of the Outback. With excellent service and a planned resort community at its base, Keystone provides a "no-surprises" experience especially suited to families. Extensive snowmaking equipment allows Keystone to capture the prize as the first or second area in Colorado to open each fall. Night skiing is offered, too. 970-468-2316; www.keystoneresort.com.

- **Copper Mountain Resort**—A ready audience of skiers and boarders appreciate the distinctly separate areas of terrain suited to all skill levels. In most cases, the unsteady, unpredictable turns of beginners don't conflict with the lightning-quick turns of experts. And everyone seems to enjoy Copper Mountain's vast 2,324 acres and 2,760-foot vertical drop. With its planned base area growing to suit the mountain, destination skiers now have shopping, dining, and accommodations to match a longer stay. 866-841-2481; www.coppercolorado.com.

Where to Eat, Drink, & Stay

BEST Historic Mountain Inn
The Peck House (Empire)

This mountain inn has the distinction of being the oldest continuously operating hotel in Colorado, and it is located an hour or so west of Denver in little Empire, Colorado. Built in 1862 by James Peck, who came to Colorado with his wife and sons to take part in the mining boom, the Peck House was originally a large home that doubled as a hotel for investors in Peck's mining company who were visiting Colorado from back East. Eventually Peck expanded his hospitality to include other travelers when he realized there were very few hotels in the area and he could make a tidy profit by catering to trav-

Enjoy the shady veranda at The Peck House Inn in Empire. PHOTO BY TAMRA MONAHAN

elers and miners. Business was so good that Peck expanded his hotel twice, once in 1873 and again in 1880.

Legend has it that James Peck settled in the small town of Empire because the people in the area were more sympathetic to Yankee politics, rather than the miners around Georgetown who held more with the Confederate philosophy.

During its 142-year history, the Peck House has maintained its Victorian charm in the architecture and furnishings. The hotel's eleven rooms are filled with antiques, some of which are original to the hotel, brought to the Rocky Mountains by oxcart. The Peck House's charming country ambiance makes it feel more like a large bed-and-breakfast than a hotel. In fact, the owners, Gary and Sally St. Claire, live in the hotel, so guests really are staying in their home. Although it may have the cozy feeling of Grandma's house, the Peck House has a large dining room and boasts an award-winning menu that includes beef, seafood, poultry, and game all carefully prepared by Gary St. Claire.

While you sit on the front porch and take in the beautiful view of the Empire Valley, you can almost feel the anticipation of the stagecoach stopping at the front door and unloading passengers. From Denver, take I-70 West to Exit 232. Go two miles on U.S. Hwy. 40 to the town of Empire. Go two-thirds of the way through town and look up on the right. 303-569-9870; www.thepeckhouse.com.

BEST Historic Night's Stay in an Elegant Hotel
The Stanley Hotel (Estes Park)

With its formal white façade and large front veranda, the Stanley hotel catches your eye every time you drive through Estes Park. The large Victorian hotel enjoys a perfect hillside perch overlooking the town, but its peaceful nature belies the fact that it was also the inspiration for a macabre horror story. After spending a weekend at the Stanley, Stephen King was inspired to write his novel *The Shining*, and the ABC miniseries based on the novel was filmed at the hotel. It's possible ghosts in the old

The stately Stanley Hotel in Estes Park was named for it's founder, F. O. Stanley, the inventor of the Stanley Steamer automobile. PHOTO BY TAMRA MONAHAN

hotel acted as King's muses since there are purported to be a few that haunt the Stanley, particularly on the fourth floor (formerly the servants' quarters) and in room 418. If you're an avid Stephen King fan, you should stay in room 217, which is where he wrote part of *The Shining*. You can also participate in murder-mystery weekends, but you may not want to stay in the Redrum!

F. O. Stanley, inventor of the Stanley Steamer automobile, built the Stanley Hotel in 1909. This wealthy entrepreneur spared no expense when he created his luxurious resort hotel, which, for the most part, is the same as it was at the turn of the century. The lobby is decorated in rich, dark wood with a sweeping grand staircase and antique Victorian furniture. The rooms are elegantly furnished, and the hotel has a wonderful spa, an excellent restaurant, and the surrounding Rocky Mountains to keep you entertained. In addition, the town of Estes Park offers a variety of shopping and sights, as well as restaurants. If you're planning a wedding, the

Stanley Hotel is a gorgeous place to get married, but don't wait until the last minute to reserve a date. With more than 400 weddings at the Stanley every year during all four seasons, the hotel books up quickly. 333 Wonderview; 800-976-1377 or 970-586-3371; www.stanleyhotel.com.

BEST Hot Dog Stand
Coney Island (Aspen Park)

It feels like something out of a nightmare as you walk inside a giant pink hot dog with all of the trimmings. In fact, this oblong restaurant in Aspen Park, about twenty miles southwest of Denver on U.S. Hwy. 285, really does serve up great dogs as well as greasy fries and burgers from its cluttered counter. You can sit inside at one of the few tight booths or, better yet, get your food to go and find a spot at one of the outdoor picnic tables. Regardless, you (and your kids) will forevermore be practically forced to say, "There's the hot dog!" as you drive past. Open year-round. 25877 CO Hwy. 285; 303-838-4210.

BEST Intimate Dining
Alpine Café (Breckenridge)

A sophisticated atmosphere permeates the various rooms of this cozy four-level restaurant located inside a Victorian-style home a half block east of Main St. in Breckenridge. Chef-owner Keith Mahoney puts a major emphasis on creative cuisine made with fresh ingredients and an extensive, well-chosen wine list. The attention to detail can be found in the folded linen napkins and an extraordinarily well-trained and knowledgeable waitstaff. A fire glows in the corner, original contemporary artworks line the walls, and you can see the vast wine selection of mostly French and California vintages displayed in racks around the lower-floor dining room and tiny bar area. The Alpine Café has earned The Wine Spectator Award of Excellence every year since 1994.

Canvas umbrellas on the outdoor deck of the Alpine Café create a natural ambience.
PHOTO BY BRUCE CAUGHEY

The eclectic menu cannot be described in detail because every day new specials appear and four times yearly it undergoes a complete revision. "The changing menu adds excitement in the kitchen and is good for our waitstaff," says one employee. "Educating customers becomes a nightly ritual and builds anticipation for the meal." Despite the menu's changeability, locals swear this place has consistently great food. The fish entrees when we visited included jerked salmon with smoked rock shrimp and mango salsa and roasted halibut with red curry *sambal*; or, choose lamb, beef tenderloin, or wild game. All dishes come with interesting pairings of wonderful sauces and side dishes. The range of cuisines represented and the expertise in the kitchen create a distinctive, memorable dining experience. For lighter appetites, the second-floor tapas bar should be your only stop. A chef behind a glass-encased counter whips up everything from sashimi to Chesapeake Bay crab cakes. Don't skip dessert, especially if you enjoy mouthwatering bread pudding.

Tapas bar seating is first-come, first-served; the main restaurant requires advance dinner reservations. For summer lunches, try the nice outdoor deck with its rattan chairs and canvas umbrellas. 106 East Adams Ave.; 970-453-8218.

BEST Home-Cooked Meals
The Happy Cooker (Georgetown)

Who has time to cook from scratch anymore? The chef-owner at The Happy Cooker does, and tourists and locals alike come out in droves to enjoy the hearty food at this restored Victorian house. Breakfast might tempt you anytime, especially the egg dishes or fluffy waffles, which come with your choice of maple, strawberry, or blueberry syrup. To really blow your diet, go for the special waffle, complete with fruit, hot fudge, and a dollop of whipped cream.

For a meal later in the day, you really cannot err by ordering one of the wonderful soups, served with thick slabs of homemade bread (the yogurt-dill bread is out of this world), or a triangular slice of a specialty quiche. Other options include creative salads, generous sandwiches, and a bowl of tasty vegetarian chili. The excellent pies are also freshly home baked (another dessert option involves walking to the shop directly across the street for a hand-packed ice-cream cone).

You will likely have ample time to enjoy the artwork and photos for sale on the wall because service tends to be on the slow side—coming here with young, hungry kids would be a bad idea. On warm days, the large front patio fills up with people soaking in the sun and the ever-present historical atmosphere of Georgetown. 412 6th St.; 303-569-3166.

BEST View from a Porch Swing
Grand Lake Lodge

"People compare it to Switzerland and Austria," says Sue James, longtime proprietor of the Grand Lake Lodge. Walking up to the national historic landmark—established in 1920 and surrounded on three sides by Rocky Mountain National Park—you know it's a special place. Parked before the large log main lodge, four restored Model A's catch your interest and set the tone. On the covered front porch, people just plop down in one of the many swings to enjoy an extraordinary view out over Grand Lake, the state's largest natural lake and the headwaters of the mighty Colorado River. Your

Grand Lake attracts sailors and sightseers to its natural beauty. PHOTO BY BRUCE CAUGHEY

panorama includes the broad shoulders of Shadow Mountain, the distinctive profile of Byer's Peak, and the Gore Range off in the distance. If you decide to stay in one of the lodge's rustic cabins, you'll be able to enjoy the same bird's-eye view from a poolside chair—an excellent option. Located a couple of miles from the town of Grand Lake, this lodge has long been a destination for visitors. Once inside the lodge, pull up a bar stool and see how the glass back bar opens to a mountain vista.

If you decide to come for dinner, lunch, or brunch, call to reserve a choice table on the covered part of the porch. The view here simply doesn't stop. If your schedule permits, seek out the Sunday champagne brunch, with fresh breads and pastries, roast-carving stations, specialty eggs, and peel-and-eat shrimp. Dinners include gourmet mountain favorites from elk to trout, skillfully cooked in an open kitchen. Simple, reasonably priced lunches are a good bet, too. For information and reservations during summer, call 970-627-3967; during the off-season, call 303-759-5848; www.grandlakelodge.com.

BEST Transformation of a Hot Springs
Hot Sulphur Springs Resort

For those who visited this hot springs in years past, you may have memories of a petri dish gone bad; the place was musty, moldy, dingy, smelly, dirty, and run-down. Thankfully, Charles Nash came along with a vision for restoring the resort into a low-key and satisfying destination. Nash made his money in Denver converting obsolete historic buildings, including churches, schools, and gas stations, into architecturally unique structures for people to live and work in. Nash says the waters here cure all kinds of ailments, and the resort remains an important historic asset for the area. In fact, when the renovation was complete, Ute Indians blessed the waters that their ancestors once used and received an open invitation to come and "take the waters."

People expecting a five-star resort spa may not find their Shangri-la. But those who want to experience unfiltered, mineral-rich water in twenty different pools (some with privacy doors, others built into an open hillside) will appreciate the soothing design and bathing options. One word of warning: the sulfur smell remains on your skin and in your bathing suit long after departing, especially if you skip a shower to let the touted minerals improve your skin. Those with sensitive nostrils should shower off vigorously with perfumed soap.

Some 210,000 gallons of natural hot water flow from the 123° F source and flow downward. Lupe's Pool, the hottest, varies from 109° to 112° F. As you move down the hill to other pools, the water gets cooler. Decks and walkways connect the pools and intermittent benches provide perfect spots to kick back and enjoy the view to the Continental Divide. The perennial favorite, called Ute Pool, features a natural rock overhang with a steaming waterfall. A filtered, kidney-shaped swimming pool lies in front of the complex. Kids are relegated to the lower, cooler pools, but adults can wander the entire premises. Suits are required except in the privacy areas. In addition to hot springs, fourteen spa rooms serve up various massages, herbal wraps, and mud-bath treatments. You can stay in one of the twenty small, clean, motel-style rooms (sans TV and phone) with unlimited use of pools. A newly refurbished cabin and an upper-floor apartment near the pools remain the choice romantic spots. 970-725-3306; www.hotsulphursprings.com.

BEST Romantic Getaway
Romantic RiverSong Bed-and-Breakfast (Estes Park)

With the multiple time demands on most couples, finding relaxing hours for romance and reconnections can be difficult. So when you do arrange to break away, you want everything to be just right. Owners Gary and Sue Mansfield designed RiverSong specifically to create spaces for couples to enjoy a certain spark from their surroundings.

Located on twenty-seven wooded acres close to the entrance of Rocky Mountain National Park, the natural environment of this bed-and-breakfast couldn't be nicer. Whether you are newlyweds, couples celebrating thirty years together, or those considering an elopement (Gary can marry couples on the spot), the warmly decorated, elegant rooms fulfill your expectations.

The Meadow Bright Suite brings tactile Western furnishings to the fore with its hand-hewn log bed, cathedral ceiling, and Navajo rugs on the gleaming wood floor. The smooth river-rock fireplace can be seen from both sides of the wall—one side in the bedroom area, the other next to a whirlpool tub built for two. Chiming Bells, the largest bedroom, creates a different ambiance with Victorian furnishings and a sunken oversized tub and redwood shower built for two. Each of the nine rooms feels private and secluded and some are located in separate cabins with private decks. The quiet settles in easily without the distractions of telephone and television. Enjoy your clean and elegant surroundings without regard to hurrying anywhere.

A full, hearty breakfast with a hot entree is served in the sunny common room each morning; candlelight dinners are available by request. No smoking. Expensive and worth it. Minimum stay requirement. 1765 Lower Broadview Rd.; 970-586-4666.

BEST View from a Lodge
Lodge at Breckenridge

You might think it's an exaggeration when they call it "Top of the World" in their printed literature. But in fact, the Lodge at Breckenridge is situated on the edge of a forested cliff, up the Boreas Pass Rd., just five minutes away from the ski town. With a full-service spa and forty-five well-appointed guest rooms, this upscale place should be on your list for a special occasion—or if you have room in your budget, any occasion! Spectacular mountain views seemingly go on forever from large picture windows in the bedrooms (be sure to ask for a mountain view) and common areas. Pricier rooms and suites offer private balconies to better enjoy sights of the ski mountain and out to the Tenmile Range, Hoosier Pass, and Mount Baldy. Hand-hewn log furniture and carefully selected Western-themed appointments help make this a unique destination.

In summer, the outdoor pool, hot tubs, and deck area offer the same sweeping views as the best rooms in the lodge. The spa area features luxurious facials, massages, herbal wraps, and other replenishing holistic and fitness-based body treatments. Comfortable common areas and a nice on-premises restaurant with floor-to-ceiling windows entice you to stay and relax awhile. For more information about this gorgeous retreat, contact 800-736-1607. www.thelodgeatbreck.com.

BEST Plush Dude Ranch
C-Lazy-U (near Granby)

If you desire a down-to-earth, rustic kind of ranch vacation, then do not book a week at the C-Lazy-U. This place brings the ranch experience up several notches in terms of sheer luxury. From the cowboy-hat-topped bellman to the monogrammed terry cloth robes in the cabins and lodge rooms, you will enjoy the mix of five-star city hotel with traditional ranch activities. An emphasis on horsemanship separates the C-Lazy-U from many ranches: expert wranglers assist you in finding the perfect horse for the duration of your stay. Visit the pool area, soak in the over-sized hot tub, play tennis, go fishing, or participate in many other organized activities. You can also head to the game room or just enjoy reading the latest novel in an overstuffed leather chair.

Kids have their own separate ranch experience, which seems odd when planning a vacation, but reveals its logic when in the midst of it—for example, the kids really do enjoy playing after-dinner games with a ranch hand while you and the other guests enjoy coffee or a brandy after a gourmet meal. Of course, the real reason to come here is to enjoy the beautiful natural environment and views of the peaks along the Continental Divide. This amenity-laden ranch brings a certain plushness to the entire experience. The activities and dining encourage camaraderie among the guests, who tend to return year after year. The accommodations bring a Western charm to the forefront without skimping. For more information, call the ranch at 970-887-3344. www.clazyu.com.

THE EASTERN PLAINS

It is perfectly plain,
destitute of every thing, even grass,
the great reliever of the eye,
and making it painful to the sight.

—SHELBY MAGOFFIN, JULY 1846,
FROM *Bent's Fort on the Santa Fe Trail*

Most people drive through eastern Colorado, not to it. What can be seen out the window of your car does not inspire awe. The South Platte and Arkansas Rivers will never be mistaken for the mighty Colorado, and the Pawnee and Comanche National Grasslands look nothing like a national forest you've come to expect. The gently rolling landscape can't hold a candle to the soaring Rocky Mountains, but poke around a little here and take a little time there, and pretty soon a fascinating picture emerges from the grasslands, farms, canyons, and waterways. On your way to somewhere else, the "other half" of Colorado has just hooked your imagination. Exploring this region of the state takes motivation, an eye for the subtle, a back-roads mentality, an appreciation for the history of the High Plains.

Along I-70 alone, we found several places you'd consider worth the stop. Stretch your legs and make the kids happy at the Kit Carson County Carousel in Burlington or pull off the road in Limon with all its services for motorists and a museum full of railroad history. I-76 is your link to immeasurable grasslands, for centuries the domain of Native American tribes. And the roadside, fresh produce stands along U.S. Hwy. 50 are a good excuse to get off the main road and continue to explore this area once traversed by the Santa Fe Trail.

From ancient dinosaur footprints and bones of the woolly mammoth to once-vast herds of buffalo; from the frontier days of Kit Carson and the Santa Fe Trail to the tragic days of Colonel John Chivington, Chief Black Kettle, and the Sand Creek Massacre; from sweet melons and spicy chiles to the delicacy of Rocky Mountain oysters, eastern Colorado beckons those willing to look beneath the surface, around the corner, and off the beaten path. In fact, outside of I-70, I-76, and U.S. Hwy. 50, no beaten path exists. Intrepid travelers discover migrating birds on the boundless prairie, age-old drawings on isolated canyon walls, and faded wagon ruts along the banks of dried-up streams.

Inhabitants of the region, rooted in the soil and seasoned by the vagaries of an agricultural economy, genuinely welcome city slickers and other passersby. Custodians of fertile ground, a proud heritage, and a prehistoric past, the people of eastern Colorado watch as the world zooms through in a hurry. Slow down and have a look around.

Cultural & Historical

BEST Equinox Phenomenon
Picture Canyon (near Springfield)

In a remote corner of southeastern Colorado, only a mile from the Oklahoma border, curious souls gather before sunrise in late March under a gnarled tree silhouetted against the early-morning glow. Standing on the west side of Picture Canyon, several people bend down to enter a narrow slot in the rock wall. Inching their way a short distance through this slender crevasse, they crouch down into cramped quarters where only four people fit. At 6:08 A.M., the sun peeks over the eastern horizon and shines its golden light directly into Crack Cave. For twelve minutes, a cryptic inscription on an otherwise darkened rock wall is the only spot illuminated by the sun's rays. Our modern travelers witness an age-old phenomenon: this ancient calendar verifies a twice-a-year occurrence—the vernal and autumnal equinoxes.

There are at least two theories about who scratched this long-ago message on a rock panel no bigger than a notebook. Most likely it was the nomadic Indians of the Southwest who inhabited these lands for centuries. Rock art depicting their way of life is widespread throughout the canyon. It's said that their intimate knowledge of nature's rhythms led to the recognition that the sun's position in the sky foretold a change of season. Others speculate that the ancient Celts from Europe somehow made their way thousands of miles inland on the North American continent. It's thought that the markings in Crack Cave do not conform to the style of art in the surrounding area. They conjecture that the writings in the cave resemble Ogam, the written language of the Celtic people. By their reckoning, the translation from that extinct tongue reads, "On the Day of Bell, the sun strikes here." That this ancient marker heralds the equinox is not in dispute, and we are left to ponder the significance of the recording of this natural event so long ago.

Picture Canyon is located in the Comanche National Grasslands, about thirty-five miles southwest of the town of Springfield. It's open all year long; check with the U.S. Forest Service office in Springfield for detailed directions. 719-523-6591. A locked gate protects the entrance to Crack Cave, which is open only for tours. Springfield hosts an Equinox Festival every spring and fall to celebrate the phenomenon. Call the Chamber of Commerce at 719-523-4061.www.springfieldco.info/index.html.

BEST View of Life on the Santa Fe Trail
Bent's Old Fort National Historic Site (near La Junta)

Pull into the parking lot and leave your car and modern life behind.
There in the distance sits Bent's Old Fort right alongside the Arkansas
River, much as it looked when it was built in the early 1830s. Long before
Denver was even on the map, this trading post was an important way station on the Santa Fe Trail. Orient yourself to the past during the five-
minute walk to the entrance of the fort. Enter the gate with the American
flag flying high above. Adobe walls enclose the plaza inside, the size of a
small town square. Imagine Mexican and American traders; Comanche,
Cheyenne, Apache, and other Plains Indians; French trappers, slaves, and
assorted mountain men gathered here in a cacophony of languages and
spirited barter. This two-story "Castle on the Prairie" was the only stop
between Independence, Missouri, and Santa Fe, then a northern city
of Mexico.

William Bent ran his trading empire from this spot on the High
Plains for no more than two decades but it was a critical era in the evolving West. Eventually his fort disappeared, rendering it but a faint memory in some history books. But in 1975, a near replica of the original was
reconstructed in the exact same spot just north of the Arkansas River, the
onetime border between U.S. Territory and Mexico. Today, it's a living
museum with people in period garb regaling visitors with first-person
accounts of life in this Old West melting pot. You'll meet Charlotte
Green, a slave of William Bent, who was respected far and wide for her
good cooking and strong spirit. A blacksmith demonstrates his skill in
fashioning wagon parts, horseshoes, and other essentials of the trail that
kept the shop busy twenty-four hours a day. The gift shop sells only
1840s-vintage goods, such as beads, beaver hats, and blocks of Chinese
tea. Up on the second level you can stand guard in the two bastions used
as lookout towers. (Bent's Fort was never attacked.)

Bent's Old Fort is open all year long. It's located several miles east
of La Junta on CO Hwy. 194. The Santa Fe Trail Encampment is held in
late July and early August. It re-creates the hustle and bustle of life as it
was during the trapping and trading days on the Santa Fe Trail. 719-383-
5010; www.nps.gov/beol.

BEST Little-Known Historic Site
Boggsville (Las Animas)

In the days when the Santa Fe Trail was still carrying pioneers and traders
to the Colorado Territory, the town of Boggsville had its moment in
time. Acquiring the land through a Mexican land grant, Thomas Boggs
and his partner, John Prowers, began raising sheep and cattle along the
Purgatoire River just south of present-day Las Animas. They provided

agricultural products to a burgeoning population during the mining boom of the 1860s. This was the beginning of modern agriculture in what would become the state of Colorado.

At its height, the settlement had more than twenty-five buildings, including a general store, post office, schoolhouse, and stage stop right along the Santa Fe Trail. Today, only the Boggs house and one wing of the Prowers house remain. As the town looked toward the future, it was also a crossroads of the past. In 1867, the legendary frontiersman Kit Carson had fallen quite ill. He moved to Boggsville to be near the post doctor at Fort Lyon, just three miles downstream on the Purgatoire River. Living in a house built earlier in the decade by Thomas Boggs, Kit Carson died in November 1868. A chapter of the Old West had closed.

When the railroad came through the area in the 1870s, the town that became Las Animas was built just a mile to the north; that spelled the end to Boggsville. Though ranching operations lasted for a while, the town disappeared. Today, the site is open to visitors from May through September, and the buildings are open from 9 A.M. to 4:30 P.M. each day. To get here, head east on U.S. Hwy. 50 from Pueblo to Las Animas. Go south two miles on Hwy. 101 and look for signs to Boggsville. For more information, call 719-384-8054. You can also find information on the Pioneer Historical Society of Bent County Web site: www.phsbc.info/boggs.htm.

BEST Indian Museum
Koshare Indian Museum (La Junta)

By the early twentieth century, the Native American way of life was vanishing. As the elders were dying off, so, too, were their age-old traditions. In the early 1930s, a concerned white man, Buck Burshears, created an organization to help preserve the colorful and rhythmic dances of Plains and Southwest tribes. The Koshare Indian Dancers have been performing ever since.

They do not pretend to be Indians. The dancers come from Boy Scout Troop 232 in La Junta, Colorado. Each boy must research the dance, make his own authentic costume, and perform only when his creation passes muster with his group. The discipline and motivation engendered by the Koshare program has produced more Eagle Scouts from this troop over the decades than anywhere in the country. Ongoing relationships with many southwestern tribes ensure authenticity and sensitivity in the dances. Under the large log roof of the ceremonial kiva, performances are scheduled all year-round at the Koshare Indian Museum. The group has performed all over the country and in different parts of the world.

As the reputation of the Koshare Dancers grew over the years, so did Burshears's collection of Indian artifacts gathered during his extensive travels. From ancient pottery and arrowheads to war bonnets and moccasins, the museum holds an impressive array of articles.

When Buck Burshears died in 1987, he was an adopted member of the Blackfeet Tribe and a blood brother of the Chippewa. He was highly respected in both the Anglo and Indian worlds that he brought together. Reach the Koshare Indian Museum by taking I-25 to Pueblo and heading east to La Junta. Go south on Colorado Ave. and follow signs to the museum at 115 W. 18th St. 800-693-KIVA; www.koshare.org.

BEST Reminder of Labor Struggles
Ludlow Memorial Monument (north of Trinidad)

Miners in the coalfields around Trinidad, Colorado, were restless. In the early years of the twentieth century, Mother Jones, a union agitator from the South, visited the area several times to offer support. The tense atmosphere between miners and mine owners erupted into the Colorado Coalfield War. The Colorado militia was sent, ostensibly to keep the peace. Some miners and their families had set up a tent colony at Ludlow, about fifteen miles north of Trinidad.

On the morning of April 20, 1914, they awoke to find machine guns set up on hills above the tents. The militia fired into the camp, setting it on fire. Women and children had been sent down into cellars for safety. The flames spread throughout the encampment above. When the smoke finally cleared, the devastation to the tent colony was complete. And in a cellar meant to keep them safe from harm, the bodies of eleven women and children were found. They had suffocated from the smoke.

In all, twenty-four people died, including a militiaman and three mine guards. Today, a poignant monument stands where those lives were lost. Open a creaking metal door to reveal steps leading underground to the small space where innocents lost their lives. Bleak and desolate surroundings mirror the sad history.

Erected by the United Mine Workers of America, this memorial hopes to remind the world that they did not die in vain. As a result of what became known as the "Ludlow Massacre," labor laws in the United States changed. During summer months, you may find archaeologists digging for artifacts that can help further reveal the story of this American tragedy. Get here by taking I-25 south past Walsenburg. Take the Ludlow exit and follow a dirt road west about a mile.www.trinidadco.com.

BEST Plains History
Centennial Village (Greeley)

"Go West, young man!" screamed the headlines in Horace Greeley's New York newspaper. It was an admonition that helped populate a utopian community in Colorado called Union Colony. Joined by his partner, Nathan Meeker, Greeley created a planned town based on temperate ideals. Adventurous easterners flocked to the northern plains of Colorado. Modern-day visitors get a sense of that turn-of-the-century life by exploring twenty-five historic buildings, most of them moved and restored from surrounding towns and ranches. Centennial Village recreates the spirit of Union Colony.

German, Swedish, and Russian immigrants were the first to farm the area, primarily growing sugar beets. Examples of their simple dwellings can be visited at Centennial Village. Tour guides lead visitors through the church, blacksmith shop, newspaper office, and other buildings that tell the story of these early settlers on the plains.

Kids especially relate to the one-room schoolhouse, where they can sit in old-fashioned straight-backed desks lined neatly in a row. Adults take special notice of the Stevens house, a well-furnished Victorian home of the time. An Indian teepee, a trail-worn chuck wagon, and even an outdoor (nonworking) privy add to the authentic feel of history.

Walking the well-manicured grounds from one building to the next gives the distinct impression of strolling through a real town. On special occasions throughout the year, the town comes to life with demonstrations, farm animals, and volunteers in period costume. Centennial Village is located at 1475 A St. on the north side of Greeley. A ticket to Centennial Village also gains entrance to Nathan Meeker's historic house in downtown Greeley. Open mid-April through mid-October. 970-350-9220; www.ci.greeley.co.us/museums.

BEST Place to Learn Not to Repeat the Past
Camp Amache (near Granada, Colorado)

Tumbleweeds blow across crumbled concrete foundations. The one-time barracks made up what was Colorado's tenth largest city in the mid-1940s. After Pearl Harbor was attacked, drawing the United States into World War II, the government ordered all people of Japanese ancestry evacuated from the nation's West Coast. Deprived of their basic rights and property, families by the thousands, mostly U.S. citizens, were shipped inland to relocation camps. On August 27, 1942, the first wave of what would number more than 10,000 souls over a period of three years arrived by train at Camp Amache in southeastern Colorado.

Surrounded by barbed wire, this settlement, along with others throughout the West, served as a misguided attempt to appease the hostility and hatred in the country for all things Japanese. Loyal and law-abiding citizens spent a bewildering part of their lives in these internment camps. Walking through the ruins of this ghost camp today, visitors to Camp Amache discover a well-maintained cemetery with gravestones of children and adults who died while being held here. One monument honors those from the camp who fought and died for the United States during the war while their families were being held against their will on this dusty plain near the Arkansas River.

Amache stands as a poignant reminder for vigilance in the protection of this country's civil rights. In the aftermath of 9-11, Muslims in America have been keenly aware of the dangers in holding an entire people accountable for the sins of those alike only in appearance. The lessons of Amache cannot be learned enough.

The site is located about seventeen miles east of Lamar on U.S. Hwy. 50, two miles west of the small town of Granada. A teacher at the high school there, John Hopper, runs the Amache

Remains of concrete foundations at Amache only hint at life in barracks behind barbed wire. PHOTO BY DOUG WHITEHEAD

Preservation Society, which involves many of his students in research and preservation of the camp. They operate a small museum in the old town hall. Visit this Web site to learn more: www.amache.org.

BEST Evidence of Dinosaurs
Picket Wire Canyonlands (south of La Junta)

Trudging through the marshy edges of an ancient sea, the feet of multiton animals sank down deep in the mud. A hundred and fifty million years later, those footprints stretch out before inquisitive eyes, beckoning the mind toward a murky, distant past. Here on the Purgatoire River south of La Junta lies one of the longest dinosaur trackways in the world.

Researchers have counted 1,300 footprints of at least 100 individual dinosaurs crisscrossing the rock ledges along the banks of the river, a onetime gathering place for herds of herbivores and carnivores. Depressions larger than two human feet were made by the huge brontosaurus (now called the apatosaurus), and the three-toed prints of a theropod even show claw marks. Step from print to print and imagine the gait of these beasts as they searched for food in the shallow reaches of an inland sea, buoyed by the water, much like a hippopotamus today.

A stark landscape in the Picket Wire Canyonlands is home to one of the world's longest dinosaur trackways. PHOTO BY DOUG WHITEHEAD

Cacti and rattlesnakes inhabit this stark canyon cut by the Purgatoire River as it flows toward the Arkansas. Cowboys couldn't pronounce the French, so the "Purgatoire" became the "Picket Wire." Called the Picket Wire Canyonlands, this remote landscape in the Comanche National Grassland reveals the sweep of time. Rock art etched on sandstone boulders and inside natural cave shelters offers hints of ancient Native American lives in the canyon. The remains of a church built by Hispanic ranchers and farmers in the 1880s include hand-carved inscriptions on the headstones of an adjacent cemetery. And buildings still stand at the old Roarke Ranch, a huge cattle operation that lasted into the 1970s.

Picket Wire Canyonlands is not accessible by car. Stop at the Comanche Grassland office of the U.S. Forest Service in La Junta for directions to the trailhead, which is about an hour's drive south of town. They offer guided tours of the area on Saturdays during spring and fall. 719-384-2181.

BEST Roadside Stop for Kids
Kit Carson County Carousel (Burlington)

Sounds from the restored Wurlitzer Monster Military Band Organ carry so far, you'd swear you can hear them all the way across the eastern plains. Here, under a white gazebo among the trees, the happy music lures kids and kids-at-heart for an old-fashioned spin on the Kit Carson County Carousel. Riding a menagerie of hand-carved, hand-painted wooden animals, you whirl back to a nostalgic past. Built in 1905, this carousel has survived the passage of time. There are fewer than 150 of its kind left in the United States.

Back in 1928, county commissioners purchased the carousel from Elitch Gardens, the famous Denver amusement park. After the depression, the carousel got new life and has been operating ever since. Today, it remains the pride of Burlington, a well-placed oasis on I-70 where road-weary travelers make a welcome stop. They get more than they bargained for in this community near the Kansas border. A fishtailed horse, a glass-eyed tiger, and all the other colorful critters of the carousel pique your imagination as the monotony of the highway melts away for only a quarter a ride.

If you've got the time, take a wagon ride over to Old Town in Burlington. Walk the streets and visit this collection of vintage buildings. Stop in at the rowdy saloon (no beer), where dancing girls kick their legs high, or check out the melodramas staged during the summer months in a big red barn. Between the carousel and Old Town, you just might have to adjust your travel schedule to give yourself a little more time. Follow signs from the exit off I-70. www.burlingtoncolo.com/tourism.htm.

DARKEST Moment in Colorado History
Sand Creek Massacre National Historic Site

Certainly "best" is not the most precise word to describe the brutal massacre by U.S. troops at an Indian encampment in eastern Colorado in the 1800s, but the event, without question, merits consideration.

On the morning of November 29, 1864, Colonel John Chivington led an attack by roughly 800 heavily armed U.S. troops, mostly volunteers, on 500 Cheyenne and Arapaho Indians camped along Sand Creek. Ignoring a white flag and a U.S. flag flown by Chief Black Kettle, the advancing soldiers left more than 160 dead, mostly women, children, and the elderly. Perhaps more than any other event of the time, the Sand Creek Massacre changed the course of history.

Tensions were running high in the summer of 1864. Near Denver, the Hungate family had been butchered by Indians, yet another atrocity perpetrated on both sides in the already vicious battle for supremacy on the High Plains. White settlers were calling for revenge. The politically motivated Colonel Chivington was happy to oblige. As news of his unconscionable act spread, even some of the most anti-Indian cru-

A lone visitor to the Sand Creek Massacre site ponders the tragic events that occurred on the southeastern Colorado plains. PHOTO BY DOUG WHITEHEAD

saders cringed at its brutality. Three separate investigations condemned the attack. Plains Indian tribes knew they were in a fight for their very existence. Over the next decade and a half, warfare raged on the plains. By 1876 and the Battle of the Little Big Horn, the Indians were fighting some of their final conflicts. In retrospect, Sand Creek was the beginning of the end for a traditional way of life that had remained intact for thousands of years.

The memories of Sand Creek are still fresh and bitterness endures in the descendants of those killed at Sand Creek. In some ways, the

Indian Wars are still being fought today. Many consider the events of Sand Creek no less than an act of genocide, but some argue that Chivington was justified in his pursuit of Indians who had committed terrible violence against white settlers. Soon, Americans will be able to visit the site and decide for themselves. The mostly dry creek bed of Sand Creek snakes through a wide plain where grasses bend in constant winds and whose borders are defined by cottonwood groves. As a result of legislation carried by former Colorado senator Ben Nighthorse Campbell in the late 1990s and early 2000s, U.S. Congress established the Sand Creek National Historic Site. As of this writing public visitation is still at least a couple of years away, but plans have begun in earnest at this place where blood stained a sad chapter in the history of the American West.

Follow progress by calling the Sand Creek Massacre National Historic Site office in Eads, Colorado, at 719-438-5916; www.nps.gov/sand. In the meantime, it is possible to visit the Bowen Ranch. This is private property adjacent to the national historic site with impressive claims to containing much of the actual battle site, complete with artifacts and historical documentation. Call Sand Creek Tours at 719-336-5082; www.sandcreektours.com. Also, check out the Colorado History Museum at 13th St. and Broadway in Denver for more information. 303-866-3681; www.coloradohistory.org.

BEST Victorian Opulence
Bloom Mansion (Trinidad)

Two houses sit side by side and about twenty years apart in the heart of historic Trinidad. Beginning in the early 1860s, Felipe Baca, one of the founders of Trinidad, lived with his family in a two-story adobe residence right along the Santa Fe Trail. A rancher, merchant, trader, and entrepreneur, Baca owned one of the fanciest and most expensive homes of the region. Tour it today and you'll see a comfortable, simple design with Greek Revival architectural elements brought from the East mixed with Hispanic folk art from the South. Built right next door, the ornate, three-story Bloom mansion tells the story of what happened in the span of twenty years.

When the wagon trails of Baca's time were replaced by railroads, Frank Bloom's burgeoning cattle operations could sell to far-flung markets. Spreading his empire to New Mexico, Montana, Texas, Arizona, South Dakota, and even Canada, Bloom built his mansion to befit a cattle king. Standing proud yet worn, the building today reveals life in the boom days. Furniture and fixtures from the era, including a grandfather clock that once belonged to the Bloom family, fill the home. When the house was being restored by the Colorado Historical Society in the early 1960s, granddaughter Alberta offered valuable information about what the original wallpaper and curtains looked like, as well as family anecdotes and history.

Housed in the original Baca barn, the Santa Fe Trail Museum transports you from the days when Native Americans occupied the land to the eras of trading, railroads, and coal mining and into modern-day Trinidad. The Bloom Mansion, Baca House, and the Santa Fe Trail Museum are all part of the Trinidad History Museum complex at 300 E. Main St. Open May through September and by appointment. 719-846-7217; www.santa fetrailscenicandhistoricbyway.org or www.colorado history.org.

BEST Railroad Museum
Limon Heritage Museum and Railroad Park

Railroad buffs revel in the nostalgia of a colorful era gone by. Vivian and Harold Lowe's passion for that past glows at this small Limon museum. As can be seen in everything from the manicured grounds to well-maintained railroad rolling stock, these caretakers of history work endlessly to preserve stories from Limon's heyday.

The Rock Island Rocket from Chicago used to split up in Limon, one half heading to Denver and the other to Colorado Springs. The Union Pacific and Rock Island lines once shared the Union Depot, which now houses photographs and artifacts from the days when trains were plentiful. One old photo shows a moveable chapel, hauled free of charge by the railroads from town to town to hold services. Money raised from offerings helped build permanent homes for local congregations. Limon's First Baptist Church credits its origins to a car called the "Evangel." A small, "N-scale" working railroad runs through a model of Limon, depicting how it looked back in 1942. On tracks behind the depot are several cars you can walk through. Sit on stools at the lunch counter in the dining car that was hauled out to crews working to clean up wrecks or repair the rail. It looks like an old main street diner complete with a working stove.

The museum plays a role in Limon's two big summer events: the Limon Western Festival and Parade in mid-June and the Heritage Celebration in early August. It is open from 1 to 8 P.M. Monday through Saturday from June through August. Limon lies ninety miles east of Denver on I-70. 899 1st St.; 719-775-2373; www.limonchamber.com/museum.html.

BEST Oddball Attraction
Genoa Tower and Museum

If one man's junk is another man's treasure, then Jerry Chubbuck is a wealthy man. From ceiling to floor on every available inch of space in twenty-two dusty and claustrophobic rooms, his riches provide an end-less stream of wonder and bemusement. You'll find weird stuff sprinkled among a myriad of old bottles, dishes, tools, arrowheads, postcards, coins, devices, instruments, rocks, and oh-so-much more. Oddities include a stuffed two-headed calf, a white rattlesnake, and a one-eyed pig preserved in a jar; rooster glasses, to protect the birds' eyes from being pecked out; and a compass mounted on a cowboy's saddle. Chubbuck points to a World War I helmet with holes in it and says, "I'll bet that guy got a headache!" He shows off one room that used to be a dance hall. The stage tilts back-ward, he says, so "if the band got drunk, they wouldn't fall into the crowd." You get the idea. This rambling repository is riddled with the strange, the gaudy, the bizarre, the mundane, the gimmicky, the one-of-a-kind.

Long before I-70 came through, C. W. Gregory built a tower in the 1920s along the old Route 24 in the hamlet of Genoa. He advertised it as the highest elevation between Denver and New York. When Chubbuck acquired the tower in 1967, he thought he could see six states from its summit. Climbing the narrow stairs to the top, he claims that on a clear day you can see all the way to the Grand Tetons in Wyoming, New Mexico, Kansas, Nebraska, and South Dakota. In desperate need of new paint, the tower stands as a lofty landmark on an agricultural landscape.

Jerry Chubbuck is no Johnny-come-lately to the collection busi-ness. While searching for arrowheads in 1956, he discovered the remains of a prehistoric mammoth in the nearby town of Kit Carson. The tusks and bones of his find are on view in the museum. He's still going strong and adding new stuff all the time. Follow signs to the tower from Genoa, exit 371 on I-70 east of Limon. It's open all year long. Small admission fee charged. 719-763-2309.

BEST Outdoor Art
City of Loveland

His strong arms stretch out and drape over the wooden yoke he carries on his shoulders. Buckets of water dangle by rope from either end as his wife helps him with his burden. "The Water Carriers" stand proud, sur-rounded by eastern Colorado cornfields. Greeting motorists heading west toward Loveland on Hwy. 34 from I-25, this larger-than-life bronze sculpture by nationally known local sculptor Herb Mignery symbolizes the resolute settlers who toiled to live on this land. This monument to Colorado pioneers serves as a gateway to what's to come.

The city of Loveland is a city of bronze. At city hall, bronze violinists and flute players form an orchestra whose music you'd swear you could hear. Drive around the south end of Lake Loveland and you'll find a happy troupe of children balancing on a log. Then there's Benson Park. Back in the late 1970s, a few sculptors asked a local foundry to pour some molds. Their resulting works were erected in Benson Park. Each year since, more and more figures from different artists began to inhabit the park. Today, the bronze population exceeds fifty statues, from the whimsical to the profound, from laughing kids on sleds to a chiseled, proud Native American face. Even if you're the only person walking through Benson Park, you don't feel alone. Human emotions exude from hard, cold metal crafted by talented hands.

Sculptors move here from all over the country to be part of this thriving artistic community. Every year in early August, the Sculpture in the Park weekend brings artists and buyers together for one of the most prominent shows of its kind in the nation. For more information, call the Loveland High Plains Arts Council at 970-663-2940. www.sculpture inthepark.org.

Outdoor Activities & Events

BEST Prairie Landscape
Pawnee National Grassland (northeast of Greeley)

Pawnee Buttes rise like twin towers 300 feet above the prairie floor, standing as the only natural landmark in otherwise gently rolling, unbroken, wide-open spaces. In *Centennial*, his novel about Colorado, renowned author James Michener called them Rattlesnake Buttes. (He wasn't kidding about the rattlesnakes. Watch your step!) North, south, east, or west, the scene hardly changes. Cut by mile after mile of dirt road, the shortgrass prairie extends as far as the eye can see. Earth meets sky on a horizon dotted only by the occasional windmill or remains of an early nineteenth-century homestead. Checkerboarded in a patchwork of private holdings, the Pawnee National Grassland preserves a landscape ravaged by the dust bowl of the 1930s.

Sunrise creates an impressive silhouette of Pawnee Buttes, the most obvious landmark in the grasslands of northeast Colorado. PHOTO BY DOUG WHITEHEAD

For all its hundreds of square miles of unceasing expanse, the Pawnee Grassland can also be experienced by what you find right underneath your feet and just in front of your nose. Grasses carpet the earth's surface, and yucca and prickly pear cactus sprout out of the ground, joined by a variety of colorful wildflowers and small shrubs. Pronghorn antelope can be seen by the hundreds. At Crow Valley, birders congregate every spring to count as many as they can of the 284 species of birds that migrate through here. The lark bunting is a plains bird. It was named the state bird in 1931, giving recognition to the "other" half of Colorado not in the mountains. In recent years, bones thought to be 35 million years old have been found in the Pawnee Grassland. Camels, three-toed horses, and turtles are just some of the animals discovered in the layers of this ancient seabed. Seasonal streams and creeks hold water for only a portion of the year, if at all, directing the waters of periodic rainsqualls toward the South Platte River.

Developed campsites are available at Crow Valley near Briggsdale. The vast grassland lies north of CO Hwy. 14 between Greeley and Sterling. Stop in Greeley at the Pawnee National Grassland office for maps and information. 970-353-5004; www.fs.fed.us/r2/arnf.

BEST Prairie Experience
Pawnee Wagon Train

Belgian draft horses pull modern-day pioneers on a wagon ride that offers a taste of life on the trail. PHOTO BY DOUG WHITEHEAD

The covered wagons don't carry you and your supplies even ten miles total, but after this three-day, two-night prairie adventure, you've lived a hint of the five-month-long, century-ago Western passage of the pioneers. Leaving weathered buildings of the bygone northeastern Colorado town of Keota in the dust, you quickly adjust to the slow rhythm of steel-rimmed wooden wagon wheels and plodding hooves of Belgian draft horses. "It's not often we live our lives at four miles per hour," says wagon mistress Jo Ann Conter. Every summer, she and husband Doug, joined by other family members, carry wannabe-nineteenth-century settlers on two authentically reproduced prairie schooners into a sea of short-grass, cactus, and wildflowers on the Pawnee National Grassland (see Best Prairie Landscape above). Guests on the Pawnee Wagon Train come nowhere close to the deprivations suffered by the real pioneers. But while there's plenty of water and shade (most able-bodied 1800s travelers walked next to the wagons; you ride), Jo Ann and Doug make sure everyone pitches in to set up tents and cots at the end of the day. Strangers just a short time ago, the Wagon Train adventurers and their guides quickly become like family, together tending the horses, organizing camp, and sitting down to a hearty Western meal. As the sun sets on a distant horizon, stories and songs of the trail emanate from this bonding circle of new friends, carried on an otherwise-silent prairie breeze to the ever-present denizens of this land. Coyotes, antelope, rabbits, and horned toads give wide berth to these human intruders. Even the grazing herd of cattle we mooed at earlier in the day is long out of sight.

Morning on the prairie brings the smell of coffee and bacon, the hustle and bustle of breaking camp, and another "Wagons Ho!" as we trundle off to the day, wondering how we would have fared on the expedition into an unknown new life in the West. Pawnee Wagon Train Vacations run from late June through the end of August. 970-522-2070; www.pawneewagontrain.com.

BEST Wildlife Spectacle
Prairie Chicken Tours (Wray)

They're wooing by booming on their leks. Enthusiasts from all over the world make the trek to the northeastern corner of Colorado every spring seeking out this rare and unusual sight. Greater prairie chickens gather at their stage on the plains, called a lek, and the show begins. Males stake out territory, make odd noises, strut their stuff, and show off colorful feathers, trying to attract the fancy of a female. Spectators of this strange mating ritual arrive at the scene at four o'clock in the cold and dark of a March or April morning. Bundled up and sitting quietly in specially designed blinds, these wildlife watchers wait patiently. Soon, eerie noises seep into the still air, rumbling like timpani from an orchestra. As day breaks, squinting eyes peer through spotting scopes to finally witness the source of this symphony of low-pitched groans. Heartsick prairie chickens puff up their jowls, inflating bright-orange air sacs like balloons. The pulsating sacs then deflate, the process creating a lustful "booming" sound, the mysterious primeval call of love to those lady prairie chickens looking for the most dominant and desirable mate.

The only way to experience this extraordinary spectacle is by signing up for tours held Saturday and Sunday mornings during the last two weekends of March and the first three weekends of April. Space is limited. Tours are run by the Colorado Division of Wildlife in conjunction with the East Yuma County Historical Society. Package deals include overnight lodging in Wray. Call the Wray Museum for more information. 970-332-5063.

BEST Sand Links
Hugo Golf Club

At first glance, barbed-wire fences and the occasional Black Angus bull are just about all you see. Then the slogan printed on the hats of players makes it clear: "Sage, Cactus, Buffalo Grass and Sand Greens." Here in Hugo, along the old Smoky Hill Trail where settlers once rode covered wagons, they've been playing golf like this since the turn of the twentieth century. A longtime member of the golf club explains, "If you can't play in the wind in eastern Colorado, you're not gonna play much golf!"

Rubber-carpeted tees and heat-shimmering views to a far horizon greet avid rural duffers who appreciate this local nine-hole course. Through natural, unmanicured "fairways," the ball finally comes to rest on brown "greens" made of sifted sand from a nearby creek and oiled to keep them from blowing away. Players smooth a path between ball and hole

A prairie golfer smoothes a path before putting on this sand green in Hugo. PHOTO BY DOUG WHITEHEAD

with a flat-edged rake. The par-five fifth hole presents the biggest challenge. It's a big dogleg to the left with cedar trees and railroad ties placed strategically to keep you from trying to take a shortcut. Out in this dry country, volunteers water what few trees exist from a surplus U.S. Army water tank. Inside the red A-frame clubhouse you'll find members playing pool or a game of cards; the old Westinghouse refrigerator is filled with pop, beer, and candy bars. Members pay $40 for annual privileges at the Hugo Golf Club, and visitors are invited to play the course for a $5 greens fee.

Take I-70 to Limon and head south on U.S. Hwy. 40/287 thirteen miles to the golf course. You'll see the flags from the highway. It's one of six sand green courses left in Colorado. You don't need a tee time in Hugo. There is no telephone.

BEST State Park-and-Putt
Lathrop State Park (Walsenburg)

Two lakes nestle in the piñon-and-juniper forest in sight of the imposing Spanish Peaks that serve as a natural landmark for miles in every direction. As you whiz by on U.S. Hwy. 160, you could easily miss the simple entrance to Colorado's first state park. Opened to the public in 1962, Lathrop State Park somehow remains one of the least known of Colorado's forty outdoor-recreation preserves.

In the midst of yucca and prickly pear cactus, waterfowl, and small game, everything you might expect can be found here: boating, fishing, waterskiing, windsurfing, swimming, camping, and hiking. All this makes Lathrop ideal for a family vacation. But there's something else you would not expect to find in a Colorado state park: a nine-hole golf course. With the backdrop of Martin and Horseshoe Lakes just below and the twin Spanish Peaks to the south, the grandeur of the Walsenburg Golf Club rivals any course in the state. As you stand on the first tee, lush fairways fall away to a pastoral palette of varying shades of green. Every year on the last weekend in June, the Walsenburg Invitational draws duffers and hackers to the area's premier golfing event. Nowhere else can you enjoy such a unique combination of the raw outdoors with the more sublime pursuits of the links.

In nearby La Veta, check out the Grandote Golf and Country Club. This eighteen-hole course is considered one of the top public courses in the state.

Lathrop State Park is located three miles west of Walsenburg on U.S. Hwy. 160; call 719-738-2376 for park information. Contact the golf course at 719-738-2730. www.parks.state.co.us.

BEST Way to Get "In the Mood"
Glenn Miller SwingFest (Fort Morgan)

An audience of at least 500 cheers when the band begins playing what broadcaster Dave Garroway once called the national anthem of World War II: "Moonlight Serenade," which wafts through the Imperial Onion Warehouse. Dinner tables empty as couples flock to the dance floor. Under a bright chandelier and a ceiling full of stars, feet shuffle softly and bodies sway with a precision that comes from decades of practice. This is the music of their lives, cemented in their psyches by the everlasting, deeply rooted emotions of youth and war. The annual Glenn Miller Festival continues to grow in Fort Morgan, the onetime hometown of the world's greatest big-band leader.

Glenn Miller fans dress for the occasion at this annual festival in Fort Morgan. PHOTO BY DOUG WHITEHEAD

The festivities begin on a Friday night at a dance where celebrants get "in the mood" with a string of Glenn Miller tunes. The audience fills out ballots for best dancers and vintage costumes. The next day, a historic tour of town takes you by homes Miller lived in between 1918 and 1921, places he worked—such as the Great Western Sugar Company—and the cemetery where his parents are buried. World War II airplanes fly in to the Fort Morgan airport, where pilots in period military uniforms offer rides in classic aircraft. The Little Brown Jug 5K/10K race takes runners and walkers through town. Here, teenager Glenn Miller's talents playing trombone, composing, and arranging flourished. Nearly twenty years later, he would achieve heights no musician—neither Elvis nor The Beatles—has equaled: forty-five hits at the top of the charts during 1942.

Glenn Miller's sudden disappearance in a plane crash over the English Channel in December 1944 left his multitude of fans the world over in shock and disbelief. On Saturday night, the Glenn Miller Orchestra, sanctioned by his family in 1946 to continue under their lost leader's name, faithfully reproduces the big-band sound, still popular today. For information about this festival, which is held during the last two weeks of June, call 800-354-8660. www.fortmorganchamber.org/gmiller.htm.

Where to Eat, Drink, & Stay

expert pick

Top Five Historic Taverns
Tom Noel, a.k.a. "Dr. Colorado"

Dr. Tom Noel is an author, newspaper columnist, professor, and all-around expert extraordinaire on Colorado history. His list of "Top Five Historic Taverns" is based on years of thorough research for his book *Colorado: A Liquid History & Tavern Guide to the Highest State* (Fulcrum Publishing, 1999). He writes, "taverns, the first and most common public buildings in frontier Colorado, served more than drinks. Among other things, they often housed pioneer governments. Saloons also doubled as theaters, art galleries, dance halls, and even housed church services."

▸▸ **Buckhorn Exchange (Denver)**—Colorado Liquor License # 1 has hung on the back bar of this liquid landmark ever since 1893. Denver had no Museum of Natural History until 1900, but saloons offered some astonishing natural and unnatural history. The best of the tavern/museums, the Buckhorn Exchange, has more than 300 stuffed mammals and birds, and a menu featuring alligator, buffalo, elk, pheasant, quail, and other wild game. 1000 Osage St.; 303-534-9509.

▸▸ **Gold Pan Saloon (Breckenridge)**—The Gold Pan Saloon has stoutly resisted the transformation of a ramshackle mining town into a cute ski and summer resort. Behind the swinging doors of Breckenridge's oldest saloon, raucous regulars fight off the invading tourist armies. The dinginess of the Gold Pan also shields it from stray tourists. This tavern consists of two tipsy clapboard buildings leaning on each other since 1879 atop wobbly log foundations. 10305 N. Main St.; 970-453-5499.

▸▸ **Gus' Place (Pueblo)**—Colorado's best-known blue-collar saloon is a small, one-story brick corner tavern that blends into a working-class neighborhood. Augusto Masciotra, an Italian immigrant, went to work at age fourteen at the nearby CF & I Steel Mills and saved to buy the house at 1201 Elm. In 1926, he added a grocery to the front of his home and, with the end of Prohibition in 1933, converted the grocery to the tavern now operated by his grandson. 1201 Elm St. (southwest corner of Mesa Ave.); 719-542-0756.

▸▸ **Kozy Corner Bar and Café (Goodrich)**—King Arthur had his round table where all were equal. So does Goodrich, Colorado, where the round table fills much of the tiny Kozy Corner Bar and Café. In this tiny, dirt-streeted village on the north bank of the South Platte River, the Kozy Corner welcomes locals and visitors to rest atop tractor seats mounted on milk-can stools. 24213 Weld CR 39 (southwest corner of CO Hwy. 144); 970-645-2064.

▸▸ **Silver Dollar Saloon (Leadville)**—This 1879 saloon is well preserved from its vintage front foyer to its back rooms for gaming, dancing, and other activities. Named for Silver Dollar Tabor, this museumlike tavern celebrates the silvery past of America's highest, wildest, and biggest silver city. 315 Harrison Ave.; 719-486-9914.

▸▸ **Teller House Bar (Central City)**—President Ulysses S. Grant stepped out of a stagecoach on April 28, 1878, to find the Teller House walk paved with silver bricks. Presumably, the cigar-chomping Civil War hero also visited the bar. Herndon Davis, a Denver artist, painted a woman's face on the barroom floor in the summer of 1936, drawing inspiration from Hugh d'Arcy's poem. This barroom is also graced by Apollo, Aphrodite with an Apple, Leda and the Swan, and five other life-size murals of Greek goddesses and gods. 110 Eureka St.; 303-582-3200.

BEST Dinner and a Show
High Plains Livestock Exchange/Drover's Restaurant (near Brush)

The rapid-fire utterings of the auctioneer are unintelligible to the uninitiated and the bids of the buyers are almost indiscernible. But stop in at the Sale Barn in Brush on a Thursday or Friday and you'll get an earful and eyeful of livestock being bought and sold in eastern Colorado.

Before taking a seat in the arena, buyers look over an array of ear-tagged cattle from the narrow gangway that stretches over the corrals out back. Taking their notes inside, they know which animals to bid on. Either individually or by lot, the livestock is paraded before this gathering as the auctioneer works quickly, pointing back and forth with the forefinger of each hand like shooting pistols at competing bidders. With a nod of the head or flick of the wrist, the price goes up until someone finally prevails. Just as soon as the sale is made, that steer or heifer is moved out of the way for the next one's fate to be determined.

As the spectacle continues throughout the day, folks get hungry. Just across the hall from the entrance to the arena, the tables of Drover's Restaurant are almost always full—and for good reason. If the daily specials don't bring 'em in (like prime rib on Saturday nights), you can still get a bottomless cup of coffee for only a quarter (that's almost a half a month's worth of java for the cost of one Starbucks!). Folks'll sit for hours, drinking one refill after another, visiting with neighbors and sharing the farm and ranch news of the day. If you walk in and don't see an empty table, just ask if you can join someone at theirs. The friendliness is genuine. Though the meals are not for the weight-conscious diner (and there's no such thing as a "nonsmoking" area), the portions are hearty, the food is fresh, and the pies are homemade.

The High Plains Livestock Exchange and Drover's Restaurant are located on U.S. Hwy. 34 just east of the town of Brush. 28601 U.S. Hwy 34; 970-842-4218; www.hplivestock.com.

BEST Colorado Melons
Rocky Ford Cantaloupe

If you ignore the farm stands along U.S. Hwy. 50 as you whiz through small eastern Colorado towns in August or September, you're missing the chance of a lifetime. Open up a melon picked from the field just hours before and treat your taste buds to the sweetest cantaloupe you've ever eaten. The reputation of Rocky Ford, the "Melon Capitol of the World," has grown for more than a hundred years.

Back in 1876, George Swink developed a seed that, when planted in the fertile soil of the Arkansas River Valley, thrives in the hot days and cool nights of a Colorado summer. Brian and Gail Knapp still raise the sweet fruit on Swink's original farm. They also grow a variety of vegetables that fill the shelves of their roadside farm market on the east end of Rocky Ford. Sweet corn, tomatoes, peppers, beans, onions, and all sorts of other veggies come from the same ground that grows the famous melons. The Knapps run just one of many farms in the region, producing fruits and vegetables sought by consumers from around the state who make a point of traveling here every year to stock up.

World-famous Rocky Ford cantaloupes fill local produce stands along U.S. Hwy. 50.
PHOTO BY DOUG WHITEHEAD

When George Swink gave away his first watermelon crop to his neighbors back in the 1870s, he began a tradition that continues to this day. Every year at the Arkansas Valley Fair held mid-August in Rocky Ford, the Watermelon Pile giveaway draws melon seekers from far and wide. Rides, rodeos, and food stands give you a reason to stay a little longer at the fair. For more information, call the Rocky Ford Chamber of Commerce at 719-254-7483.

BEST Restaurant for Unusual Local Cuisine
Bruce's (Severance)

Whatever you call 'em—bull fries, Rocky Mountain oysters, swinging steaks—they always make for a memorable conversation between bites. Despite the cringe effect on the squeamish, they really do taste great. You might even venture away from the bull-harvested variety and try tender turkey oysters for a change of pace. Whatever you decide, co-owner Betty Schott will encourage you to "have a ball!" If you can't even imagine doing that, then why not settle for a perfectly cooked steak, some deep-fried seafood, or a reasonably priced burger?

Bruce's remains a great place to take guests from out of the country for a truly cultural experience. Located in the former recreation center of the aptly named town of Severance, just northwest of Greeley, Bruce's still caters mostly to a local crowd. Slide into a booth or share a long wooden table, which seats about twenty, with some newfound friends. Western dress, cowboy hats, and boots are the norm. And when the country-and-western band kicks off its first set on Friday and Saturday nights, you'll know that this is the only place to swing. 345 1st St. in Severance, east of I-25 on CO Hwy. 74. 970-686-2320.

BEST Out-of-the-Way Hotel
The Plains Hotel & Wedding Chapel (Cheyenne Wells)

If you know Cheyenne Wells at all, it was probably from the time you were stuck here during an eastern Colorado snowstorm. Few travelers ever have much reason to come this way. But the renovated Plains Hotel can make a destination out of this town where residents admit there's really not much to do but notice how much and how hard the wind blows.

Donna Pennington bought this historic but dilapidated old building (built in 1919) and has turned it into a charming home-away-from-home bed-and-breakfast where she does all the work. Seven individually decorated rooms upstairs have a distinctively nostalgic feel with original light fixtures, claw-foot tubs, and many of Donna's treasured family photographs on the shelves and walls. The lobby is like a comfortable living room and the parlor an inviting gathering place with a full-service bar. Without the distractions of a busy vacation, couples find time to reconnect here, book lovers find time to read, and breakfast alone would be reason enough to seek out the comforts of the Plains Hotel.

Planning a small wedding? The tiny chapel just next door can handle twelve people, including the bride and groom, and Donna will do it all: accommodations for the wedding party, rehearsal dinner, Saturday breakfast, candlelight dinner, wedding cake, decorations, Sunday brunch, and any other help you might want. Take U.S. Hwy. 40 south from Limon through Kit Carson to Cheyenne Wells near the Kansas border. 171 E. 1st St.; 719-767-5550; www.theplainshotel.net.

BEST Resort on the Plains
The Runaway Inn (Joes)

Looking south from U.S. Hwy. 36 just past Joes, the silhouette of a barn and a windmill about a mile away catch your attention. Follow your eye and run on out to the Runaway Inn. This is no mountain resort. Here it's a prairie way of life made accessible to us poor city slickers, a way to see the world through a flatlander's soul.

Carl and Barbara Comer's enthusiasm for sharing their world is infectious. They welcome weddings, reunions, retreats, or romantics looking for a weekend away. Horse-drawn carriage rides down country roads at sunset, fishing for bass and trout, skeet and trap shooting, outdoor barbecues, even a nine-hole chip-and-putt golf course will keep you occupied out here. If all you want to do is sleep, the beds are so comfortable, the nights so quiet, you might never wake up. But there's so much to do, rest may be the last thing on your mind. There are surprises at the Runaway Inn. Pilots can fly in to the private airport, from which you can get a bird's-eye view of the plains on a sightseeing flight. And bird hunters flock here, traipsing through fields full of pheasant, chukar, and quail. They raise hunting dogs or will help you train your own. It's quite a sight watching those bird dogs at work. If hunting's not your thing, they still welcome your family dog, or you can board your own horses and ride the trails.

You won't go hungry. Two stone fireplaces in the dining room set the mood for gourmet meals, and the Covey Cantina is the place in these parts to watch a football game, eat burgers and brats, and tip a few. You can also play darts or pool. Carl and Barbara, along with their partners, David and Kathleen Poole, serve up genuine prairie hospitality.

Take I-70 to the small town of Byers, east of Denver, and pick up U.S. Hwy. 36. You'll go through Last Chance, Akron, and Cope before you reach Joe. Just east of town follow signs to 8762 CR 5. Call the Runaway Inn at 970-358-4567. www.runawayinn.com.

BEST Rest in the Old West
Chicosa Canyon Bed-and-Breakfast (north of Trinidad)

If you had visited W. C. Riggs's place way back in this rugged canyon, you might have rubbed shoulders with Kit Carson or Bat Masterson. Riggs mentions them and other historical figures in a detailed diary he kept at the ranch he homesteaded in 1870. The sturdy stone home and fences he built survive today on sixty-four acres in Chicosa Canyon as a quiet, remote, and unique bed-and-breakfast.

In the cool confines of the original house, three individually appointed rooms are furnished with period antiques, quilts, and comforters. Photographs of the Riggs family and their original ranch adorn the walls of the Western-style living room. In an addition to the original stone house, you can relax in the sunny solarium or soak in a soothing hot tub. In the restaurant business in Denver for years, innkeeper Keena Unruh knows how to get your day off to a great start with an elegant breakfast. The bunkhouse for the cowboys on Riggs's ranch has been renovated as secluded quarters for guests looking for privacy and romance. The original wood-slat exterior has been preserved while the interior was gutted to build a cozy room with a queen-size bed, a kitchen, a loft for two single beds, and a porch with views of the canyon.

In keeping with the rustic nature of Chicosa Canyon, horse lovers can board their animals in the old red barn on the ranch. Riders explore miles of scenic trails through sandstone canyons where whispers of the Old West blow on a nostalgic breeze. The ranch's proximity to Trinidad (about fourteen miles to the southeast) encourages guests to spend time investigating the museums, restaurants, and shops of a historic town on the old Santa Fe Trail. They're open from Labor Day through Memorial Day. The bunkhouse is available year-round. 32391 CR 40; 719-846-6199; www.bbonline.com/co/chicosa.

SOUTH-CENTRAL

The vistas here stretch the eyes,
enlighten the heart,
and make the spirit humble.

—JOHN GUNTHER, FROM *Inside U.S.A.*
(HARPER AND BROTHERS, 1947)

Unique and distinct geographic domains sprawl through southern Colorado, where wide basins and broad river valleys fit together like pieces of a puzzle. Headwaters of the South Platte, the Arkansas, and the Rio Grande originate here, draining snowmelt from extensive mountain ranges that flows into many states beyond. The twin Spanish Peaks are a formidable landmark between Trinidad and the Cuchara Valley. At the heart of secluded, forested country, the rolling Wet Mountains open up to sweeping alpine views. From the top of Kenosha Pass, South Park drops away dramatically, a vast bowl with a far horizon, ringed by rocky peaks. From Leadville, the Arkansas River begins with a trickle then quickly gathers momentum as it rushes south past a curtain of 14,000-foot snowcapped summits before veering east to cut the Royal Gorge. And from Poncha Pass, the immense San Luis Valley stretches and spreads to the New Mexican border, its eastern wall a jagged spine called the Sangre de Cristos, to the west the rugged San Juans.

Colorado's hard-rock history seeps from the vanishing ghost towns and dilapidated mining structures of this region where gold and silver fueled a fever for riches. Hordes of people fled the destruction and economic ruin of the Civil War and poured west on wagon trails, filling mining camps and creating new towns almost overnight. Fairplay's South Park City preserves remnants of that past in an authentic Old West town and Leadville's Route of the Silver Kings winds through the mining district that produced the wealth of Molly Brown and Baby Doe Tabor. Much of southern Colorado's past, however, comes not from the east, but from the south. San Luis, Colorado's oldest town, and the valley of the same name date to the days of the Spanish Empire. After wiping out the Aztecs in the early 1500s, the Spanish expanded north, eventually claiming Ute Indian territory all the way up to the Arkansas River and the San Luis Valley. Mexico continued the trade routes through Colorado when it won independence in 1821, before ceding the area to the United States in 1848. That 500-year legacy is reflected today in the lives and traditions of residents of the southern reaches of the state.

Mountain biking along the Continental Divide and rafting on the Arkansas River provide access to incredible vantage points you won't reach any other way. And you'll cover lots of miles in your car to experience the "best" of this wide and varied country.

Cultural & Historical

expert pick

Top Five Ghost Towns
Kenneth Jessen

More towns have vanished in Colorado than exist today, and no one knows those old ghost towns better than Ken Jessen. Accompanied by his wife, Sonje, Jessen has spent years searching the ruins of places where dreams soared and crashed, often within the short space of a year or less. Three volumes of Jessen's *Ghost Towns: Colorado Style* (JV Publications, 1998–2001) document a short-lived but lively past quickly fading into a once-bustling landscape. His top five ghost towns include some places that have never quite died and some where there's very little left.

▸▸ **Ashcroft (Aspen area)**—Located along Castle Creek south of Aspen, Ashcroft is one of the best-preserved ghost towns in Colorado. As an added feature, it is accessible via a paved road in the very heart of towering mountains, some exceeding 14,000 feet. A parking lot with a trail though the town was constructed by the Forest Service. Interpretive signs allow visitors to learn about this town built during the 1880s.

▸▸ **Caribou (Nederland area)**—In an 1873 photograph taken by renowned Colorado photographer William Henry Jackson, Caribou had more than eighty structures sitting in a high meadow at 10,000 feet. This town of more than 500 included the three-story Sherman House, one of its several hotels. With winds greater than 100 miles per hour, many of the structures, including the schoolhouse, had to be braced by large timbers. Today, visitors can view the walls of two stone structures at the Caribou site by traveling west over a graded dirt road from Nederland.

▸▸ **Crystal (Marble area)**—The picturesque power plant below Crystal sits by a small waterfall and is among the most photographed structures in Colorado. The town got a post office in 1882 and grew to include more than seventy homes and a good number of saloons. Some of these homes remain standing and are seasonally occupied. Crystal is east of Marble and requires driving over a rough, moderately difficult four-wheel-drive road that is open only during the short mountain summer.

▸▸ **St. Elmo (Buena Vista area)**—Out of all of the mining towns west of Buena Vista in the Chalk Creek drainage, the one that lasted the longest was St. Elmo. Its row of abandoned buildings is enhanced by a backdrop of high mountain peaks, possibly making it the most visited ghost town in the state. Based on a nearby deposit of gold and silver ore, St. Elmo got its start in the 1870s as Forest City. It was later renamed by residents for the title of a novel, *St. Elmo* by Augusta J. Evans.

▸▸ **Teller City (Rand area)**—This North Park town was the largest settlement in the area, and today, more than two dozen foundations can be found among a dense stand of lodgepole pines. It was founded in 1879 by Madore Cusman, locally known as "Old Cush." Teller City boasted Grand County's first newspaper and reached an estimated population of more than 1,000. By 1885, Teller City was all but abandoned, including its two-story hotel, the Yates House, as well as the town's four saloons.

BEST Religious Shrine
Stations of the Cross (San Luis)

On a hill overlooking Colorado's oldest town, an age-old story unfolds. Following a narrow, winding path uphill from the small town center of San Luis, pilgrims stop to reflect at each of fifteen bronze sculptures telling of the crucifixion, death, and resurrection of Jesus. At each Station of the Cross, inspired images crafted from the hands of local sculptor Huberto Maestas are set against a backdrop of town below and mountains beyond. Shadows from the sun accentuate a crown of thorns, a weary face, a hammer nailing Jesus to the cross. A flower might be placed in His hand. Rosaries, candles, and other offerings lie at the base of each depiction of Christ's passage. With every step nearer the crest of the hill, Christ's story nears its crescendo until, at the top, you reach the figure of His ascension into heaven. Completing the experience, the faithful find a place for reflection and meditation at La Capilla de Todos los Santos, or All Saints Chapel, a beautiful refuge at the top of the hill.

This project was inspired by local parish priest Father Pat Valdez, helping to fulfill his dream of making San Luis an artistic and spiritual destination. Catholicism has been rooted here for 400 years, and the Stations of the Cross are just the latest manifestation of Catholic faith in this area. When the Church lost influence in the far-flung reaches of the Southwest during the 1800s, the faith was preserved in towns such as San Luis in the *moradas*, or small chapels of the Catholic brotherhood known as the Penitentes. And while attending Colorado for World Youth Day in 1993, Pope John Paul II became the most notable visitor to San Luis and these Stations of the Cross.

Reach the Stations of the Cross by taking I-25 south to Walsenburg. Go west on U.S. Hwy. 160 to Fort Garland and then south sixteen miles on Hwy. 159 to San Luis. For additional information, call Sangre de Cristo Catholic Church at 719-672-3685 or Huberto's Sculpture Studio at 719-672-3022.

BEST Spiritual Convergence
Crestone

Like individual streams combining to create a mighty river, assorted spiritual paths converge in Crestone to form an irresistible magnet for mind, body, and soul. At the eastern edge of the world's largest alpine valley, below the majestic spine of the Sangre de Cristo Mountains, this remote burg offers sanctuary to seekers of truth. From ancient observances to New Age rites, a medley of mysticism, Eastern thought, and Christian tradition plays to a host of spiritual wanderers. Here is just a partial list of what can be found in Crestone:

▸▸ **The Spiritual Life Institute at Nada Hermitage**—The contemplative life is practiced by the monks, men, and women of this Carmelite monastery created in the Roman Catholic tradition. As at similar hermitages in Ireland and Nova Scotia, private weeklong retreats offer solitude and reflection close to nature. Write to Nada Hermitage, P.O. Box 219, Crestone, CO 81121. 719-256-4778; www.spiritual lifeinstitute.org.

▸▸ **Haidakhandi Universal Ashram**—Here you can join the daily activities of a spiritual community based on the teachings of Haidakhan Babaji, a teacher from India. Prayers are sung twice a day at the Divine Mother Temple. An energy efficient "Earthship" and straw-bale greenhouse are examples of followers' attempts to live with sustainable resources. Witness a sacred fire ceremony offered on the full and new moons. 866-686-4185; www.babajiashram.org.

▸▸ **Crestone Mountain Zen Center**—For six months out of the year, cloistered Zen Buddhist monks train in the tradition of Shunryu Suzuki-roshi. During the "guest season" from May through October, you can participate in Zen

Buddhist study and meditation. Visit, among other things, a statue of Sho Kannon, the bodhisattva (similar to a saint) of infinite compassion. The only other statue like it sits in the rotunda of the Hiroshima Peace Museum in Japan. Overnight accommodations are available. 719-256-4692; www.manitou.org/MF/centers/zen.html.

▸▸ **Karma Thegsum Tashi Gomang**—This center for the study and practice of Tibetan Buddhism offers instruction in meditation, teachings, and prayer activities. A "stupa," or traditional Tibetan shrine, serves as a symbol of enlightenment. 719-256-4764; www.kttg.org.

BEST Ongoing Construction Project
Bishop Castle (north of San Isabel)

The engine of an old green Dodge pickup truck strains loudly as Jim Bishop lurches it back in reverse. A rope tied to the front bumper tightens over a pulley hitched from scaffolding more than two stories high. On the other end, a bucket full of rocks hoists into the air level with the wooden planks that run like a gangway around a portion of an outside wall. Setting the brake, the lean and muscular Bishop climbs like a man half his age up steel supports. Balancing precariously on this rickety perch, carefully laying each boulder in place, he adds yet a few more pieces to the more-than-thirty-year-old puzzle he calls the world's largest one-man construction project.

It is big. You can see parts of Jim Bishop's castle through the trees as you make the short walk from the highway. The enormity of his medieval monstrosity hits you only as you stand before it, neck craned skyward, taking in the sight of this unlikely concoction of iron and stone in the heart of the Wet Mountains. Bishop's enthusiasm for his castle has not diminished one bit since he began putzing around in the summer of 1969. If anything, it has grown with each addition to his dream-in-progress. On ground level you pass under stone arches and through narrow passageways to dungeonlike rooms. Climb the stone steps of a cramped spiral staircase to the second level, where it feels like a giant cathedral with stained glass and high ceiling, a monument to the unceasing vision of this ornamental-iron worker from Pueblo. All the while, Bishop explains the details of what he has created so far and his intricate plans for the future. Shaking your head in awe, you continue the ascent to higher levels, stepping out on narrow ledges looking out over the turrets and spires, trees and mountains that surround this Colorado Camelot. Back on the ground, Bishop excitedly points out an inspired touch. Sitting high atop his creation is the steel head of a dragon gleaming in the morning sun. Disappearing for several minutes, Bishop negotiates the back ways of his three-story-high labyrinth until he reappears on the uppermost roof. Crawling out on the mythical beast, he reaches into its mouth and lights a propane torch. Rising up and waving like a schoolboy, Bishop stands untethered and laughs as the dragon spits orange fire into the blue Colorado sky.

There is a gift shop next to the castle. Bishop does not charge admission but gladly accepts donations. Park on CO Hwy. 165 along the Frontier Pathways Scenic Byway. You'll see signs for Bishop Castle several miles north of San Isabel. It's open every day. 719-485-3040; www.bishopcastle.org.

BEST Scenic Byway
Los Caminos Antiguos (San Luis Valley)

In a state predominantly defined for tourists by its Old West image, an Old World history unfolds in the San Luis Valley. Once the northernmost frontier of the Spanish Empire in the Americas, these lands are soaked in a legacy unbroken since the sixteenth century. Sensing that tradition through your car window can be elusive, but travel Los Caminos Antiguos Scenic Byway and you'll journey deep into the soul of Hispanic Colorado.

These "Ancient Roads" lead to many of the beautiful manifestations of the region's Catholic faith, such as Our Lady of Guadalupe Church in Conejos, the state's oldest parish, and the stunning bronze statues of the Stations of the Cross (see Best Religious Shrine above, page 138) in San Luis, the state's oldest incorporated town. You'll stand where Don Juan de Onate crossed the Rio Bravo del Norte (the Rio Grande River) as he claimed these lands for the Spanish crown. Remnants of early Hispanic settlements appear like ghosts along the byway. Fort Garland Museum (see Best Cultural Crossroads on page 147) tells the story of how three cultures—Indian, Mexican, and American—came into uneasy and inevitably violent contact in the 1800s. The Cumbres & Toltec Scenic Railroad (see Best Steam-Engine Train Ride on page 145) highlights the intense push into the Colorado mountains as America flexed its industrial muscle into the twentieth century. Besides the rich human history, Los Caminos Antiguos Byway helps visitors discover fantastic natural wonders and teeming wildlife, such as the Great Sand Dunes (see Best Desert in the Mountains on page 156), the annual migration of Sandhill Cranes (see Best Bird Spectacle on page 154), Bighorn Sheep, Zapata Falls, and the rugged Sangre de Cristo mountain range. Even a more-modern creation such as the Colorado Alligator Farm (see Best Out-of-Place Reptiles on page 157) brings unique character to this southern Colorado circuit.

Pick small sections of Los Caminos Antiguos Scenic Byway for day trips but allow at least several days to explore its length and breadth. For more in-depth information, call 719-379-3512. www.loscaminos.com.

BEST Collection of Scenic Drives
Cañon City Area

Drive your car from Cañon City toward almost any point on the compass and within minutes you'll find yourself in another world. Each route presents its own special history and landscape. Following are some of the best day tours in the region. Call the Cañon City Chamber of Commerce for more info. 800-876-7922; www.canoncitycolorado.com.

➤➤ **Gold Belt Tour**—As the crow flies, it's about twenty miles between Cañon City and the historic mining towns of Cripple Creek and Victor. Three distinct, winding routes connect the two areas. Several miles east of Cañon City from U.S. Hwy. 50, Phantom Canyon Road follows a narrow railroad route that once hauled out rich ore from the thriving mines. Remnants of those days remain along the way, including a tunnel, high trestle, and ghost town. The Shelf Rd. leaves Cañon City and leads to the Garden Park Fossil Area, where the world's most complete stegosaurus skeleton was uncovered. Farther along, the red-sandstone formations of Red Canyon Park remind you of Garden of the Gods in Colorado Springs or Red Rocks Park in Denver. Following the narrow road on a shelf high above the streambed, drivers reach the Shelf Road Recreation Area, where rock climbers scramble up more than 100 routes in a series of limestone canyons (see Best Vertical Rock on page 152). The High Rd., farthest west on the Gold Belt tour, follows a more mellow, rolling course with views of the Royal Gorge Bridge below.

➤➤ **Temple Canyon Park**—Heading south on 1st St., a maintained dirt road leads about seven miles to this Cañon City mountain park. Only about one square mile in area, the park is filled with steep rock walls, sage-covered arroyos, and a roaring springtime creek that seems deeper than it is wide. Native American legends of the area make this an interesting exploration.

A rolling, one-way road traces the hogback ridge of Skyline Drive above Cañon City.

PHOTO BY DOUG WHITEHEAD

▸▸ **Skyline Drive**—In the early 1900s, convicts from the state penitentiary in Cañon City built a rolling road along the hogback above town to create a scenic drive originally traveled by horse and carriage. The one-way route turns off U.S. Hwy. 50 just a couple of miles west of Cañon City. The road climbs quickly and follows an undulating spine with views falling off in both directions. The ten-minute drive offers a view into the prison yard before dropping back down into a residential section of town.

▸▸ **Royal Gorge Bridge**—Travel west on U.S. Hwy. 50 and follow signs to the world's highest suspension bridge, towering 1,053 feet above the thundering Arkansas River. If you're just looking for scenery, beware. The rim of the canyon has also been built-up into a full-fledged tourist park. Adults pay a $20 entrance fee; kids are $16, which includes all the carnival rides, petting zoo, wildlife park, Incline Railroad, gondola rides, theater, and more. For an added price, you can strap in to the "skycoaster" and swing out over the gorge. (It is possible early morning and late day to pay a lesser price just for the bridge and view of the Royal Gorge; we think they've gone overboard here with all the tourist clutter at the rim.) On the road out to the bridge, Buckskin Joe traps tourists at a Hollywood's-eye view of the Old West.

BEST Old West Town
South Park City (Fairplay)

The honky-tonk sounds of a player piano burst through the swinging doors of the saloon and drift down the main street past the bank, the jail, the blacksmith shop, and the livery stable. In fact, you'll see just about anything you'd expect to find in a thriving mining town of the 1800s. In South Park City the past oozes from every nook and cranny.

The buildings have been salvaged over the years from ghost towns with names that read like an obituary from Colorado's past: Dudley, Leavick, Garo, Ophir. Restored from various stages of deterioration, more than thirty buildings now form this two-block re-creation of an Old West town in present-day Fairplay. Furnished with items from the times, each spot tells a rich story. Implements from the dentist's office would scare anyone with a toothache today, and Grandma might remember products from her childhood stocked on the shelves of the mercantile. Wandering down the wooden boardwalk from place to place, you can spend an entire afternoon in South Park City and never get bored. Because it is run as a museum rather than as a tourist trap with "gunfights" in the street, the experience rings authentic, the history real. It doesn't take much to imagine living in those rough-and-tumble times.

In recent years a new visitors center has opened with displays featuring the history and heritage of Park County. South Park City is located one block off of CO Hwy. 9 in downtown Fairplay at 100 4th St. It's closed in the winter. 719-836-2387; www.southparkcity.org.

BEST Historic Mining District
Route of the Silver Kings (Leadville)

It all happened quite by accident. Two prospectors looking for gold up California Gulch found silver in 1875, and the Leadville mining boom was on. Today, a patchwork of dilapidated remains are scattered as if a tornado had ravaged the hillsides. Legendary fortunes were born where the ruins lie like broken dreams on the Route of the Silver Kings.

Turn east on 4th, 5th, or 7th Sts. from downtown Leadville and within minutes you're in the heart of a mining district that transformed the high-altitude hamlet into a thriving cultural center of the West. James J. Brown's Ibex Mine created the wealth enjoyed by Molly Brown. The Little Pittsburgh reaped riches for Horace and Baby Doe Tabor, and the Robert E. Lee produced more silver than any other mine in the area. The reign of the Silver Kings, however, did not last long. When silver prices crashed in 1893, Horace Tabor, the king of Silver Kings, lost everything but the Matchless Mine. Upon his death he instructed Baby Doe, his socialite wife, to hang on to it in the belief that it would one day produce wealth again. For thirty-five years, Baby Doe lived in increasing poverty at the Matchless. In the winter of 1935, a deliveryman found her frozen body in the cabin. Her tragic death starkly symbolized the end of an era.

On the Route of the Silver Kings you can visit the Matchless Mine and the many other ruins of the Leadville Mining District. You can also explore the area on your bicycle as you pedal the 3.5-mile loop of the Mineral Belt Trail. Pick up maps at the Leadville Chamber of Commerce on 809 Harrison Ave. 800-933-3901; www.leadvilleusa.com.

See skeletons of old mine workings along the Route of the Silver Kings. PHOTO BY DOUG WHITEHEAD

BEST Steam-Engine Train Ride
Cumbres and Toltec Scenic Railroad (Antonito, Colorado, to Chama, New Mexico)

Black smoke, blue skies, white steam. Add deep greens from alpine forests and rainbow hues of wildflowers for a vivid ride on America's highest narrow-gauge railroad. Passengers are in no hurry on this sixty-four-mile, six-and-a-half-hour trek from Antonito, Colorado, to Chama, New Mexico. Twisting and curving across the state line eleven times, this historic train clackety-clacks along tracks first laid down in 1880 to haul gold and silver out of the San Juan Mountains.

Classic steam engines and railroad cars of the Cumbres and Toltec Scenic Railroad roll through remote country. The adventure includes several high-trestle crossings, including an exhilarating run 137 feet above Cascade Creek. When the old wooden trestle was first built before the turn of the century, one railcar apparently derailed high upon the bridge. Not to worry: the railroad insists it has never happened again! Two engines pull uphill to the 10,015-foot summit of Cumbres Pass,

The Cumbres and Toltec Railroad crosses a high trestle in rugged country along the Colorado–New Mexico border. PHOTO BY DOUG WHITEHEAD

refilling at vintage water towers along the way. One unhooks at the top and the remaining engine does the downhill duties the rest of the way. Expert guides patrol the aisles, offering history lessons and answering questions. The ticket price includes hot lunch, salad bar, and homemade desserts at the Osier, Colorado, dining hall. It's not easy to feed a trainful of hungry travelers all at once, but they do a good job. Try the turkey dinner with dressing, yams, and green beans. Yum.

The train runs Saturday through Thursday mid-May through mid-October. Leave from the depot in either Antonito or Chama and a bus will carry you back to where you began. Any way you ride it, the Cumbres and Toltec is a must. Reservations are highly recommended. 888-CUMBRES. Check out their Web site at www.cumbresandtoltec.com.

BEST Ride and Dine
Royal Gorge Route Dinner Train (Cañon City)

With several blasts of the whistle the diesel locomotive pulls west out of
Cañon City. Within minutes the train snugs up next to the Arkansas
River and enters the rugged embrace of the Royal Gorge. Packed with
riders craning their necks to see the famous Royal Gorge Bridge spanning
the canyon a thousand feet above, the popular railroad now adds the
option of a gourmet meal to the experience.

As the sinking sun reflects off waters rushing just outside the windows, dinner rolls out in the elegant dining cars. Lengthening shadows
envelop the narrowing chasm as the waitstaff, expert at negotiating narrow aisles, begins serving appetizers, complimentary champagne, and
green salad with homemade blue-cheese dressing and fresh bread. A cash
bar is available. The two-and-a-half-hour round-trip excursion allows
ample time to savor each course with walks in between to the open-air
car to take in the scenery. Waving to the last white-water rafters of the
day coming down the Arkansas, diners dig in to the main entrees, prepared in the specially designed kitchen car. Whether you choose the
prime rib with baked potato and vegetables or salmon with wild rice and
vegetables, you won't be disappointed. The Royal Gorge Route Dinner
Train has perfected the art of food and service. On our ride, the head
chef was complimented with a hearty round of applause from his dinner
guests as they found room for scrumptious cheesecake.

The Royal Gorge Route also offers lunch runs on the weekends.
Or you can ride one of the daily excursions without a meal. The Dinner
Train is very popular, so reservations are a must. The railroad operates
year-round from the Santa Fe Depot at 401 Water St. Check schedules
online at www.royalgorgeroute.com or call toll free 888-RAILS-4U.

BEST Monument to a Sports Hero
Jack Dempsey Museum and Park (Manassa)

In a small log building where "The Manassa Mauler" was born, mementos,
newspaper articles, and photographs from a celebrated boxing career adorn
the walls. Display cases hold memorabilia, including gloves from the Firpo
fight and shoes from the Tuney fight. These prized possessions were given
to the small museum by a bigger-than-life sports hero, Jack Dempsey.
Known early in his career as "Kid Blackie," the budding boxer fought in
small towns all over Colorado. As Dempsey went on to capture the Heavy-
weight Championship of the World, author Damon Runyon dubbed him
"The Manassa Mauler," after the town where the champ grew up.

The sleepy town of Manassa in southern Colorado has never forgotten its favorite son. In summer 1999, in front of the museum, local
sculptor Bob Booth unveiled a life-size bronze likeness of Jack Dempsey

in a fighting pose. Dedicated to Dempsey's mother, to whom he lovingly gave credit for raising him with strong values, the sculpture honors a small-town kid who made it big. As the guest book in the museum attests, supporters from all over the world have made the pilgrimage to his hometown. Well off the beaten path, Manassa hopes to continue luring fight fans here with this statue that immortalizes the power and grimace of a backwater fighter who became an American hero.

The Jack Dempsey Museum is open 9 A.M. to 5 P.M. Memorial Day through the end of September. There is no admission fee. It's located on CO Hwy. 142 in Manassa, south of Alamosa. Call the Manassa Town Hall for information. 719-843-5207; www.museumtrail.com/Jack DempseyMuseum.asp.

BEST Cultural Crossroads
Fort Garland Museum

The West of the 1800s was in flux. Lands traditionally held by Native American tribes were changing hands from the Spanish to the Mexicans to the Americans. Historical forces brought them all together in a restless mix of competing interests. Over a period of twenty-five years, from 1858 until 1883, Fort Garland became a cauldron of cultures in Colorado's San Luis Valley. Today, within the original thick adobe walls of this old Western outpost, a museum tells the story of the last surviving nineteenth-century military fort in Colorado.

Entering each building of the four-sided fort visitors explore detailed dioramas, maps, and displays of historic artifacts. Troops from Fort Garland fought in the Battle of Glorieta Pass, saving Colorado for the Union in the Civil War. The famous scout Kit Carson commanded Fort Garland in 1866 and 1867. And the museum sheds light on an often-overlooked chapter of the American West: the all-Black regiments that became involved in the Indian campaigns following the Civil War. The 9th Cavalry was stationed at Fort Garland from 1875 through 1879, where it served the U.S. Army with distinction. Indian foes regarded the Black troops' skills with respect, calling them "buffalo soldiers." Several buffalo soldiers received Congressional Medals of Honor for their service.

The Fort Garland Museum today is home to a summer program where the cross-cultural tradition carries on. Urban kids come to live for a time in this rural setting to learn about other people, history, and life in the San Luis Valley. The museum is an important cog of Los Caminos Antiguos Scenic Byway. The bookstore contains an impressive collection of books about the West. It's located in the town of Fort Garland just south of the intersection of U.S. Hwy. 160 and CO Hwy 159 between Walsenburg and Alamosa. 719-379-3512; www.loscaminos.com/fort garland.html.

Outdoor Activities & Events

expert pick

Top Five Peaks
Gerry and Jennifer Roach

Gerry has climbed the world's highest peaks on every continent on Earth, including Mount Everest. His book *Colorado's Fourteeners* (Fulcrum Publishing, 1999) is a classic. Jennifer has the distinction of climbing every 13,000-foot peak in the state. Along with Gerry, she has written *Colorado's Thirteeners* and *Colorado's Lost Creek Wilderness: Classic Summit Hikes* (Fulcrum Publishing, 2001). More detailed information on their "Top Five Peaks" can be found in these books.

▸▸ **Longs Peak (14,255 feet)**—Dominating all within sight of it, Longs Peak is the monarch of northern Colorado's Front Range. Longs is the highest peak in Rocky Mountain National Park and is also the northernmost Fourteener in Colorado and the Rocky Mountains. Its summit attracts thousands of people each year, and Longs is one of the most popular peaks in the western United States. The reason for its popularity is its tremendous east face, which enraptures all but the most heartless soul. Longs has many routes, and the easiest—the Keyhole Route—is a full-day hike and scamper that has challenged many feet.

▸▸ **Bison Peak (12,431 feet)**—While 14,000 feet is magic elsewhere in Colorado, 12,000 feet is magic in the Lost Creek Wilderness. Only forty miles southwest of Denver, Bison Peak is the highest peak in the Tarryall Mountains and the Lost Creek Wilderness. It carries this honor well and is justifiably popular. Bison's large summit area is festooned with picturesque Jurassic rocks. Good trails reach high on the peak, and Bison is not hard to ascend. If you have climbed all of Colorado's Fourteeners but have never ascended Bison, make it your next outing.

▸▸ **Mount Massive (14,421 feet)**—Colorado's second highest peak, Mount Massive, is eleven miles southwest of Leadville, and together with Colorado's highest, nearby Mount Elbert, this is Colorado's apex. While Elbert is a few feet higher, Massive is massive, and the mountain's name captures its essence. Unlike Elbert, Massive is in the Collegiate Peaks Wilderness and has five summits above 14,000 feet on a three-mile-long summit ridge. Massive is not just a peak; it is a region. If Massive were truncated at 14,000 feet, the area of the resulting plateau would be nearly half a square mile! No other peak in the forty-eight contiguous states has a greater area above 14,000 feet, and by this measure, Massive reigns supreme. A good trail leads up Massive's east slopes, and the ascent of this giant is a long, rewarding hike.

» **Mount Adams (13,931 feet)—** Shapely Mount Adams is a few miles north of the famous Crestones in the central Sangre de Cristo Range. Compared to the majestic Crestones, Adams offers a relatively easy ascent via a variety of routes, but remember that Adams's ease is

The snowy shoulders of Mount Massive, Colorado's second highest peak, tower over the headwaters of the Arkansas River.

PHOTO BY BRUCE CAUGHEY

relative to some of Colorado's hardest peaks. Adams's slopes are still steep, and a distinctive summit cap guards the summit. Adams is usually climbed with a backpack to Horn, Willow, or South Crestone Lake, but for the fit, it makes a nice day climb.

» **Jagged Mountain (13,824 feet)—**Jagged is in the appropriately named Needle Mountains, which are some of Colorado's most rugged and remote peaks. Surrounded by miles of the San Juans's wildest country, Jagged is the most remote of Colorado's highest peaks, and Jagged is usually done with a backpack. Climbing Jagged is a combination of a sublime wilderness approach and a steep, serpentine climb that sometimes turns technical.

BEST River Rafting
Arkansas River

Technical, steep, and continuous rapids through huge boulders in the Pine Creek section of the upper Arkansas River leave no margin for error. Make a mistake in this Class V white water and the consequences are severe. But you do have alternatives. In an outdoor sport that classifies its degrees of difficulty by how likely you are to damage your health if you mess up, rafters flock to the Arkansas for good reason. For every terrifying, exciting Class V run such as Pine Creek, the Numbers, or the Royal Gorge, long sections of more moderate Class II and III waters attract floaters of all abilities. Add scenic beauty, easy accessibility, and incredible variety and you have one of the premier rivers in the country for white-water rafting.

From narrow canyons where the view goes straight up to wide vistas of the Collegiate Peaks and the Sangre de Cristos, the Arkansas River cuts a silver swath through Colorado's midsection. Some of the state's pioneer river outfitters set up shop along its banks, offering anywhere from half-day to multiday adventures.

Just as soon as winter's snow starts melting from high peaks and valleys, you'll find someone paddling on the Arkansas. Anglers take to the river in early May during the famous caddis hatch. With the warming weather, these flying bugs fill the air, providing brown trout with a ready meal. Around mid-June, Salida's long-running "FibArk" river festival celebrates the region's lifeline with a weekend of music, arts and crafts, and races on the river.

Rafters negotiate rapids of the Arkansas River just north of Buena Vista. PHOTO BY DOUG WHITEHEAD

The Arkansas Headwaters Recreation Area regulates use of the river and provides put-in and take-out facilities along the 148-mile stretch from Leadville to Pueblo. Call 719-539-7289. The Arkansas River Outfitters Association lists member outfitters. Check out their Web site at www.aroa.org.

BEST Single-Track Biking
Monarch Crest Trail

On trails once traversed only by foot, mule, or horseback, Colorado's backcountry today is made accessible by the ubiquitous mountain bike. It's the conveyance of choice for a whole new generation of lovers of the outdoors. Quite a few books are available that document a web of trails all over the region, but we think one trail is hill and dale above the rest for beauty, challenge, length, accessibility, and single-track purity: the Monarch Crest Trail.

Beginning at 11,312 feet on the summit of Monarch Pass, park your car, grab your bike, and hit the trail. Following the Continental Divide, the Monarch Crest Trail rises gradually at first through a forest of Douglas fir and ponderosa pine. The narrow path leaves just enough room for only one set of fat-tire tracks at a time. After a few short but steep climbs, you're already riding through rarefied air above treeline, trekking through fragile tundra that demands you keep your bike on the trail. One scar on this delicate, high-altitude landscape can take years to heal. Nearby 13,000-foot peaks come into view as your bike hugs the ever-rising contours of this awesome alpine ribbon. The higher the elevation, the wider the vista. Famous Colorado mountain ranges appear in all directions: the Sawatch Range, Sangre de Cristos, San Juans, and West Elks.

After fourteen miles in this top-of-the-world environment, you arrive at Marshall Pass, whose dirt road you follow down to U.S. Hwy. 285 and back to Poncha Springs. The amazing thing about this trail is that a family of intermediate ability can do this ride if they're not in a hurry, or a hot-shot mountain biker can cover it in a couple of hours. Mountain bikers should always defer to horses and hikers on the trail. Check with the High Valley Bike Shuttle in Poncha Springs at 800-871-5145; www.monarchcrest.com. They'll haul you and your bike to the top of Monarch Pass to begin the trail.

BEST Way to Lighten Your Load
Spruce Ridge Llamas Adventure Treks

Tired of hauling your camping gear into the backcountry? Well, let llamas do the heavy lifting. In fact, let Dan Jones and his llamas do all the work, so you and your family are free to hike, pack free, into the beautiful high country of south-central Colorado. Not only does Spruce Ridge Llamas Adventure Treks cook your meals, bring tents and sleeping bags, and provide a professional guide, you'll also learn to love the quirky personalities of the llamas, sure-footed beasts of burden originally bred to traverse the rugged Andes region of South America. Each trip is custom designed for your group or family, and the llamas quickly become your best friends. You may never want to carry that pounding weight by yourself again!

From Dan Jones's ranch just east of the Continental Divide near Poncha Springs, the llama treks set out in a variety of directions, from day hikes to four days out, leading into the heart of the Sawatch Range with its gaggle of 14,000-foot peaks. Follow the llamas up narrow trails to pristine lakes in lush mountain meadows or head up above timberline where the views open up to sweeping vistas of the upper Arkansas River Valley or the Sangre de Cristo range to the south. After your hike, camp becomes a welcome respite from an active day at altitude and you're probably as hungry as a llama. (They eat a lot of greens along the way to fill their three stomachs.) Thanks to the hauling ability of these good-natured members of the camel family, you fill your stomach with good, fresh, healthy food; no freeze-dried entrees here. Nighttime in your high-country camp is lit only by the stars and the flickers of your marshmallow-roasting campfire. Their rates are reasonable: kids ages six to twelve get in for half price and those who are five and under are free. They operate from June into October. Call Spruce Ridge Llamas Adventure Treks at 888-MTN-TREK. www.spruceridgellamas.com.

BEST Vertical Rock
Shelf Rd. Recreation Area (near Cañon City)

With knuckles taut and curled, a climber's hand grips a crack in the rock surface with nothing but his fingertips. Belly to the wall and neck craned upward, one leg swings carefully as his foot searches blindly for its next toehold. Sensing an infinitesimal perch, he pushes himself another six inches higher, spread-eagled like a spider on a sheer stone face. He is but a speck in a labyrinth of limestone canyons known to rock climbers around the world as the Shelf Road Recreation Area.

Given names such as Lizard with a View, Not So Killer Bees, and Primal Scream, hundreds of routes have been pioneered since the mid-1980s on cliffs called Sand Gulch, the Gallery, the Dark Side, and the Gymnasium, to name a few. Located in a banana belt, this climbing area in the piñon-and-juniper forest is accessible all year long. With an extensive network of cliffs and walls, climbers never feel crowded. A well-coordinated effort between aficionados of the sport and the Bureau of Land Management has led to more than 400 established climbing routes in this landscape between Cañon City and Cripple Creek. Expansion bolts strategically placed open up all manner of technical pitches, bulges, cracks, and slabs. Climbers spend little time getting to these easily accessible routes and most of their time climbing them.

The area is located about nine miles north of Cañon City on CR 9, part of the Gold Belt Tour Scenic Byway (see Best Collection of Scenic Drives on page 142). Bureau of Land Management campsites are available in the area, or more refined accommodations can be found in nearby Cañon City or Cripple Creek. Call the Bureau of Land Management in Cañon City at 719-269-8500. www.goldbeltbyway.com.

BEST Rock Scrambling for Kids
Penitente Canyon (near La Garita)

Hiking a short trail along the canyon floor, visitors to Penitente Canyon enter an enchanted world. Softly rounded rock formations billow like clouds to form the walls of this secluded playground. Volcanic ash from an ancient eruption around 30 million years ago hardened, creating the rough, but not loose, texture of these rocks. The perfect combination of good friction and steep, bolted routes attracts hard-core technical climbers from all over the world who scurry up with a single belay from below. But Alex Colville, a longtime local climber from nearby Del Norte, explains that Penitente Canyon is also a perfect place for kids.

"Kids can't get lost, you can always see them" in this readily accessed, flat-bottomed canyon, says Colville. Boulders of various sizes lie scattered about, offering all sorts of nooks and crannies easily explored by youngsters as young as three or four years old. As they get older and want to try climbing with ropes, kids find plenty of easy and moderate routes to practice on. Here you'll find one-stop shopping, a place to grow from beginner to expert. Be sure to keep an eye out for the now-fading image of Our Lady of Guadalupe painted years ago on one of the rock walls in Penitente Canyon.

Travel north from Del Norte on CO Hwy. 112 about three miles and follow signs on a dirt road toward La Garita and Penitente Canyon. There are no fees required to enter this Bureau of Land Management land. There are some camping spots near the parking area.

BEST Animal Sanctuaries
Mission: Wolf (near Gardner) and Indigo Mountain Nature Center (near Lake George)

Howls carry through the still air of an otherwise silent night, awakening primal memories of a wilderness lost. Wolves disappeared from many parts of the West years ago, but here in isolated country near the San Isabel National Forest, wayward purebreds and hybrids find refuge. They arrive here as washed-up "movie actors" from Hollywood or onetime pets to unsuspecting owners unaware that wolves cannot be domesticated. They live out their lives in dignity in acre-size fenced-in enclosures with the dedicated, passionate help of Mission: Wolf.

For years now, Kent Weber and his staff have made public education a top priority. Intrepid visitors to the remote Mission: Wolf site find a visitors center that provides a good introduction to this wild animal. A full-time caretaker escorts you around the property, where intimate encounters with more than forty resident wolves and wolf hybrids make an indelible impression with their stature, grace, strength, and beauty. From piercing eyes and noble countenance to huge, wide paws like snowshoes, it's a rare image of cunning

Six-week-old wolf dog pup Takoda enthusiastically greets Mara Whitehead at Indigo Mountain Nature Center. PHOTO BY DOUG WHITEHEAD

creatures ideally suited to range freely in a landscape today made inhospitable to them by pressures of the modern world.

Mission: Wolf is open to the public from 9 A.M. until sunset year-round. Camping is allowed. No admission fee, but donations are appreciated. It's located south of the small town of Westcliffe, or from CO Hwy. 69, it's located north and east of Gardner on dirt roads. For exact directions and educational opportunities, visit their Web site: www.mission wolf.com.

In addition to long-established Mission: Wolf, we also want to recognize Indigo Mountain Nature Center. Sue Cranston and Carol Scarborough worked for years at other refuges, helping to save wolf hybrids, bears, mountain lions, and other exotic captive-born wildlife. Not happy with how some of those places operated, they set out to do it better. Since 1997, these two dedicated women have been rescuing abused, abandoned, and neglected animals from around the country and bringing them to Indigo Mountain. Large, fenced-in enclosures in a natural landscape, similar to Mission: Wolf, provide a sanctuary where these animals can live out their lives in safety and dignity. Public tours are by reservation only. Indigo Mountain Nature Center is located south of Lake George off of U.S. Hwy. 24. Call them at 719-748-5550. www.indigomtn.org.

BEST Bird Spectacle
Monte Vista National Wildlife Refuge

It's an ancient call that echoes from snow-covered peaks. Still and silent mornings are pierced with the rusty honks of thousands of sleek birds on the wing. The scene evokes images of the great preserves of Africa. Every spring for millennia, the skies of the San Luis Valley in Colorado are filled with the migration of sandhill cranes. Wave upon wave arrive from Mexico as their feet droop down for a pterodactyl-like landing in the wetlands of the Monte Vista National Wildlife Refuge. During their two-month stay here along this time-tested flyway, the birds load up on abundant food sources in the valley as they prepare to continue the long flight to summering grounds in Idaho.

From late February until mid-April, Monte Vista is alive with this annual spectacle. The Monte Vista Crane Festival, on a long weekend in March, offers opportunities for naturalist-led tours, seminars, and workshops. With markings of red and black, the charcoal-gray cranes stand as tall as four feet. A delicate dance can be observed in the fields as they flutter and dip in their unique mating ritual. It's a rare sight to see this majestic crane with an eight-foot wingspan in flight. The Monte Vista National Wildlife Refuge is located at 6140 CO Hwy. 15 south of U.S. Hwy. 160. For information about the spring festival, call 719-852-3552. www.cranefest.com.

BEST Fossilized Bugs
Florissant Fossil Beds National Monument
(near Florissant)

Millions of years ago, Colorado's climate resembled a tropical paradise. Ancient mudflows created a huge lake, covering giant sequoias, cedars, and pines. Tons of ash trapped layer after layer of thousands of insects that thrived in the warm, humid climate. Almost like ancient photographs, exquisite forms of delicate bodies and wings are preserved on thin sheets of shale. More than 1,000 species of butterflies, caterpillars, spiders, and other long-gone bugs can be seen along with petrified redwood stumps and a huge variety of cones, leaves, flowers, and twigs. It all contributes to this world-renowned snapshot of a onetime Colorado swamp.

Geologists estimate there are probably eighty or ninety petrified tree stumps in the park, most of them still buried underground. The one-mile Petrified Forest Loop Trail takes you past stumps up to seventy-four feet around, and other trails meander through this natural park. In addition to the geologic history of the Florissant Fossil Beds, Adeline Hornbek's cabin, barn, shed, and root cellar preserve human history in the valley. This single mother brought her children here in 1878, becoming one of the first women in the West to take advantage of the Homestead Act. Take U.S. Hwy. 24 west from Colorado Springs to the small town of Florissant. Follow signs south to the fossil beds. 719-748-3253; www.nationalparks.org.

BEST Wheelchair Outdoor Experience
Wilderness on Wheels
(Pike National Forest)

Roger West spent a lifetime in the outdoors with his dad. When his elderly father became wheelchair bound, his heart sank. How would his father ever enjoy smelling the scents of the forest or landing a rainbow trout again? How could any physically handicapped person take part in outdoor activities the rest of us take for granted? Out of his grief, an idea was born. Now, for more than a decade, Wilderness on Wheels has provided the answer.

Visitors to Wilderness on Wheels enjoy an autumn stroll through the Pike National Forest. PHOTO BY DOUG WHITEHEAD

Built with lots of heart on years of volunteer labor and generous donations from places such as lumberyards and hardware stores, an eight-foot-wide boardwalk winds for more than a mile through the Pike National Forest on the south side of Kenosha Pass. With a gentle grade and numerous pullouts (sort of like scenic rest stops with picnic tables), people in wheelchairs work their way up the hillside, rolling past a mountain stream, casting a line into a fishing pond, or setting up camp in the pine forest. Quite a few tent platforms and two wheelchair-accessible cabins allow anyone to stay several nights in the woods. Wilderness on Wheels has also been discovered by once-active elderly folks who, even if it's with a walker, have a way to reconnect with the outdoors. All ages with every kind of disability find a sense of independence here.

One spur of the boardwalk descends to an outdoor amphitheater with a stage for concerts and room for 300 people to gather for an outside event. With boardwalks becoming increasingly popular, more and more physically handicapped people are gaining access to the outdoors. Wilderness on Wheels hopes to be a model for other efforts around the country and the world. Even though Roger West's father did not live to visit what his son created, the legacy of their bond will live on here for generations to come. Wildernees on Wheels is located 3.8 miles west of the small town of Grant on U.S. Hwy 285. 303-403-1110; www.wilder nessonwheels.org.

BEST Desert in the Mountains
Great Sand Dunes National Park and Preserve (near Alamosa)

The Great Sand Dunes lie in sharp contrast against the Sangre de Cristo Mountains.
PHOTO BY BRUCE CAUGHEY

It's a scene out of *Lawrence of Arabia.* Strong and steady winds blow over an ever-changing landscape of shimmering dunes of sand. Here the dunes lie thousands of miles inland surrounded by 14,000-foot snow-covered peaks. Great Sand Dunes National Park and Preserve lies at the base of the Sangre de Cristo Range on the eastern edge of the San Luis Valley.

Ages ago, the entire valley was a swamp. Today, with the water not very far beneath the surface of the ground, giant mounds of sand are held in place by the moisture. Constant wind currents run up against a wall of mountains, depositing airborne sand particles at this very spot. In the springtime, visitors to the dunes wade across the wide and shallow flow of Medano Creek. Every twenty seconds or so, it surges as constantly building dams of sand on the bottom of the creek can no longer hold, setting loose gentle waves of water downstream. Hikers then approach the dunes that reach up to 700 feet high. With each sliding step, the perspective of time and distance is lost in the shifting sands of undulating hills and dales as you climb ever so slowly toward distant ridges. Jumping, rolling, and sliding back down make it worth the effort.

In September of 2004, what was a national monument officially became Colorado's fourth and newest national park and preserve. The area's entire ecosystem is protected by recent land acquisitions in the mountains above and the valley below. One hundred eighty first-come, first-served campsites sit at the edge of the dunes, where deer, elk, and other wildlife also visit. Take U.S. Hwy. 160 west from Walsenburg to Hwy. 150. Go sixteen miles north to the entrance of the park and the new visitors center. 719-378-6399; www.nps.gov/grsa.

BEST Out-of-Place Reptiles
Colorado Alligator Farm (north of Alamosa)

A gaggle of gators wait to be fed as they bask in the thermal waters of the San Luis Valley. PHOTO BY DOUG WHITEHEAD

Mama, don't let your babies grow up to be ... alligator wrestlers! Lynne Young didn't follow that advice, but her son, Jay, doesn't seem to mind. In fact, he's pretty comfortable with the gaggle of gators that live outdoors at the Colorado Alligator Farm. These critters, more likely seen in a Louisiana bayou, may seem a little out of place in the San Luis Valley. That's precisely why they're such a novelty.

The alligators weren't intended to be the main attraction. The Young family raises tilapia here, a tropical perch consumed by people around the world. Alligators were brought in as garbage disposals to clean up dead fish and waste from processing. The same geothermal waters that make it possible for the fish to survive brutal Colorado winters also act as a kind of gator spa. A well produces water at a constant 87° F at this farm seventeen miles north of Alamosa, making it an ideal environment for these otherwise warm-weather creatures.

When locals became fascinated with the presence of alligators in their neighborhood, the Youngs realized they needed to cater to the public. You can feed the nasty-looking things and even get your picture taken holding a real live baby gator. The first alligator hatched in Colorado, Sir Chomps O' Lot, and other hatchlings can be seen here. Since they introduced the gators in 1987, the Young family has added iguanas, turtles, pythons, rattlesnakes, and even two sharks to its menagerie.

The annual Gatorfest attracts thousands of visitors on a summer weekend to see alligator wrestling, shark feeding, turtle racing, and other special events. You can even wrestle a gator yourself! There's a gift shop with all sorts of T-shirts and gator memorabilia. The Gator Farm is located at 9162 CR 9 about 17 miles north of Alamosa just east of CO Hwy. 17. 719-378-2612; www.gatorfarm.com.

BEST Thermal Waters
Cottonwood Hot Springs

After many arduous hours soothing, relaxing, comparing, and rechecking, we found the task of picking the "best hot springs" in a region almost flooded with thermal waters to be draining. Every avid soaker knows each place has its own personality; to each his own. But over recent years we've found the rock-lined pools of Cottonwood to be the most inviting. While the main building with its Old West wooden boardwalk and simple motel-style rooms is circa 1950s, the soaking is strictly twenty-first century, with New Age nuances.

They've put a lot of effort into improvements to the pools, grounds, and public changing rooms at Cottonwood. Five main pools, each with a different shape, size, and temperature, give you a choice. A creekside pool has been added, accessed by a stone stairway, mixing the cold waters of Cottonwood Creek with geothermal waters that come gurgling down from their source just above this spa at the base of the Collegiate Peaks. Several cabins are available along the creek, each with its own private soaking pool. In addition, there's a smorgasbord of modes of self-realization and body/mind techniques, including a dizzying array of massage. Cottonwood is comfortable—hardly upscale, which is precisely why we like it. If you want a different sort of experience, choose from Mount Princeton Hot Springs, Valley View Hot Springs, or Joyful Journey, which all can be found within about an hour's drive. Take U.S. Hwy. 285 to Johnson Village and go north on U.S.

Bathers warm up on a cold winter day at Cottonwood Hot Springs. PHOTO BY BARB WHITEHEAD

Hwy. 24 to the stoplight in Buena Vista. Find the springs by following the Cottonwood Pass Rd. west five miles to 18999 CR 306. 719-395-6434; www.cottonwood-hot-springs.com.

BEST Music Festival
Jazz in the Sangres (Westcliffe)

It started in a downpour. When a few jazz bands played from a flatbed wagon in 1984, the heavens opened up. Everyone crammed into the Feed & Seed Restaurant to get out of the rain, and the music played on. A few years later, the Big Tent went up in Westcliffe's Town Park—and weather hasn't been an issue since. On lawn chairs and blankets, about 1,800 fans gather every summer in the shadow of the Sangre de Cristo Mountains for an intimate weekend of Jazz in the Sangres.

The list of musicians who've played here over the years reads like a "Who's Who" of jazz: Spike Robinson, the Wallace Roney Quintet, Herbie Mann, Spyrogyra, "Sweets" Edison, Dotsero, Queen City Jazz Band, and Hot Tomatoes Dance Orchestra, just to scratch the surface. Beginning Friday night (with a simultaneous wine-tasting party) and continuing through the weekend, you'll hear every variation of this indigenous American music—traditional, Dixieland, swing, blues, and classical. As a long-standing tradition at the festival, "The Heavenly Echoes" belt out gospel tunes on Sunday morning with majesty to match the mountains. With a mix of local and regional acts and national headliners, Jazz in the Sangres attracts topflight talent. Musicians love the nine-foot Steinway piano that graces the stage, and the sound system always seems to carry the music loud and clear. Jazz fans mingle with musicians in the autograph tent, and artists from around the region display their works. With food and drink concessions and a playground for the kids, this is a well-organized family weekend of music.

Festivities begin with a free concert Friday night of the second weekend of August. For tickets , call 719-783-3785. www.jazzinthesangres.com.

BEST Snowcat Skiing
Monarch Ski and Snowboard Area

White, fluffy flakes pile up every winter on the Continental Divide at the southern end of the Sawatch Range. Monarch Ski Area has always been known for its abundant snow and small crowds, but now, thanks to snowcats, 900 acres of backcountry terrain make deep, untracked powder available to hard-core skiers and boarders in the Waterdog Lakes region of the San Isabel National Forest. Avoiding the chairlifts and groomed trails at this alternative to Colorado's mega-resorts, schussers and shredders drop a thousand feet on the runs of this private playground that gets almost thirty feet of annual snowfall.

With Crested Butte more than an hour to the west and Ski Cooper and the resorts of Summit County well to the north, Monarch sits like an alpine oasis in Colorado's winter paradise. Though the area makes for a good family outing with lower lift prices and uncrowded, easy, and moderate trails, its reputation for extreme snowboarding and skiing continues to grow. With the addition of snowcats to the scene, the smooth, soft, steep snow in more remote reaches of the area presents new challenges to hearty downhillers.

Reservations are required. The area is located on U.S. Hwy. 50 near the top of Monarch Pass, about fifteen miles west of Poncha Springs. 888-996-7669; www.skimonarch.com. (For other snowcat alternatives, check out Claudia Carbone's expert picks on page 179.)

Where to Eat, Drink, & Stay

BEST Real Mexican Meal
Calvillos Mexican Restaurant & Bar
(Alamosa/Monte Vista)

Here in the San Luis Valley, where so much history and heritage comes from south of the border, it makes sense the most authentic Mexican cuisine is truly Mexican. José Lopez and his family came to Alamosa from the city of Calvillo, Mexico. With only $4,000 they opened a small restaurant in 1997. News of their mouthwatering recipes spread by word of mouth. They moved to a bigger building, and today the reputation of Calvillos Mexican Restaurant reaches far and wide.

Order from the menu if you must, but the daily buffet teems with every spice and flavor you may crave. Freshly prepared food pours out of the kitchen. When one dish disappears from the buffet line, another new entree takes its place. Dine slowly to allow time for all the possibilities. Green chile, posole, relleno casserole, burritos, fajitas, chicken, beef, pork, guacamole, *pico de gallo*, salads, fruit, sopaipillas ... the list goes on and on. As José delivers shrimp to our table with three different sauces to taste, he regales us with stories of his mother's cooking when he was growing up. We try the shrimp scampi (a garlic and butter sauce), *la ranchera* (a mild spicy sauce with vegetables), and *a la diabla* (a zesty hot sauce). Each bite bursts onto our taste buds, a fiesta of flavor. We savor the seasonings and realize we're lucky to be the beneficiaries of that Lopez family culinary legacy. In fact, nearly 80 percent of the recipes come directly from the family's matriarch. José boasts of the ultimate compliment from a Mexican visitor: "This food is better than in Mexico!" We don't doubt it.

Calvillo's Mexican Restaurant is located at the edge of downtown Alamosa at 400 Main St. The buffet is open every day from 10 A.M. until 9 P.M. Breakfast is served at 7 A.M. Look for their other restaurants by the same name in Monte Vista and Center. Save room for dessert. 719-587-5500.

BEST Southwestern Fare
Emma's Hacienda (San Luis)

Because three generations learned to cook their tasty recipes right here in San Luis, they don't refer to their cuisine as "Mexican." They say they prepare their "food of the Southwest" the way they do at home: from scratch. We went back just to make sure just how good it is. In Colorado's oldest town, the town's oldest restaurant serves the region's best local fare. San Luis was founded in 1851, and for more than half a century a small brick building in the center of town has been home to Emma's Hacienda. On our latest visit, Emma Espinoza's granddaughter Yolanda was doing the cooking. "It'll stay in the family for eternity. We've got a pretty good start at over fifty years!"

We can attest to their consistency. The burritos, enchiladas, rellenos, tacos, tamales, and green chile are fresh, the flavors distinct. Ever since opening the restaurant in 1947, Emma has maintained her unwavering dedication to quality, roasting her own chiles and mixing in fresh tomatoes, herbs, and spices. So particular is Emma that she's been known to send a whole truckload of chiles back to New Mexico because they weren't quite right. The dishes at Emma's Hacienda leave a vivid, lingering taste in your mouth without a heavy feeling in your stomach. Sopaipillas, made from their own special dough and spread with homemade honey butter, leave a lasting impression at the end of your meal. The food at Emma's Hacienda always tastes good.

Spry and effervescent, well-dressed and always in high heels, eighty-something Emma still greets her customers like old friends, and many of them are. Even on your first visit, you'll feel like you're part of the family. 355 Main St.; 719-672-9902.

BEST Steak House
True Grits (Alamosa)

It doesn't look like much from the outside, but judging from all the parked cars, this is a popular spot to eat. Even inside, with basic decor and tables packed tightly together, you wonder what you're in for. But you can trust John Wayne. His pictures, omnipresent on the restaurant walls, testify to the hearty meal you're about to enjoy.

Order from a wide variety of steak combos, with shrimp or chicken or catfish as the second choice on your plate. When the salad arrives and the signature soda bread is placed on your table, you might think that's meal enough. The portions could satisfy "the Duke" after a long day in the saddle. But even his eyes would roll at the Texas-size steak and grapefruit-size baked potato that show up for the main meal. Somehow, of course, you find room for this Colorado beef and locally grown spuds. And after you can hardly move anymore, you're pleasantly surprised by the check. Prices are reasonable at this Alamosa institution. True Grits is located on U.S. Hwy. 160 on the east edge of town at 100 Santa Fe. Reservations suggested. 719-589-9954.

BEST Hydroponic Veggies at a Snack Bar
Sand Dunes Swimming Pool (Hooper)

Kind of silly, you say? Best concession stand? From years of experience as kids eating popcorn and candy from swimming pool snack shops, and now as fathers of kids, we can declare with authority this one beats them all. At this open-air pool filled with thermal waters with views of the Great Sand Dunes across the valley, the snack shelves are stocked with a dazzling array of every kind of chocolate bar, sucker, chip, soda, slushy, ice cream, frozen yogurt, gum, rope, cookie, and candy you dream of in your youth. But what really sets this place apart makes the most antisugar adult drool with delight.

The signature menu item at the Sand Dunes Swimming Pool is the tomato-and-cucumber salad. Grown in adjacent greenhouses heated year-round by the same hot water well that fills the pool, this hydroponic, organic produce is as fresh as you can get. We've also found for sale fresh chiles, peaches, and other Colorado-grown fruits and vegetables, when they're in season. In addition, you can choose from a full list of favorites, the quality far better than fast-food joints and greasy spoons: hamburgers, hot dogs, corn dogs, fries, onion rings, nachos, pizza, and more.

Take CO Hwy. 17 north from Alamosa to Hooper. Look for the sign just north of that small town and follow the road about two miles to the Sand Dunes Swimming Pool. You might as well take a dip while you're there. 719-378-2807; www.sanddunespool.com.

BEST Dining in the Boondocks
Tennessee Pass Cookhouse

You can't get there by car. In the winter, it's reached only by skis or snowshoes. Leaving the Piney Creek Nordic Center at the base of Ski Cooper near the top of Tennessee Pass, it's a good thing you work up an appetite on the moderate mile-long trail. Your stomach starts to growl as you glide through the trees of the San Isabel National Forest, and you can almost smell the four-course gourmet dinner-in-the-hills that awaits.

Hungry cross-country skiers await the first course of their high-altitude meal at the Tennessee Pass Cookhouse.
PHOTO BY DOUG WHITEHEAD

Arriving at a Mongolian-style yurt called the Tennessee Pass Cookhouse, you kick off you skis and take in the expansive view of the wild country spread out before you. As the sun begins to set, you enter the candlelit romantic ambience of the yurt and sit down to a soothing glass of wine. Sound good? That's just the start. Creative appetizers, fresh salads, and tempting soups are brought by attentive servers. No one seems to be in a hurry. You order your entree when you make your reservation. The food is hauled to the yurt by snowmobile, but everything is cooked fresh by chefs in the small kitchen of the cookhouse. The menu reminds us of fine dining in the city: Colorado rack of lamb with rosemary-pistachio pesto, baked salmon in tangerine teriyaki, oven-roasted chicken with wild-mushroom stuffing, and grilled elk tenderloin with blueberry, sage, and port wine. There's also a vegetarian choice available. For dessert, fresh fruit pies. When the meal finally comes to an end, the diners of the Tennessee Pass Cookhouse step outside into the brisk mountain air, strap on skis, and don helmets with headlamps to light their way back down the trail. On nights with a full moon, no artificial light needed.

From I-70 at Copper Mountain, take CO Hwy. 91 to Leadville. Head north on U.S. Hwy. 24 and follow signs to Ski Cooper. The Piney Creek Nordic Center sits just next to the parking lot of the ski area. Call the Tennessee Pass Cookhouse for reservations winter or summer: 719-486-8114. If you're not up for the hike, they'll take you up by snowmobile in the winter or by jeep in the summer. www.tennesseepass.com.

BEST Cheap Burgers and Malts
The Owl Cigar Store (Cañon City)

Pete Santilli was a pretty good poker player. Stationed in Italy during World War II, he sent his winnings back to his brothers in Colorado. When Pete got home in 1947, they had enough money to buy a Cañon City institution. The Owl Cigar Store has been in the family ever since.

Passing through town and sick of fast food? The most expensive item on the menu, a thick malt, costs only $2.50. At one time you could buy a hamburger for $.10, but today burgers are still a good deal, starting at $1.25. The hearty "Triple Triple," three patties and three cheeses, costs $2.30. You come here for the prices and the nostalgia. Sitting at the worn marble counter on a red swivel stool, you wish you could put a quarter in the old "Wall-O-Matic" jukeboxes, but they're only for decoration.

James Santilli reminisces about his brother Pete and the memories they created running Owl Cigar Store for more than five decades. PHOTO BY DOUG WHITEHEAD

There's more than a bar, a few vinyl-covered booths, and some pool tables. Mounted deer, antelope, and a bighorn sheep shot by long-gone patrons stare down from the walls. Big fish, historic photos, old advertisements, and dated license plates (one is from 1929) finish out the decor. This has been a local watering hole since the turn of the century.

Pete Santilli died in August of 2003. It was the biggest funeral they'd seen around here for a long time. His son and nephew run the place now. Daughter Susan still works behind the counter. Pete's brother James stops by most days. He misses his old business partner. "We did everything together, side by side, all our lives." Stop by, say hello to the family, and tip a malt for Pete Santilli. If you can't find The Owl Cigar Store in downtown Cañon City, just ask somebody. Everyone knows where it is. Smoking is allowed. 626 Main St.; 719-275-9946.

BEST Drive-in without a Car
Movie Manor (Monte Vista)

It's your basic Best Western Motel with nice rooms and decent rates, but Movie Manor, on the outskirts of Monte Vista, is unlike any motel in the world. As the sun goes down, you get your popcorn, turn up the volume, settle back, and wait for the movie to start. A drive-in? Well, yes, but you're not in your car, you're in your motel! With a speaker in each room and the big screen outside the window, guests simply open the curtain, watch the movie with sound piped right into the room, and then settle in for a good night's sleep.

George Kelloff remembers pumping a player piano at his mother's silent movie theater when he was a kid, so the movies are in his blood. He built the drive-in theater in 1955 and then got the idea to add the motel nine years later. Each door of all sixty rooms is labeled with the name of old Hollywood stars, such as Humphrey Bogart, Marilyn Monroe, John Wayne, or Ann-Margret. Posters and paintings of Hollywood's greatest decorate the walls.

Guests at Movie Manor can watch a drive-in movie screen from their motel room.
PHOTO BY DOUG WHITEHEAD

While drive-ins seem to be a vanishing American institution, Movie Manor may be the only place in the country that has actually added a second screen. Now, for the price of a room, the kids can watch a G- or PG-rated movie from the motel while Mom and Dad go outside, sit in the car, and watch an R-rated flick on a screen just out of view of the motel windows. Not a bad value.

The Foundation of Motion Picture Pioneers honored Mr. Kelloff with a Golden Movie Pass that gives him free access to any movie theater in America. Well into his eighties, he now lets his son run the business. But George says he loves being back where he started. During the summer, you'll find him selling tickets and threading the film. Movie Manor is located at 2830 W. U.S. Hwy 160 about two miles west of Monte Vista. 800-771-9468; www.coloradovacation.com/motel/movie.

BEST Small-Town Bed-and-Breakfast
El Convento (San Luis)

You don't have to be Catholic, or even religious, to stay overnight in this refurbished convent. From the 1930s until 1957, the Sisters of Mercy taught grade school and high school in this two-story historic building. In what looks like a class picture, a photograph of the nuns in their black-and-white habits hangs in a hallway. Today, the local parish runs El Convento as an inn, welcoming travelers for a good night's rest. Located next to Sangre de Cristo Catholic Church in San Luis, it's only a block from the trail that leads up to a hill above town following the Stations of the

Cross (see Best Religious Shrine on page 138).

Large windows and high ceilings allow light to pour into each of the four spacious rooms on the second floor of this building, built in 1905. With simple wooden furniture, wood floors, and hanging plants, these quiet lodgings feel like home. Two of the rooms include an adobe-style, nonworking fireplace for a little Southwest ambiance. You won't find a phone in your room, but you can watch TV. Walking down the steep staircase to the first floor in the morning, you smell the coffee brewing and breakfast cooking. Sit down in the dining room to your choice of juice, fruit, cereal, eggs, sausage, and toast. To get there, take I-25 south to Walsenburg. Go west on U.S. Hwy. 160 to Fort Garland and then south sixteen miles on Hwy. 159 to San Luis. Contact the rectory of Sangre de Cristo Church for reservations. 512 Church St.; 719-672-4223.

BEST Vestige of History in a Gambling Town
Imperial Hotel (Cripple Creek)

Back-to-back fires nearly destroyed Cripple Creek in 1896, but just as soon as the wooden buildings burned to the ground, the town was rebuilt brick by brick. With more than 25,000 residents and fifty-six passenger trains arriving daily in the world's richest mining district, a grand hotel rose from the ashes in the heart of this thriving boomtown. For more than a hundred years, the history of Cripple Creek has passed through the doors of the Imperial Hotel.

Around the turn of the century, industrialists, politicians, and celebrities enjoyed the opulence of the Imperial, one of the few places in the country to feature the modern convenience of electricity. Little at the hotel has changed since then. With no elevator, crooked staircases today lead to rooms on the second and third floors, some with shared bathrooms at the end of the hall and some with private facilities. Many of the original light fixtures hang from the ceilings; telephones and televisions are about the only contemporary appliances. Antique furniture, claw-foot bathtubs, and steam-heat radiators contribute to an atmosphere unchanged since Grover Cleveland was president of the United States and Albert W. McIntire was governor of Colorado. Though the classic rooms are clean and comfortable, the Imperial Hotel appeals to those looking not for the latest amenities but to experience an era gone by.

With a bustling casino, popular Friday and Saturday buffets, and a Sunday brunch, the Imperial now caters to gamblers hoping to strike it rich in the town that once produced great fortunes from the mines. It's located near the corner of 3rd St. and Bennett Ave. at 123 N. 3rd St. 800-235-2922; www.imperialcasinohotel.com.

SOUTHWEST

The world seems tinted blue in truth.
Sky, flowers, distant mountains all are stained with it.

—JAMES GRAFTON ROGERS,
FROM *My Rocky Mountain Valley*

White-capped peaks do glimmer in the rarefied air of the "Shining Mountains." Known by that name for centuries by the native Ute Indians, the
San Juan Mountains have long enticed people to their almost-incompre-
hensible dimensions, elevation, and grandeur. Raging rivers, high meadows, and immeasurable forests provided an abundance of wildlife to the
Utes, age-old caretakers of their pristine homeland. During a few short
decades in the 1800s, though, the Utes lost everything to white settlers'
thirst for gold. Today, the landscape lies riddled with the dramatic
accomplishments of an industrial invasion into these sacred hills. With
backbreaking labor, mine shafts were sunk and narrow-gauge tracks were
laid in seemingly inaccessible mountain locales so steam engines could
haul out the ore holding incredible wealth. Those old trails now provide
travelers with a way to explore the remote backcountry of the San Juans,
marveling at the achievements that fueled the growth of the United
States and changed forever the fortunes of the Utes.

The San Juan Skyway, a ribbon of road connecting much of this
region's resources, provides a continuous source of amazement as it loops
through high mountains and drops through river valleys. You can spend
all your time along U.S. Hwy. 550 in Ouray, Silverton, and Durango, but
that would be just scratching the surface! Enjoy a different festival every
week during the summer in Telluride or explore Colorado's third national
park, the deep-and-narrow chasm called the Black Canyon of the Gunnison. Wildflowers burst into brilliant colors in Crested Butte, Colorado's
official Wildflower Capital. The list goes on and on.

The burgeoning population of southwest Colorado has never
reached the numbers present in antiquity. The extraordinary remains of
the Anasazi, ancestors of modern Pueblo tribes, offer testament to a thriving culture. The ruins of Mesa Verde, Hovenweep, Chimney Rock, and
the Ute Mountain Tribal Park, along with similar sites in adjoining states,
reveal a highly organized, flourishing civilization. The abrupt end to the
Anasazi in A.D. 1300 remains a mystery to this day. The cliff dwellings,
towers, kivas, potsherds, and rock art left behind provide plenty of clues
but few answers. The wealth of nature and history in the San Juan Mountains of southwest Colorado can never be fully explored, not even in a
lifetime. But even one visit can spawn a lifetime of interest.

Cultural & Historical

BEST Walk among the Ancients
Ute Mountain Tribal Park (Towaoc)

A Ute guide climbs a ladder to reach remote ruins in Ute Mountain Tribal Park.
PHOTO BY BRUCE CAUGHEY

The most spectacular examples of the Anasazi cliff dwellings are found at Mesa Verde National Park, but the most intimate experience with the "Ancient Ones" comes at Ute Mountain Tribal Park.

A rugged landscape of flattops, cones, and needles stretches miles in every direction on your approach south from Cortez. As you travel a dusty road eastward, a Ute Indian guide points out potsherds that lie strewn across the canyon floor and rock art chipped out of the desert varnish on sandstone and shale. The slender Mancos River snakes its way through bottomlands lined with cottonwood trees. Then, rising to the mesa top, the road carries you through piñon-and-juniper forest to the brink of narrowing arroyos and canyons. From here, you tread the same paths, toe the same chiseled footholds, climb down the same steep canyon walls, and enter the same doorways of shelters once inhabited by the ancestors of modern Pueblo tribes. Fingerprints from builders remain pressed in adobe bricks. From this cliffside perch, you see similar homes in equally improbable locations tucked in shallow caverns up and down the canyon. The forces that bound people together in this unlikely neighborhood may never be fully understood, but your mind's eye is freer here to contemplate those ancient lives without the crowds of visitors found at Mesa Verde to the north.

To get here, take U.S. Hwy. 160 west through Durango to Cortez. Go south on U.S. Hwy. 160 through the small town of Towaoc, which is the tribal headquarters of the Ute Mountain Ute Indians. Continue south several miles to the small Ute Tribal Park Museum. You'll get an introduction to the park from the artifacts, photographs, and artwork in this one-room museum. Begin your guided tour here. Tours offered daily May through October. To make reservations, call 800-847-5485. www.ute mountainute.com/tribalpark.htm.

BEST Anasazi Tour
Trail of the Ancients (Cortez vicinity)

A thousand years ago, more people lived in the Four Corners region of the southwestern United States than call it home today. Evidence of a flourishing civilization, ancestors of modern Pueblo tribes, remains in canyons and arroyos, on mesas and mountaintops, along remote stretches of river, and on parched plateaus. What happened to the Anasazi? It's the biggest mystery of Colorado's past. The remains of their once-thriving culture are found across southwest Colorado and the Four Corners region. It's impossible not to wonder about the circumstances that led to these extraordinary communities and why they were abandoned around the year 1300. Tying many of the Colorado sites together for the modern motorist, the Trail of the Ancients Scenic Byway reveals a fascinating history, each place with its own unique story to tell about the ancestors of modern Pueblo Indian tribes. (Note: the term *Anasazi*, a traditional Navajo word meaning "ancient ones" or "ancient enemy," refers to the ancient Pueblo people. Many now use "Ancestral Peubloans" to refer to the occupants of these ancient archaeological sites. We use the terms interchangeably here.)

▸▸ **Mesa Verde National Park**—Mesa Verde can overwhelm your senses by the sheer scale and majesty of its architectural achievement. Designated a World Cultural Heritage Site by the United Nations in 1978, this national park contains extensive ruins of spectacular cliffside communities tucked into steep walls of rugged canyons. On Chapin Mesa, hike the self-guided trail to Spring House ruins, take the ranger-led visit to Cliff Palace, or take the challenge of the Balcony House tour, where rangers lead you up a thirty-two-foot ladder, through a twelve-foot tunnel, and up more ladders and steps to reach the ruins. The Chapin Mesa Museum provides a good starting point for your education here. Also consider making the drive out to Wetherill Mesa, where far fewer visitors venture. Rangers guide groups into more remote canyons to Long House and Step House ruins. The year 2006 marks the centennial anniversary of Mesa Verde as a national park. Look for special programs and events at the park and in the Four Corners region all year long. Look for the entrance near the town of Mancos on U.S. Hwy. 160 between Durango and Cortez. For park information, call 970-529-4465. Also try these Web sites: www.nps.gov/meve or www.mesa.verde.national-park.com.

▶▶ **Anasazi Heritage Center**—Continue west toward Cortez on U.S. Hwy. 160, then head north on CO Hwy. 145 to the small town of Dolores. Signs will lead you to this museum and research center, which was created when the nearby McPhee Reservoir was built. Before 1,600 ancient sites were flooded, more than 2 million artifacts were gathered, cataloged, and stored to provide a broad picture of the lives of these ancestors of modern Pueblo and Hopi Tribes. Hands-on opportunities and thought-provoking exhibits make this worth the visit. They ask only a small entrance fee. A twenty-minute uphill trail leads to ruins and views of McPhee Reservoir just above the facility. 27501 Hwy. 184 in Dolores; 970-882-5600; www.co.blm.gov/ahc.

▶▶ **Lowry Pueblo**—From Dolores, take CO Hwy.184 west to U.S. Hwy. 491. Go north to Pleasant View and follow signs west about nine miles to this national historic landmark. Surrounded by wide-open ranch land, you'll see the Great Kiva, one of the largest of circular ceremonial structures to be found in the Four Corners region. Forty rooms sitting three stories high once housed a community here. The unique Painted Kiva survives with several layers of murals preserved on its walls. Lowry Pueblo is part of the Canyons of the Ancients National Monument with headquarters at the Anasazi Heritage Center (see listing above).

▶▶ **Hovenweep National Monument**—Take the McElmo Canyon Rd. west from Cortez into Utah and follow signs to Hovenweep, which straddles the Utah-Colorado border. A footpath follows the rim of a gentle arroyo along which Square Tower Ruins lie. This gathering of castlelike structures strikes a mysterious pose on a solitary landscape. Chances of meeting large crowds here are slim, allowing a more private encounter with the past. Check the bulletin board at the visitors center for daily nature programs. Several other Hovenweep sites can be accessed by trail or by dirt road back across the Colorado border. Call 970-562-4282. www.nps.gov/hove.

▶▶ **Ute Mountain Tribal Park**—From Cortez, go south on U.S. Hwy. 160 past tribal headquarters at Towaoc to the Ute Mountain Tribal Park. (See Best Walk among the Ancients on page 168.)

▸ **Crow Canyon Archaeological Center**—Just north of Cortez on U.S. Hwy. 491, a sign will point you a mile west to this place where daylong and weeklong programs offer amateurs a chance to join ongoing archaeological digs at various Anasazi sites. (See listing below.)

BEST Way to Dig into the Past
Crow Canyon Archaeological Center (Cortez)

As you carefully brush away the dirt, layer by layer, a faint pattern appears in the ground. It's the fragment of a design painted on a potsherd, a small piece of the ancient puzzle you are helping to reveal. Your eyes are the first to gaze on this work of art, crafted by human hands, in at least 800 years. That simple yet profound act of archaeology can overwhelm your mind with more wonder about the past than a library full of books. Crow Canyon Archaeological Center offers anyone, not just scholars and professionals, the chance to make that direct connection to lives of antiquity.

Students master the ancient art of throwing an atlatl, a weapon once used for hunting game. PHOTO BY DOUG WHITEHEAD

Crow Canyon is a research and educational institution that organizes digs at various sites throughout southwest Colorado to continue the search for knowledge about the ancestors of modern Pueblo Indian tribes. They encourage the public to take part in their projects. Archaeologists teach basic skills to students, families, groups, and individuals, allowing them to become part of the team in programs that last a day or up to a week in duration. Digs can last for several years or longer, each project with a particular research goal in mind. Practicing what they call "conservation archaeology," Crow Canyon then fills the site back up with dirt at the end of the project, leaving the land as it was when they began. In that way, the resources are protected for future archaeologists who will be armed with more advanced technology and research techniques.

Back on the Crow Canyon campus, participants take classes, meet at the lodge for homemade meals served cafeteria style, and stay overnight in dormitories or hogans, which are small Indian-style cabins. The quality of teaching and the richness of subject matter combine for an intense and rewarding learning experience. What you take away here will enhance your travels to other Anasazi sites in Colorado and the Four

Corners region. Call Crow Canyon Archaeological Center in Cortez to learn more about the programs they offer. 23390 Rd. K in Cortez. 800-422-8975; www.crowcanyon.org.

BEST Archaeo-Astrology Site
Chimney Rock Archaeological Area
(West of Pagosa Springs)

Two rock towers rise high above the valley floor, prominent landmarks for travelers both modern and ancient. Today, we're pulled by our imaginations to the ruins that surround these pinnacles, full of questions about the people who came here for reasons we will never fully know. Led by interpretive guides, we explore what's left of stone walls, the remains of a community built by those who ventured away from abundant water and fertile lands below to occupy this much more inhospitable elevation. Why?

For all the theories, the most intriguing explanation speaks of a celestial phenomenon called the "Lunar Standstill." Astute observers of the skies, the Ancestral Puebloans followed the rhythms of heavenly bodies, including the moon. They knew it took about eighteen years for the moon to complete a giant round-trip journey across the night sky, arcing from south to north and then back again. Nearing the one-way end of that sweep and about to begin its return in the other direction, the moon seems to "stand still." At its northernmost point, the moon comes to "rest" in the window created between the twin spires of Chimney Rock. Visitors to this place follow a narrow path that rises along a rocky spine up to the area's highest structure. The Great House Pueblo was built the same time as the Lunar Standstill that began in 1076. Archaeologists say an addition to the original structure dates to 1094, exactly eighteen years later, at the completion of the cycle.

The twin spires of Chimney Rock rise above the Piedra River in southwest Colorado. PHOTO BY DOUG WHITEHEAD

What significance did the Anasazi give to that event? Is it just coincidence that the Great House Pueblo and its addition were built precisely during the years of this phenomenon? Was it the venerated keepers of that sacred knowledge who created a monument to this vital occurrence, protecting their own status as sage leaders? Ask yourself these questions when you visit Chimney Rock. Take U.S. Hwy. 160 west from Pagosa Springs, go south a few miles on CO Hwy. 151, and follow signs to the visitors center. Guided tours through September are reasonably priced. May 15 through September 30, call 970-883-5359. www.chimney rockco.org.

BEST Mountain Drive
San Juan Skyway (Ouray, Durango, Telluride)

This wide loop of paved highways would take about six hours if you drove nonstop, but the trip will be so much better if you give yourself a lot more time. Circling the circumference of the heart of Ute Indian homelands, the San Juan Skyway passes through some of the most rugged and scenic country in Colorado. Victorian mining towns and modern ski resorts, Anasazi ruins and bubbling hot springs, luxury accommodations and backcountry camping, and historic mountain passes with steep, winding descents all combine for a breathtaking, inspiring, almost-overwhelming journey.

This view from Dallas Divide can be seen along the San Juan Skyway. PHOTO BY BRUCE CAUGHEY

Leaving the hot-springs pool of Ouray behind, U.S. Hwy. 550 follows a route pioneered by Otto Mears, Colorado's "Pathfinder" who blazed trails in the 1800s. A series of switchbacks climbs past ruins of mines and mills surrounded by towering mountain peaks. The avalanche-prone road crests at 11,018 feet at the summit of Red Mountain Pass and drops down to Silverton, surrounded by the remains of mines and mills from the gold- and silver-mining days. The highway rises again over Molas Pass, passing Trimble Hot Springs and Durango Mountain Ski Resort. Then you enter Durango, capital of the Four Corners region and southern terminus of the Durango and Silverton Narrow Gauge Railroad (see Best Ride on the Rails on page 174). U.S. Hwy. 160 heads west past Mesa Verde (see Best Anasazi Tour on page 169) to Cortez, where CO Hwy. 145 begins its northward trek over Lizard Head Pass to Telluride, home to a thriving destination ski resort. The trip continues to Placerville, where CO Hwy. 62 heads back east over Dallas Divide, with its incredible views of Mount Sneffels to Ridgway, where Orvis Hot Springs lies just ten miles north of your starting point of Ouray.

With miles of hikes, four-wheel-drive roads, museums, mine tours, and much, much more, explorations along the San Juan Skyway could take a lifetime. The route is best enjoyed during the summer and fall months. Portions of the route are sometimes closed during winter. Chambers of Commerce: Ouray: 800-228-1876; Silverton: 800-752-4494; Durango: 800-GO-DURANGO; Cortez: 800-253-1616; Telluride: 800-525-3455.

BEST Ride on the Rails
Durango and Silverton Narrow Gauge Railroad

When the whistle blows, you can hear it all over town. Look for its source by the black smoke belching into the sky. Follow your nose to the hustle and bustle of the depot and climb onboard the historic railcars of the Durango and Silverton Narrow Gauge Railroad. Steam hisses, the whistle blasts again, and the coal-fired steam locomotive lurches forth to begin the forty-five-mile pull into the San Juan Mountains, all the way to Silverton, for one of the world's great scenic railroad adventures.

Smoke pours from a Durango and Silverton Narrow Gauge steam engine along the Animas River. PHOTO BY DOUG WHITEHEAD

From downtown Durango, the train snakes north along the Animas River through forested glades. Soon enough, steel wheels on narrow tracks hug the ledges of canyon walls high above the roaring river below. Following the same route that once saw precious ore being hauled out from the abundant mining districts farther north, you begin to sense the incredible manpower and chutzpah it took to construct this marvel of engineering. With coal cinders flying, passengers in both enclosed and open-air railroad cars gasp at the sheer drop-offs and stunning scenes that greet them around every twist and turn of the track. At times, the canyon is so narrow you can reach out and touch the rock. At other times, you're eye-to-eye with river runners as the train chugs alongside the white-water rapids of the Animas River. Mile after mile, the Durango and Silverton Railroad carries you through wilderness accessible only by track, river, or trail. After three hours, the train pulls into the depot of the hard rock–mining town of Silverton. Passengers flock to the souvenir shops, candy stores, and restaurants of this mountain burg that once hummed with the raucous comings and goings of miners blowing their dollar-a-day wages on a once-a-month furlough.

In the summer months, the round-trip from Durango to Silverton and back takes about seven hours. You can save some time by taking a bus one way and riding the train the other. The train operates in the winter for the two-hour trip from Durango to Cascade Canyon and back. To make reservations on the Durango and Silverton Narrow Gauge Railroad year-round, call 888-TRAIN-07. The Durango depot is located at 479 Main Ave. www.durangotrain.com.

BEST Boat Ride
Black Canyon Boat Tours (west of Gunnison)

This adventure begins on a stairway to paradise. Paradise is the majestic Black Canyon. First you descend 200 wooden steps following Pine Creek as it tumbles down to the Gunnison River. After you drop 1,000 feet to the canyon below, a great chasm looms ahead. Walk about a mile along the worn narrow-gauge railroad bed where the "Scenic Line" once carried nineteenth-century tourists. At the end of a leisurely trek, you board a boat, not a train, for this modern-day scenic excursion.

Between the Blue Mesa and Morrow Point Dams, the *Curecata II* slices through calm, cold green waters past steep, gray canyon walls. Under an azure Colorado sky, a cool breeze blows on faces turned toward the canyon rim high above. A tour guide describes how, for millennia, the river cut through this Precambrian rock, the world's oldest, on this journey through the basement of geologic time. Camera shutters whir as the open-air pontoon boat passes close to the spray of a waterfall that

Steep canyon walls loom high above the pontoon boat that leaves a wake in the smooth waters of Morrow Point Reservoir.
PHOTO BY DOUG WHITEHEAD

pours a silver stream from a rocky ledge. Anglers on smaller fishing boats show off their catch to the applause of passengers on this canyon cruise.

Then, rounding a bend in the river, the Curecanti Needle appears. This natural monument of stone, a trademark of the old "Scenic Line," juts into the sky as it dominates a breathtaking panorama already saturated with towering stone. The needle is easily seen from the canyon rim, but there's no substitute for the view from the river below.

The boat finally turns around and winds its way back to the dock. The hike out and up the wooden stairway leaves plenty of time to contemplate the wonders you have just witnessed. Black Canyon boat tours run from late May through August. For reservations, call the Elk Creek Marina on Blue Mesa Reservoir at 970-641-0402.

BEST Ghost Town
Animas Forks (north of Silverton)

Like so many other ghost towns from Colorado's past, there should not be much left of Animas Forks. Decades of long winters with heavy snows should have weathered these century-old buildings into the ground. Rusty nails, maybe a few bricks from a foundation, or the wooden planks of a sagging wall might have survived. But here many of the buildings still stand, in various stages of collapse, preserved for posterity, offering a glimpse of a fleeting yet intense moment in Colorado history.

Arriving in Animas Forks, you wonder how this town could exist in such harsh conditions at such high altitude in such a remote location. Exploring the ruins of mines and mills in surrounding valleys even higher up and yet more remote, you realize that this mountain hamlet was actually a thriving hub of activity, a capital of sorts for a flourishing mining district in the heart of the unforgiving San Juan Mountains. At more than 11,000 feet in elevation, nearly 500 people, two newspapers, plenty of saloons, and rock-solid determination made up this town in the 1870s. A landmark to that prosperity still stands in Animas Forks today. The bay window of a two-story house owned by a successful businessman in town overlooks the rushing headwaters of the Animas River. Because the structure has been shored up and stabilized by the Bureau of Land Management and the San Juan County Historical Society, visitors can once again stand in its living room and look through the window's three-paneled frame. Elsewhere in town, the jail survives, as do extensive remains of the buildings where raw ore was processed. The ore was delivered to this mill in buckets strung high on a cable that ran between a series of towers reaching far up to surrounding mines.

By the mid-1880s, Animas Forks was already in decline, but it died a slow death, because for some the dream of riches lingered for decades. The last full-time resident occupied an old house well into the 1940s. Preservation projects over the years have helped save many of the buildings. As mountain winds carry voices of the past through Animas Forks, this town will remain rooted in its hard rock–mining history for generations to come. Take U.S. Hwy. 550 south from Montrose through Ouray and over Red Mountain Pass to Silverton. Go through town and look for CO Hwy. 110, the well-maintained dirt road to Animas Forks. Take your four-wheel-drive vehicle about twenty miles to the ghost town. The route is drivable only in the summer months, but can be accessed by snowmobile in the winter. Get more information by calling the Silverton Chamber of Commerce. The visitor center is located at the intersection of U.S. Hwy 550 and CO Hwy 110. 800-752-4494; www.silvertoncolorado.com.

BEST Stagecoach Ride
Mancos Valley Stage Line

Steel-rimmed wood-spoke wheels spin faster and faster. The coach picks up speed down the rough and steep "Devil's Dive." Dirt and dust kick up from the hooves of four horses in full gallop as they pull your stage along a rutted road. Hold on tight for this bump-and-rumble ride. Finally, the road levels out past a dilapidated barn and old wooden silo. Riding the Mancos Valley Stage Line is just like the real thing.

Operating in a distant corner of southwest Colorado since 1994, Dennis and Carole Bartels make the experience as genuine as possible. They've done a lot of research into the old stage lines. Their thirty-something-year-old son, Eric, decked out in cowboy hat, boots, and duster, sits up top, driving a team of horses as he regales you with stories from the historic Overland and Butterfield Routes. The coaches are built by Will Stone, a local man from Mancos whose attention to detail produces authentic reproductions of stagecoaches from the 1800s. You can choose several different rides. There's a one-hour trip or you can sign up for the two-and-one-half-hour Lunch Tour. The latter follows a county road for five miles into remote Weber Canyon, where wild turkeys trot through the piñon-and-juniper forest. You arrive at an old homestead with a chicken coop, stables, and other outbuildings. Two bachelor brothers also built tiny cabins where each of them lived in the 1800s. To these weathered structures the Bartels family has added a rustic log cabin where lunch is served: sandwich and a salad. Later in the day, you can take the Sunset Steak Dinner Tour and they'll whip up a hearty steak-and-potatoes dinner in this Old West setting. Nearby, guests explore Anasazi ruins similar to those in adjacent Ute Mountain Tribal Park and Mesa Verde (see Best Walk among the Ancients on page 168 and Best Anasazi Tour on page 169).

Stagecoach passengers hang on for an authentic ride into Weber Canyon. PHOTO BY DOUG WHITEHEAD

The Mancos Valley Stage Line operates from May through September. The office is 4.5 miles south of the town of Mancos on CR 41. 800-365-3530; www.thestagecoach.com.

BEST Indian Museum
Ute Indian Museum (Montrose)

In 1880, the Utes were officially removed by the U.S. Army from their homelands in the young state of Colorado—despite a federal treaty guaranteeing their ownership of tribal lands. Chief Ouray died earlier that year. He had lived the final year of his life with his wife, Chipeta, on a homestead near the present-day city of Montrose. The Ute Indian Museum occupies that site today.

A monument to Ouray and Chipeta was erected by the State of Colorado in 1926. It sits on the grounds of this museum, which contains one of the most extensive collections in the United States concerning one particular tribe. In recent years, the Ute Indian Museum has undergone a renovation of spirit and space. The building has been expanded and improved, and the museum's mission has new energy from its director, C. J. Brafford, a Lakota Sioux. Brafford's Native American heritage enables her to offer authentic interpretations of Ute history. Their story is honestly told through exquisite artifacts and thought-provoking exhibits. You'll see ceremonial garb the controversial Ouray wore during negotiations in Washington, D.C. He was empowered by the U.S. government to represent the Ute Nation, even though the various bands of the tribe did not themselves recognize his authority to do so. He was, however, a respected and powerful leader. In addition to his story and Chipeta's, you'll learn about traditional life, such as the Bear Dance, one of the oldest continuous ceremonies of the Ute people.

The story of the Utes is woven into the fabric of the mountainous terrain of southwest Colorado. For the first time in history, flags of the three Ute tribes—Southern, Ute Mountain, and Northern—fly together in unity, carrying the Ute story into the future. The museum is open year-round; hours are shorter in the winter. A regular series of educational programs is offered. The museum is also home to the Montrose Visitor Information Center, so stop in for all you need to know about the area. The museum is located a few miles south of Montrose, just off of U.S. Hwy. 550, at 17253 Chipeta Rd. 970-249-3098. Check the historical sites section of the Colorado Historical Society Web site: www.coloradohistory.org.

BEST Navajo Weavings
Toh-Atin Gallery (Durango)

When Jackson Clark went to work for the Durango Pepsi-Cola distributor in the mid-1950s, one of his first accounts was the Two Grey Hills Trading Post on the Navajo Indian Reservation in northern New Mexico. He noticed some beautiful weavings in a back room. Trading soft drinks for rugs, he returned home with a carload and, in one night, was able to sell the traditional, handcrafted works to friends. Thus began a relationship that created a gallery that has grown into one of the top dealers in the world for Navajo weavings.

Weaving styles had been identified for years by the trading post from which they came, but the Jackson family started to distinguish the individual artists. As a result, names such as Helen Begay and Mae Jim, among others, have become nationally known in the world of Navajo art. The Toh-Atin Gallery eventually branched out to include all kinds of Native American art. The pottery of Maria Martinez rekindled recognition of pottery as an art form. The jewelry of Ben Nighthorse Campbell was represented at Toh-Atin long before he became a U.S. senator from Colorado. In a stunning array of color, texture, form, and medium, rugs, baskets, kachinas, jewelry, sculpture, paintings, and other fine art now fill the gallery with works by top artists in their fields.

Today, the Toh-Atin is run by Jackson Clark Jr. and his sister, Antonia. Traveling with their father while they were growing up, they acquired a knowledge and respect for Native American art unsurpassed by any other dealer. The gallery is located at 145 W. 9th St. in Durango. 800-525-0384. Just around the corner, Toh-Atin's Art on Main carries prints and posters, greeting cards, and even Western clothing. It's located at 865 Main Ave. www.toh-atin.com.

Outdoor Activities & Events

expert pick

Top Snowcat Operators
Claudia Carbone

We decided to ask Claudia Carbone, the author of *Women Ski* (World Leader Corporation, 1996), about her favorite snowcat ski escapes. An indefatigable skier herself, Carbone shot back within a few days with a list of her favorite snowcat operators. Any of these three companies will make absolutely sure you get the most out of every moment, whether it's the camaraderie in the cat or savoring the experience of schussing downhill without the hum of the ski lift or anyone else in sight. This wholesome activity pleases every sense, leaving you exhausted and dreaming of your next backcountry excursion.

Every ski season, passenger snowcats prowl the mountains from Steamboat to the San Juans, carrying adventure seekers to the best powder stashes in the state. As the organizer for my powder pals, I pick operations where I know the cats will be comfortable, the terrain challenging, the guides knowledgeable, and the snow soft and deep. That last part isn't always easy, because not all powder trips yield freshies and face shots. Weather is the ultimate decider. Nevertheless, I do have my favorites.

Powder hounds ski unbroken snow on Chicago Ridge at Ski Cooper atop Tennessee Pass. PHOTO BY DOUG WHITEHEAD

Number one is the San Juan Ski Company based at Durango Mountain Resort. Spread out over 35,000 acres in the rugged San Juan National Forest, it is the largest cat-ski operation in the state. With that much room, owner Bob Rule promises that we never have to cross another person's tracks. 800-208-1780; www.sanjuanski.com.

A close second is Chicago Ridge Snowcat Tours at Ski Cooper outside of Leadville. The cat climbs as high as 12,600 feet on top of the Continental Divide, and the open-bowl skiing from there is as delicious as poof powder can get. 719-486-2277; www.ski cooper. com/chicago. (For more information about snowcat skiing at Monarch Ski and Snowboard area, see page 160.)

BEST White-Water Adventure
Upper Animas River (Silverton)

When the snow starts melting in the San Juan Mountains, the hearts of river runners begin to pound. Gathering momentum as it flows south from the Victorian mining town of Silverton, the Animas River drops faster and steeper than almost any other river in the state. Adventurers on rafts and kayaks float for two days and twenty-eight miles on almost-unending white water through spectacular Colorado scenery.

The roar of the rapids is overpowered only by the wail of the whistle as the Durango and Silverton Narrow Gauge steam locomotive winds its way alongside the river. Fourteen-thousand-foot peaks loom overhead as rafts splash through bellowing waves of water and bounce through seemingly impenetrable gardens of rock. Several stretches of the most difficult white water challenge even experienced river guides, who know there is no room for error in these rough waters. The precarious course through No Name rapids takes the skill of an expert to negotiate the powerful forces of the river through a narrow drop of giant boulders. At the halfway point, rafters camp for the night in remote surroundings at Needleton. No road exists anywhere near this backcountry. Next day, the big rapids of Broken Bridge and Soda Pop Falls await any flotilla of river rats bold enough to tackle one of the wild rivers of the West. The canyon finally becomes so narrow that rafts can no longer pass through, requiring takeout at Rockwood, almost thirty miles north of Durango. The train stops to let the river runners load their gear on a freight car and then hop onboard to ride the rails the rest of the way out. We went with Mountain Waters Rafting in Durango at 800-585-8187. Their Web site is www.mtnh2o.com. Find other outfitters by logging on the Colorado River Outfitters Association Web site at www.croa.org, or call 303-280-2554 for a brochure.

BEST Single-Track Mountain Biking
Gunnison National Forest

Step out the door, hop on your mountain bike, and within a few blocks you're riding a section of what some believe is the best 900 miles of single-track trails anywhere. Of all the roads that lead to Crested Butte, only one is paved. The rest are dirt trails over mountain passes and ridges connected by a web of single-track paths, many developed by mountain-biking pioneers.

Bicyclists ride single file along the Lower Loop Trail just outside of Crested Butte.
PHOTO BY DOUG WHITEHEAD

A short twenty years ago, hard-core locals started riding their one-speed Schwinn clunkers for thrills downhill. Since those legendary early days of the sport, mountain-bike technology has made quantum leaps, enabling riders to venture farther into sometimes-challenging and always-spectacular terrain.

The Upper Loop trailhead at Crested Butte Ski Area careens down a couple of steep drops through aspen groves, over a creek, and into miles of meadow filled with wildflowers and wide-open views. At the west end of Teocalli Ave. in town, the Lower Loop follows an old railroad bed toward the alpine scenery of the Paradise Divide. Check with local bike shops for extensive trail maps of the area.

Crested Butte holds the world's oldest Fat Tire Festival every June. The Mountain Bike Hall of Fame and Museum in town documents the rapid development of this ever-growing sport. Vintage bikes, photographs, memorabilia, and highlights of historic races and events fill this museum on Crested Butte's Elk Ave. The Hall of Fame inducts pioneers of the sport every year. The annual Pearl Pass Tour to Aspen each September is the oldest organized mountain-biking event in the world. For information, call the Crested Butte Chamber of Commerce at 800-454-4505. www.mtnbikehalloffame.com.

BEST Four-Wheel-Drive Adventure
Alpine Loop Scenic Byway (Lake City, Ouray, Silverton)

We have the '59ers to thank for the rugged network of roads that spread out like a spider web through the Colorado mountains. With the discovery of gold in 1859, fortune seekers were motivated to find the shortest distance between rags and riches. The routes they left behind to the high-elevation gold and silver mines are today bone-jarring passages offering entrance to an alpine world.

Harrowing stories of four-wheeling abound from mountain passes with names such as Black Bear, Imogene, and Ophir. But Engineer Pass and Cinnamon Pass in the heart of the San Juans cut the widest path. Both roads begin in the old mining town of Lake City. They follow two different routes through the high mountains to form a jolting loop that connects Lake City with the historic mining towns of Ouray and Silverton. The roads ascend past dilapidated ruins of once-thriving mining operations disintegrating from decades of harsh weather. On long, rocky, winding climbs to the tops of Cinnamon and Engineer, the intense blues and whites of the columbine, Colorado's state flower, are reflected in the summer sky and year-round snowfields at elevations reaching more than 13,000 feet. From the summits, a panorama of jagged peaks blankets the view for 360°. Both roads then descend to the ghost town of Animas Forks (see Best Ghost Town on page 176). From here, where creeks converge at the headwaters of the Animas River, the road continues past still more historic mines and on into Silverton. Above Animas Forks on the west side of Engineer Pass, an even more difficult and treacherous spur of the byway drops down into Ouray.

The Alpine Loop Scenic Byway is only passable by high-clearance four-wheel-drive vehicles for three or four months out of the year, from mid-June through mid-October. For more information, contact the Silverton Chamber of Commerce toll free at 800-752-4494; www.silverton colorado.com. Lake City: 800-569-1874; www.lakecityco.com. Ouray: 800-228-1876; www.ouraycolorado.com.

BEST White-Knuckle Drive
Black Bear Pass (Telluride)

In the San Juan Mountains, where treacherous four-wheel-drive roads outnumber paved highways by a long shot, Black Bear Pass claims the title "King of the Hills." The beginning of this notorious one-way passage to Telluride can be deceiving. The dirt road climbs quickly and easily enough from the top of Red Mountain Pass on U.S. Hwy. 550 (see Best Mountain Drive on page 173) to incredible vistas in all directions. Cresting the summit and rumbling down the west side past year-round snowfields gets a little dicey, but you probably aren't holding your seat in a death grip quite yet. As the faraway town of Telluride appears like Shangri-la in the valley below, you might still be wondering what gives Black Bear Pass its nasty reputation.

Suddenly and frighteningly, there's no turning back. Dirt road transforms to solid rock. The grade drops severely, following a once-meandering creek that now plunges abruptly in a torrent. Calling this the "Stair Steps," veterans of the drive stay in ultralow gear, tapping carefully on the brakes, inching their way down. Tires crunch and slide in a heartstopping descent as the driver directs the wheels precariously high on the edge, dodging disaster by keeping the transmission from being torn to shreds on menacing boulders in the middle of the road. Finally through the worst, you're immediately met with a series of sharp,

Black Bear Pass provides a challenge to four-wheelers near Telluride. PHOTO BY DOUG WHITEHEAD

steep switchbacks that demand the driver back up two or even three times to make it safely around each corner. Once again, catastrophe is averted by avoiding the sheer drop-offs at every turn.

Approaching the end of this white-knuckle adventure, stop and catch your breath in the cool mist of Colorado's longest waterfall, Bridal Veil Falls. The roar of water plummeting 325 feet somehow soothes the nerves for the final few twists and turns down to Telluride. Go with a tour operator first, then decide if you want to try it yourself. We recommend San Juan Backcountry in Silverton: 800-4X4-TOUR; www.sanjuan backcountry.com. Or Dave's Mountain Tours in Telluride: 970-728-9749; www.telluridetours.com. Local chambers of commerce can supply a list of other reputable outfitters: Silverton: 800-752-4494; www.silverton colorado.com. Ouray: 800-228-1876; www.ouraycolorado.com. Telluride: 800-525-3455; www.visittelluride.com.

BEST Natural Wonder
Wheeler Geologic Area (near Creede)

It's no Sunday drive to get here, but the destination inspires the awe of a parishioner. First recorded in the diaries of Spanish explorers carrying Christianity from Mexico deep into the New World, these monumental rock formations are unlike any others found in Colorado. A cathedral of stone is surrounded by dense spruce forest in the La Garita Wilderness near Creede. Tall spires and mosque-shaped domes made from ancient volcanic ash tower in the distance.

After a seven-mile hike, you finally turn a corner to be met with an extraordinary sight. Standing on a wilderness stage, a natural amphitheater created by eons of erosion through the soft volcanic "tuff" fills your view. High above, a jagged outline of rock extends across the horizon; below, deep crevasses widen out to an array of terraces, twisted and tortured conglomerations. As you explore what seems like a lunar surface, fragile rock crunches underfoot. Narrower grooves that carry small rivers of runoff fan out across an open expanse. Twenty-foot-high mounds of cementlike stone lie scattered, as if dripped from a volcanic cauldron of lava and frozen in place. A more serene mountain panorama falls away into the distance from this spectacular scene Teddy Roosevelt designated a national monument.

To get here, take U.S. Hwy. 160 to the town of South Fork in the San Luis Valley. Go north toward Creede on CO Hwy. 149 to Wagon Wheel Gap. Follow the dirt road about twelve miles to Hanson's Mill. From here, hike seven miles into the Wheeler Geologic Natural Area or continue another twelve miles on a rough four-wheel-drive road to the boundary of the La Garita Wilderness. Camping is allowed only in designated sites. No campfires. Call the Creede office of the Divide Ranger District of the Rio Grande National Forest at 719-658-2556.

BEST Canyon
Black Canyon of the Gunnison National Park

Sheer, narrow, dark, and deep. Powerful and grand. Cut by erosion more than 2 million years ago by the steady forces of the Gunnison River, this gash in the Earth's surface is, perhaps, one of the least-known natural wonders of the West. The Black Canyon of the Gunnison dwarfs those who venture to its jagged rims, where human figures shrink to a speck against massive walls that drop, at the highest point, 2,689 feet to the roaring river below. Golden eagles, red-tailed hawks, turkey vultures, and peregrine falcons negotiate the air currents of this canyon that has remained, with few exceptions, all but impassable.

The Black Canyon splits open a mesa top in rugged country high above the Uncompahgre Valley. The popular South Rim Rd. winds to a series of overlooks and nature trails that lead to the precipitous walls of the canyon. A hiker can walk through shoulder-high gambel oak unaware of the abrupt drop-off just strides away. Standing as if perched on an aerie, one beholds a scene too large to take in all at once. Peripheral vision competes with the view straight ahead as you strive to perceive unfathomable depths and faraway vistas at the same time. The East Portal Rd. follows a circuitous, 16 percent grade to the river near the park's southeast boundary. Many a car's brakes have burned on the way down, so use your lowest gear. The North Rd. traverses a more remote side of the Black Canyon, leading to equally stunning and fantastic views. Though no marked trails down into the canyon exist, a backcountry permit allows hikers to descend on primitive, winding routes best described by park rangers.

There are two campgrounds available at the Black Canyon, one on each rim. Stop at the visitors center on the South Rim for all the information you need, including maps and books. A half-hour video shown throughout the day reveals the sweep of geologic and human history in the canyon. In the fall of 1999, the Black Canyon of the Gunnison was granted new status, joining Mesa Verde and Rocky Mountain and becoming Colorado's third national park. The south entrance is fifteen miles east of Montrose from U.S. Hwy. 50; the North Rim can be reached from CO Hwy. 92 on an eighty-mile dirt road from Crawford. 970-641-2337; www.nps.gov/blca.

BEST Float Fishing
Gunnison Gorge

This could be the most beautiful, productive fifteen miles of river you'll ever get to fish. Located between the Black Canyon of the Gunnison National Park and the North Fork, this dramatic rock canyon creates isolated beauty and some of the best float fishing around. In addition to mere fishing, enjoy the many bird species and wildlife-viewing opportunities.

You can get to various points of this gorge by trail, but nothing compares with floating at the same pace as your fly, just waiting for a large trout to strike. The water flow can vary quite a bit—especially in May and June, thanks to the dams above—but even when the river is running high, the fishing can be good. Unfortunately, with many side canyons and little creeks, a quick rain shower can leave the river murky and the fishing slow going. But when it's raining clean, be on the lookout for deep pools, eddies, and riffles to throw your caddies, green drakes, or pale morning duns. If you catch the salmon fly hatch in June, nothing compares to the thrashing that occurs when you lay down a properly placed sofa pillow. Large rainbows and browns comprise most of the native trout on this Gold Medal stretch. A list of commercial outfitters with permits to operate in the Gunnison Gorge National Conservation Area can be found at this Bureau of Land Management Web site: www.blm.gov/ggnca/gorgeoutfit.htm.

BEST Scenic Reservoir
Taylor Park Reservoir (northeast of Gunnison)

Okay, so picking "most scenic" is like choosing "best pie" at the Cherry Pie Bake-Off. They're all pretty darn good. But we'll try. Winter never really quite goes away during summer high up on Cottonwood Pass. Melting snowpack in the alpine basin, which stretches all the way over to Taylor Pass, provides a constant flow of precious water to the Taylor River. Where the wide-open park cinches down into a narrow canyon, a small dam creates a large lake. Taylor Park Reservoir glistens under the white peaks of the Sawatch Range.

Sheer cliffs rise out of the water near the dam, reflecting their grandeur on the mirrorlike surface of the lake. Trolling in boats, anglers cast their lines in search of brown and rainbow trout and even kokanee salmon. But some aren't satisfied with anything but the famous Mackinaw trout, which reach sizes upward of twenty-one pounds. On the far side where the river enters the lake, fly fishermen work their way upstream for some more good fishing.

You feel as small as a drop of rain in a downpour in this high-altitude mountain bowl. Within a mile below the dam, Gold Medal waters produce rainbow trout so big that even a five-pounder is considered small by Taylor River standards! Farther downstream, several outfitters float the boulder-strewn river for some challenging white-water rafting.

Take the Cottonwood Pass Rd. west through Buena Vista over into Taylor Park, or take CO Hwy. 135 north from Gunnison to Almont and follow the Taylor River up to the reservoir. The Taylor Park Marina sits at the edge of the lake and offers bait and lures, boat rentals, and snacks. Several national forest campgrounds dot the area. The marina operates from mid-May through mid-October. 970-641-2922; www.taylorpark marina.com.

BEST Accessible State Park
Ridgway State Park (south of Montrose)

Even if it weren't one of the most accessible parks in the country for wheelchairs, Ridgway State Park would still rank as one of the best anywhere. Spread out in the Uncompahgre River Valley about twenty miles south of Montrose, the park sits between the San Juan Mountains to the south and the Cimmarons to the east. With Ridgway Reservoir as its centerpiece, this park acts as base camp for excursions into southwest Colorado's outdoors.

The modern design of Ridgway State Park encompasses a network of gently sloping paths and a total of more than 260 campsites dispersed in different areas of the park, the majority of them accessible to wheelchairs. Picnic areas, the swim beach, and visitors center can all be utilized by disabled visitors. The Dakota Terrace campgrounds are situated within easy walking distance just above the swimming area. An accessible fishing deck is especially designed for people in wheelchairs. From RV hookups and a camper-services building with laundry, showers, and flush toilets to fishing access on a specially designed trail along the river below the dam, there is very little here that wheelchair-bound campers cannot do.

Heading south on U.S. Hwy. 550 from Montrose, look for entrances to three separate areas of the park: Dallas Creek, Dutch Charlie, and Pa Co Chu Puk. 970-626-5822; www.parks.state.co.us. The Ridgway Marina can be reached at 970-626-5094. www.ridgway marina.com.

BEST Time to See Wildflowers
Crested Butte Wildflower Festival

Spring and summer don't last very long in the Colorado high country, so Mother Nature takes full advantage of what little time she has. Wildflowers bloom with a brilliance and intensity that sparkles in terrain already brimming with deep-blue sky, lush, green foliage, and silver-gray mountains. What people in Crested Butte have known for years, the Colorado legislature made official in 1989: Crested Butte was declared the Wildflower Capital of Colorado.

The unmistakable purple-and-white petals of the columbine, Colorado's state flower, spread throughout the aspen forests and high meadows, reflecting the majesty of surrounding snowcapped peaks. Every flower imaginable sets the hillsides ablaze with color: lemony yellow mule's-ear sunflowers, orange-scarlet gilia (hummingbirds love them), pink wild rose, blue lupine, and violet flax. For one week each July, the town celebrates its botanical abundance with the Crested Butte Wildflower Festival. Along with daily hikes and tours, experts offer workshops in everything from photography, butterflies, painting and drawing, herbal medicine, natural history, and gardening to slide shows, lectures, concerts, and the annual Wildflower Art Show and Sale.

With a variety of accommodations and a wealth of local restaurants (see Best Small-Town Dining on page 195), this onetime coal-mining town offers a weeklong feast for the senses at the Crested Butte Wildflower Festival. 970-349-2571;www.crestedbuttewildflowerfestival.com.

BEST Collection of Festivals
Telluride

Before other Colorado ski towns figured out what to do at the end of winter, Telluride was filling its schedule with a summer of festivals. With Bridal Veil Falls at one end of the valley, this is a picture-postcard setting for these gatherings surrounded by the jagged peaks of the San Juans. Here you can leave your car parked and take advantage of the gondola, the free public transportation that carries riders up and down between Mountain Village and the well-preserved town of Telluride. If you go for the four-wheeling, hiking, horseback riding, camping, climbing, and the like, don't let the festivals keep you away. They tell us that, with just a couple of exceptions, there's always plenty of room in town for visitors of all kinds. But the festivals can add a special, unique excitement to summers in Telluride. For the entire rundown, get in touch with the Telluride Visitor Center at 800-525-3455. www.visit telluride.com. Here are some highlights:

A happy couple ties the knot at the Telluride Balloon Festival. PHOTO BY BRUCE CAUGHEY

▸▸ **Telluride Bluegrass Festival**—Toes have been tapping at this four-day festival for more than a quarter century. Offering both traditional and modern music, the event has included Doc Watson, Emmylou Harris, Willie Nelson, Kasey Chambers, Tim O'Brien, Bela Fleck, and a host of nationally known artists. Held the last part of June. 800-624-2422; www.bluegrass.com.

▸▸ **Telluride Jazz Celebration**—Since 1976, hot jazz has been heating up cool mountain air with daytime performances outdoors at Town Park and nighttime jams in downtown clubs. Performers have included Leon Russell, Larry Coryell, and the Steve Nygaard Quartet. Held the first weekend in August. 970-728-7009; www.telluridejazz.com.

▸▸ **Telluride Blues & Brews Festival**—They call it "lots of blues, barrels of brews, and mountains of bliss." World-famous performers flock here for one of Telluride's fastest-growing festivals. Since the mid-'90s, the festival has seen performers such as B. B. King, Buddy Guy, Hazel Miller, Joe Cocker, and Blues Traveler. 866-515-6166; www.tellurideblues.com.

▸ **Telluride Chamber Music Festival**—For more than thirty years, this mid-August classical classic has begun with a free sunset concert surrounded by mountain peaks and ended in the historic elegance of the Sheridan Opera House. Ensembles, orchestras, bands, and more play at venues all over town. Tickets are available through the Telluride Visitor Center. 800-525-3455; www.visittelluride.com.

▸ **Telluride Film Festival**—After more than thirty years, this has become one of the world's most important film festivals. *The Crying Game, Bullets over Broadway*, and *The Piano* are just some of the films that have premiered in Telluride. Limited passes go fast, so get yours early. Free films are offered in an outdoor theater. Held Labor Day weekend. Call festival headquarters at 603-433-9202. www.telluridefilmfestival.org.

BEST Agricultural Festival
Olathe Sweet Corn Festival

Sink your teeth into sweet kernels on the cob. Roasted or boiled, upwards of 80,000 ears of this golden treat get gobbled up at one of the Western Slope's largest events. One day every August, the tiny town of Olathe (population 1,500) swells to nearly 25,000 people, all of them here to celebrate the community's cash crop. When harvesttime comes, Olathe Sweet becomes the corn of choice for corn lovers far and wide. At the Olathe Sweet Corn Festival, the corn flows freely and free, all-you-can-eat, all day long.

A wacky early morning parade with a new theme every year starts things off. (In 1999, "Corn to Be Wild" brought out some pretty corny floats.) Free shuttle buses carry festivalgoers to Olathe Community Park along U.S. Hwy. 50 just south of town. Contests such as corn eating, cornhusking, and kernel spitting challenge adults and kids alike to show their skills. Musical acts and dance teams perform on the main stage in between karaoke singers trying to impress the audience. Live music on the Western Slope Ag Center Stage keeps fiddles fiddling and toes tapping.

Almost 200 vendors peddling food, drink, and arts and crafts provide plenty of diversion for adults, and the Corny Kids Club keeps younger ones busy with games and prizes. As the sun sets, a big-name concert rounds out the day. The 2004 festival featured the rock 'n' roll band Styx, along with Denver bands Toast and Groove Society. A huge fireworks display sends the corn-fed crowd home happy at the end of the day.

In 1992, economically depressed local farmers agreed to plant a hybrid corn seed developed by David Galinant, and the rest is history. At the big tent up on the hill at the festival, volunteers hand out free cobs of Olathe Sweet like candy to eager eaters.

The Olathe Sweet Corn Festival is held the first part of August. Reasonably priced day passes include the featured evening concert. 877-858-6006; www.olathesweetcornfest.com.

BEST Out-of-the-Way Culture
Creede Repertory Theater

You wouldn't expect to find much of a general store, much less a nationally known repertory theater, in tiny Creede. But in this growing, out-of-the-way corner of Colorado, with sheer canyon walls as a backdrop, you can enjoy the talents of young actors who converge here from around the country. The Creede Repertory Theater has been building a stellar reputation each summer since 1966.

This former silver-mining boomtown used to attract 300 newcomers a day, which contributed to the town's reputation for wild nightlife. In

This out-of-the-way theater in Creede is nationally known for the quality of its productions. PHOTO BY DOUG WHITEHEAD

1892, publisher Cy Warman penned a memorable poem to celebrate the town's attractions, called "And There Is No Night in Creede." Although this town has quieted down, you can still find memorable nightlife—in the form of energetic musicals, light comedies, and historical dramas.

Visitors come to enjoy this unlikely slice of culture at the historic and nicely restored Creede Opera House right on the town's main street. Here, you can count on seeing some outstanding performers because, as the company's reputation has grown, so, too, has the number of auditions—some 2,000 actors, directors, costume designers, stage managers, and more compete for only fifty or so summer slots. Mandy Patinkin, Emmy and Tony award–winning actor and singer, star of the TV series *Chicago Hope* and the movie *Princess Bride*, is among their most notable alumni. Many of the plays sell out early, so be sure to reserve tickets in advance. Five different productions on three main stages and two smaller ones are offered six nights a week (Mondays off). They've also added a shorter fall season in September. For information, call 866-658-2540. www.creede rep.org.

BEST Celebration of Ute Culture
Council Tree Pow Wow and Cultural Festival (Delta)

Oh, if the Council Tree could talk! In the shade of this now-200-year-old cottonwood near the banks of the Gunnison River, tribal elders would meet to discuss affairs of the Ute nation. After the Ute people were removed to reservations in the 1880s, the Council Tree was abandoned as an important meeting place. A farm and ranch community grew up around it, but the eighty-five-foot-tall tree's role in Ute life was never forgotten. Beginning in 1995, the City of Delta invited the Ute tribes back to their ancestral lands to the annual Council Tree Pow Wow and Cultural Festival.

Dancers participate in the Grand Entry to kick off the Council Tree Pow Wow in Delta. PHOTO BY DOUG WHITEHEAD

"The tree is happy. We are back home." That sentiment, expressed by a modern Ute elder, captures the spirit of this three-day gathering in late September. Beating drums provide the rhythm for the weekend, colorful dances the pageantry. Crowds gather at the Arbor, a circular cedar-log outdoor arena, as the Grand Entry kicks off the festivities each day and night. Dancers of all ages, in handmade costume, showcase traditional styles, competing for prize money and prestige. Sometimes the public is invited to join in, learning steps such as the time-honored Bear Dance. About fifty vendors offer a wide choice of Indian arts, jewelry, clothing, leatherwork, and, of course, food. The popular Tipi Village contains at least fourteen traditional lodges, some of which can be rented for overnight stays during the festival at a reasonable price.

In addition to the Southern, Ute Mountain, and Northern Utes, other tribes from across the United States and Canada join with non-Indians in this unique cultural celebration.

The Council Tree Pow Wow and Cultural Festival is held during late September at Confluence Park in Delta, located on U.S. Hwy. 50 between Montrose and Grand Junction. Call Wilma Erven at 800-874-1741. www.counciltreepowwow.org.

BEST Fall Colors Drive
Kebler Pass (Crested Butte)

Every autumn, for a brief moment in time, nature's brush paints a brilliant Colorado canvas. Mountainsides burst from forest green to every shade of orange, yellow, and gold. Aspen and scrub oak leaves glow intense colors that have only a short time during this season to grab your attention. From early September through mid-October, gold seekers hit the road to capture that perfect combination of deep-blue sky, crisp, cool air, and fluttering aspen leaves. No road approaches perfection like Kebler Pass.

The thousands of trees of an aspen grove are actually shoots from the root system of one giant living organism. For thirty miles on a well-maintained dirt road between the distinctive peak of Crested Butte and the North Fork of the Gunnison River, Kebler Pass traverses one of the largest contiguous aspen forests in the world. Travelers follow a well-worn route as the road rises from the mountain town of Crested Butte toward the old ghost town of Irwin, where 5,000 people once made their living mining silver.

Irwin's cemetery sits on top of Kebler Pass. An inscription on the gravestone of seventeen-year-old Mary Bambrough, Irwin's first death, in 1881, offers this advice: "My good people, as you pass by, as you are now, so once was I. As I am now you soon shall be. Prepare yourselves to follow me." That somewhat somber message is replaced by nature's uplifting inspiration as the road leads into a wide-open valley where the changing aspens spread like a carpet of color over the landscape. The West Elk Wilderness falls away to the south, and the Raggeds Wilderness juts up to the north. They act as a rugged border to this broad vista of burning autumn hues.

An entire valley turns gold during the fall season up on Kebler Pass. PHOTO BY DOUG WHITEHEAD

Reach Kebler Pass by taking U.S. Hwy. 50 to Gunnison. Go north on CO Hwy. 135 to Crested Butte. On the north side of town, follow signs to Kebler Pass. You can also catch the road on the west side north of the small town of Somerset near Paonia Reservoir. Call the Crested Butte Visitors Center at 800-545-4505. www.visitcrestedbutte.com.

BEST Hot Springs
Pagosa Hot Springs

It's a welcome sight to mountain travelers. Clouds of steam hover in the alpine air as pure, hot waters gurgle to the Earth's surface. From these soothing and healing waters, aching muscles and weary souls have found relief for centuries. Here along the banks of the San Juan River in the town of Pagosa Springs, a series of fabricated grottos dots the hillside.

Even on the coldest winter night, bathers clad only in bathing suits meant for the sunniest beach walk narrow, rocky pathways to any of seventeen pools built into the embankment. From the uppermost pool, with water around 99° F, you look down on an array of outdoor dens of different sizes and temperatures. The "Lobster Pot" tests your mettle at 112° F. Some pools are connected to others by small rivers of thermal waters. With faces turned upward into a warm cascade, visitors revel in one waterfall that pours from the stream above. Couples sneak a little privacy in a pool tucked into rocks over on the side. From the lowest pool, hearty swimmers leave their hot-water pocket to ease into the cold and invigorating currents of the San Juan River. A floating boardwalk with heavy ropes as handrails acts as a pathway across a shallow warm-water pond from one side of the hot springs to the other. After an active day in the mountains, this is the place to recharge.

The Pagosa Hot Springs pools are open twenty-four hours a day. The owners of the springs resort are continually improving the pools and buildings, giving this place a Mediterranean-style feel. Access to the waters is included in the price of your room or suite. Otherwise, there is a charge. Call them at 800-225-0934; www.pagosahotsprings.com. To find Pagosa Hot Springs, take U.S. Hwy. 160 west over Wolf Creek Pass to the town of Pagosa Springs. Look for steam rising right in the middle of town.

BEST Ice Climbing
Ouray Ice Park

As if the town called "The Little Switzerland of America" doesn't get enough snow and ice in the middle of a San Juan Mountains winter, Gary Wild started making more ice! He set up a series of sprinklers along the edges of a narrow crevasse known as Box Canyon, spraying water down canyon walls, creating sheets of ice a hundred feet in length that stretch to the Uncompahgre River below. The result: ice climbers flock to Ouray the way mountain bikers swarm to Moab, Utah.

Ice climbing was once the province of adventurers seeking remote backcountry cliffs where the hike in can be at least as difficult as the climb itself. Here at the easily accessed Ouray Ice Park, climbers spend all of their energy on the ice. With each move up the frigid wall, climbers knock off chunks of ice that shatter like glass on the canyon floor. They climb with jagged spikes strapped to their feet, swinging ice axes to get a grip on the frozen surface. Onlookers have plenty of perches to watch as belayers hold ropes for protection. Even beginners, under the watchful eye of experienced guides, dare to tackle the challenge, employing seldom-used muscles on the icy ascent.

Even though the ice is manufactured, the setting is hardly artificial.

Summer crowds hike deep into this river-cut chasm to its roaring water-fall, but the picturesque town used to go into hibernation when the cold weather set in. These days, the ever-growing Ouray Ice Festival high-lights the winter season. Every year around the third weekend in January, climbers and spectators bring the town alive with a celebration of ice. www.ourayicepark.com. Or try the annual Ouray Ice Festival Web site at www.ourayicefestival.com. 970-325-4288.

BEST Powder Skiing
Wolf Creek Ski Area

When Colorado's other ski areas are busy making artificial snow, Wolf Creek tends to get dumped on by Mother Nature. So reliable are the 465 inches of annual snowfall, this ski area in the southern San Juan Moun-tains should be the pick for powderhounds, especially those who like to tackle the steep glades and chutes along the Continental Divide.

Extreme skiers and snowboarders get shuttled by snowcat to Knife Ridge, an area of breathtaking vertical exposure at an elevation of more than 11,000 feet. Floating on clouds of dry, light, fluffy powder, adven-turers find their rhythm down the deeply blanketed inclines of this high-altitude playground. Strong intermediate skiers may want to try the milder but no less awesome terrain of Water Fall.

Beginners can take advantage of the green runs down by the base. Skiers on the slopes of this small, family-owned-and-operated ski area sacrifice nothing in quality while they avoid the long lift lines of Col-orado's larger resorts. And with reasonably priced all-day adult lift tick-ets, Wolf Creek remains one of the best bargains in the state.

Wolf Creek Ski Area is located on U.S. Hwy. 160 near the top of Wolf Creek Pass. Lodging is available in South Fork and Pagosa Springs, on either side of the pass. For updated snow conditions, contact 800-SKI-WOLF. www.wolfcreekski.com.

BEST Steep-and-Deep Skiing
Telluride

No place in Colorado compares so favorably to the Alps as the incredible views from the ski mountain at Telluride. A mining boomtown from more than a century ago, Telluride again has boomed and now entices skiers and snowboarders to the long, steep front of the mountain and its mellow back side. Contrasts continue between the mountain and the two separate bases. The front of the mountain connects directly to the funky, historic town with its refurbished miners' homes and picturesque main street. The back side, hidden three miles away by road, ties via gondola with Telluride Mountain Village, an upscale development of million-dollar homes, condos, and its own golf course. Regardless of where you choose to stay, you will appreciate the variety of skiable terrain that lies in the middle.

With a vertical drop of more than 3,100 feet and a base elevation of 8,725 feet, the snow here remains some of the best in the state. Weather patterns often favor this high-mountain area, providing ample amounts of light, dry powder. Warning: this area's expert runs truly require expert skills. When you see a black diamond, it means you had better have honed skills for the physically demanding slopes. Those who enjoy the steeps will find few places that compare to the front of Telluride, with its ungroomed legends of Spiral Stairs and The Plunge. Massive bumps combined with a steep pitch will make you feel like you somehow got placed atop a slow-moving jackhammer. Take your time, stop to catch your breath, and enjoy the sweeping views over the historic town and out to surrounding 13,000- and 14,000-foot peaks. It may be the only way to get down, other than by toboggan. 800-525-3455; www.tellurideskiresort.com.

Where to Eat, Drink, & Stay

BEST Small-Town Dining
Crested Butte

In a business that sees restaurants open and close as often as the hungry mouths they feed, Crested Butte is an aberration. For sheer longevity, the high quality eateries and the variety of cuisine in this mountain town hold distinction. Many restaurants have been around for decades, but even the newer ones strive for the standard set by those who came before. For the complete scoop, log on to www. visitcrestedbutte.com. Here's a sampling:

Historic downtown Crested Butte boasts some of the finest dining in the state.
PHOTO BY DOUG WHITEHEAD

▶▶ **Bacchanale**—Northern Italian cuisine has been served at this restaurant since the early 1970s. Veal dishes, cannelloni, specialty desserts, and Italian wines. Dinner served nightly. Reservations accepted. 208 Elk Ave.; 970-349-5257.

▸ **Donita's**—Known for its homemade salsa (you can buy it and take it home), this Mexican restaurant has long been a Crested Butte tradition. The chile rellenos are especially good, or try the fajitas. Open only for dinner, it's located on the corner of 4th St. and Elk Ave. 970-349-6674.

▸ **Le Bosquet**—This family-owned-and-operated restaurant has been serving delicious French cuisine since 1976. Entrees such as elk, duck, and salmon are presented with delectable sauces. Reservations recommended. Located at 6th St. and Belleview Ave. in the Majestic Plaza. 970-349-5808.

▸ **Soupçon**—The continental menu changes every day, as the chef uses fresh, in-season ingredients. Shrimp, oysters, lamb, salmon, homemade soups, and desserts. Located behind the Forest Queen Hotel. Reservations recommended. 127 Elk Ave.; 970-349-5448.

▸ **Slogar**—Pass the chicken, pass the potatoes. This family-style restaurant uses a "recipe famous for great flavor since 1915" in preparing skillet fried–chicken dinners. Grilled steaks are tasty, too. Nice atmosphere. 517 2nd St.; 970-349-5765.

▸ **Secret Stash**—Crested Butte's newest favorite spot is cozy and fun. Even the locals are excited. Sit on the deck outside, at café tables on the main floor, or on pillows at low tables upstairs. Gourmet pizza, salads, wings, and wraps with a variety of libations. 21 Elk Ave.; 970-349-6245.

BEST Unique Cuisine
Metate Room (Mesa Verde National Park)

A national park is not the first place you think of for fine dining, so the Metate Room at Mesa Verde comes as quite a surprise. Here's a sampling of the entrees: barbecued quail, hickory-smoked buffalo ribeye, coriander-crusted ahi tuna, Navajo spiced free-range chicken, maple-chile–glazed pork tenderloin. How about these appetizers: cactus dip with spinach and artichokes, poblano chile relleno stuffed with *asadero*, cheddar, and cream cheese, or blackened shrimp saguaro with a Mexican *remoullade* sauce. Not only is this the most unique menu we've ever found, but we're impressed with the philosophy behind it. Executive Chef Todd Halnier has expanded on this restaurant's tradition of using sustainable, "eco-friendly" ingredients. Keeping with an "Ancestral Puebloan" theme, the dishes were designed with regional flavors in mind, derived from plants and animals of the Southwest. Trying as much as possible to use organically and locally grown food, the idea is to "restore and preserve the Earth to the beauty and abundance enjoyed by Mesa Verde's original inhabitants." The menu includes herbal teas, specialty coffees, and an interesting choice of wines.

The Metate Room, located in the Far View Lodge, is surrounded by large picture windows, allowing great views of the mesa tops and faraway landscapes. Wondering about dessert? There's Cactus Crème Brulee, a prickly pear custard with candied cactus fruit, or the Cliff Palace Crisp, "the house favorite," a flour tortilla filled with mascarpone cheese and chunks of dark chocolate, deep-fried, dusted with cinnamon-sugar, and served with vanilla ice cream and mocha sauce. Treat yourself.

BEST Pizza
Farquart's and Pizza Mia (Durango)

We went back just to make sure. After all, pizza can be like wine. Connoisseurs are very picky. And things change. But this place still seems to be as popular as it ever was. Owner Toby Peterson started making his homemade pizza in 1972. Today, what has consistently been voted by locals as "Durango's Best" is still one of "Colorado's Best."

The whole-wheat crust of Pizza Mia's pizza at Farquart's is a long-standing tradition. Not too thick or heavy, this pizza holds all the toppings you'd imagine. Looking around this restaurant with its high ceiling and brick walls covered by old posters and photographs, you notice that pizza is not the only popular offering at Farquart's. Huge meatballs sit atop linguini smothered in marinara sauce, and spicy chiles add flavor to big portions of Mexican entrees. Salads are fresh, and there's a bar full of domestic and imported beers. And for an added treat, try the homemade s'mores. They'll bring a plate full of graham crackers, chocolate, marshmallows, and a small flame over which you hold your marshmallow to create your own dessert. Customers will tell you, though, that first you've just got to try the pizza. 725 Main St.; 970-247-5440.

BEST Steak House
Ole Miner's Steakhouse (east of Pagosa Springs)

Weathered lumber makes the building look like an old mine high in the Colorado mountains. Enter the doors and you immediately feel like you're in a mine shaft. Wait for your table in a sitting room that seems like the mine boss's home, with comfortable couches and chairs, a fireplace, and paintings on the wall. Many parties can be seated at once, yet each table feels private. Of course, when you're in a steak house, order steak.

"In twenty-two years, I've never said I don't want to come to work." Paul Aldridge has been owner and chef at the Ole Miner's Steakhouse since 1982, and he sees no end in sight. He cuts every New York strip, top sirloin, and filet fresh for each order. Each is as tender a steak as we've found. The menu also includes kabobs, seafood, a variety of chicken entrees, Cornish game hen, and quail. The salad bar is well stocked with fresh vegetables and fixings. On our last visit we had filet, teriyaki chicken, and charbroiled shrimp. Come here hungry. They choose not to serve alcohol, which makes for a family-friendly atmosphere. While you're waiting for your table, look around the small mining museum with photographs, implements, and other historical memorabilia. Open for dinner only, closed Sundays. The Ole Miner's Steakhouse is located on U.S. Hwy. 160 two miles east of Pagosa Springs. 970-264-5981.

BEST Historic Hotel
Strater Hotel (Durango)

The four-story redbrick building with white trim on the corner of 7th and Main Sts. stands like a monument to Durango's past. It's anything but a relic. Operating continuously since 1887, the Strater Hotel preserves the opulence of a rich history, renovating and updating all along the way. What Henry Strater built and nurtured, three generations of the Barker family have improved upon since 1927.

Each of the ninety-three rooms at the Strater is individually decorated and furnished. Antique four-poster beds, marble-top dressers, custom-made drapes, and everything else in the room create an elegant experience of days gone by. The lobby, staircases, and hallways serve as a museum, with displays containing items from the 1800s, such as combs, watches, dolls, and toys. Even some original hand-painted photographs by the famed Western photographer William Henry Jackson hang on the walls. But history here doesn't just lie still. Ragtime tunes dance from the piano in the raucous Diamond Belle Saloon. Cheers, boos, and hisses emanate from the Diamond Circle Theater. Every summer six nights a week since 1961, professional melodramas and vaudeville revues entertain crowds looking for a slice of Old West entertainment.

Rooms at the Strater Hotel do not come cheaply, but they do include a full breakfast buffet heaped with fresh fruit, muffins, pastries, pancakes, waffles, eggs, and other fixings. Henry's Restaurant also features a fine dinner menu prepared by a world-class chef. Located in the heart of downtown Durango, the Strater can be used as a headquarters for exploring southwest Colorado. 699 Main St.; 800-247-4431; www.strater.com.

BEST Bed-and-Breakfast
Blue Lake Ranch (near Hesperus)

The Garden of Eden has nothing on Blue Lake Ranch. Fragrant flower gardens, quiet footpaths through the trees, a well-stocked lake, and cozy dwellings tucked in secluded, forested nooks combine to make this 200-acre paradise an elegant retreat for work-weary city dwellers looking for a break.

"This is the place to do nothing," says Shirley Isgar. She and her husband, David Alford, have turned this onetime homestead into a one-of-a-kind country inn. David's got the green thumb at Blue Lake Ranch. Hollyhocks, asters, columbine, and a canopy of flowers color and grace the grounds of each of sixteen handicapped-accessible cabins, cottages, casitas, and rooms. On our latest visit, we found that the Main Inn has been renovated, with several private suites added, an expanded dining room, and improved facilities to handle weddings up to fifty people. We stayed at Lower

Fragrant flowers inundate the grounds of Blue Lake Ranch west of Durango. PHOTO BY DOUG WHITEHEAD

Spring House, a luxurious home away from home with a large living room, big picture windows, private bedrooms, and a beautiful setting.

A short walk through the piñon pine leads to trout-filled Blue Lake, where faraway views of the La Plata Mountains stretch to the horizon. Overlooking this scene, the "Cabin on the Lake," with its wraparound deck and stone fireplace in the living room, offers enough room to sleep up to eight people comfortably. The cultivated accommodations of Blue Lake Ranch fit in harmony with its natural surroundings. Before you leave, be sure to stock up on the owners' own brand of flower seeds, jam, and honey.

If you plan to do more than "nothing," the staff is well versed on how to best make use of your time touring southwest Colorado. The ranch is located at 16000 CO Hwy. 140, 6.5 miles south of Hesperus, about fifteen miles from Durango, near Mesa Verde and Cortez. 888-258-3525; www.bluelakeranch.com. The owners also run beautiful inns in Santa Fe, New Mexico (The Don Gaspar) and Farmington, New Mexico (Casa Blanca Inn).

BEST Small-Town Lodgings
Ouray County

For such a small, year-round population, Ouray County can sure put up a lot of people, and they do it with style. From historic Victorian buildings and chalets to more modern southwestern architecture, the National Historic District of Ouray is replete with charming and fascinating lodgings. For a complete list, call the Ouray Chamber Resort Association at 800-228-1876; www.ouraycolorado.com. Here's a sampling of our favorites:

▸▸ **Wiesbaden Hot Springs and Lodgings**—If you don't want to share the waters of Ouray's public hot-springs pool, the Wiesbaden features its own enclosed, private outdoor hot tub and geothermal vapor caves accessible right from the lobby. Suites with kitchens available. 625 5th St.; 888-846-5191; www.wiesbadenhotsprings.com.

▸▸ **Manor Bed-and-Breakfast**—This three-story renovated house in Ouray has a Georgian/Victorian mix of architecture and is on the National Register of Historic Places. Each room is individually decorated. Parlor, patio, and outdoor hot tub. 317 2nd St.; 800-628-6946; www.ouraymanor.com.

▸▸ **Main Street House**—Two century-old homes in downtown Ouray have been completely redone with elegant furnishings. In between you'll find a gazebo in a nice little courtyard. A separate cottage sits out back. Open mid-May through early October. Reasonable prices. 334 Main St.; 970-325-4871; www.mainstreethouse.com.

▸▸ **Chipeta Sun Lodge & Spa**—Wrapped with a wall of windows, this bright, imaginative adobe-style building in Ridgway, ten miles north of Ouray, offers great views of the San Juan Mountains. They've got a full menu of spa services here. A creative, healthy breakfast is served in the plant-laden, two-story solarium. Check out the hot tub in an adobe turret on the third floor. 304 S. Lena St. in Ridgway; 800-633-5868; www.chipeta.com.

ALPHABETICAL LISTING OF PLACES & ACTIVITIES

INDEX

COLORADO'S **BEST**

ABOUT THE AUTHORS

A fourth-generation native Coloradan, **Bruce Caughey** is coauthor, with Dean Winstanley, of the best-selling book *The Colorado Guide*, which, over five editions, has served as the most comprehensive, visitor-friendly travel sourcebook to the Centennial State. Bruce has contributed to the Rough Guide Series in London and is coauthor of the hiking guide *Crete: Off the Beaten Track* (Cicerone Press), in addition to many other freelance projects. He can be found hiking, fishing, skiing, and biking in the mountains of Colorado, or spending time at his family's cabin near Deckers. Bruce is communications director and legislative liaison for the Douglas County School District. Bruce and his family live in the south Metro Denver area and, whenever possible, they share adventures out on the open road.

Bruce Caughey. PHOTO BY BARB VAN EPPS

Since 1992, **Doug Whitehead** has served as producer, writer, and photographer for the award-winning television series, *Colorado Getaways* (Saturdays on CBS 4), a weekly program highlighting the many outdoor and travel-related, historical, and cultural aspects of the state. A Colorado resident since 1971, he has acquired more than a passing knowledge of Colorado, experience that has formed the basis for many of the contributions to this book. Doug and his family live in Denver, Colorado.

Doug Whitehead. PHOTO BY BARB VAN EPPS

More **GOLDEN** opportunities in Colorado
from Fulcrum Publishing

Valley of the Dunes
Great Sand Dunes National Park and Preserve
Bob Rozinski AND Wendy Shattil
WITH TEXT BY Audrey DeLella Benedict

ISBN 1-55591-523-X
11¼ x 9 • Full-color photographs • 152 pages
$19.95 pb

Rise & Dine
Breakfast in Denver & Boulder
Joey Porcelli

ISBN 1-55591-509-4
4¼ x 6¾ • 224 pages
$12.95 pb

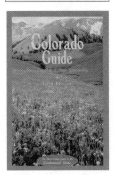

The Colorado Guide
Revised, Fifth Edition
Bruce Caughey AND Dean Winstanley

ISBN 1-55591-576-0
6 x 9 • b/w photographs • 672 pages
$19.95 pb

FULCRUM PUBLISHING
WWW.FULCRUM-BOOKS.COM

16100 Table Mountain Parkway, Suite 300, Golden, CO 80403
To order call 800-992-2908 or visit www.fulcrum-books.com.
Also available at your local bookstore.

Fulcrum \'Fùl-krəm\:l a:PROP; specif:
The point at which motion begins